War and Its Discontents

War and Its Discontents
Pacifism and Quietism in the Abrahamic Traditions

EDITED BY
J. PATOUT BURNS

GEORGETOWN UNIVERSITY PRESS, WASHINGTON, D.C.

Georgetown University Press, Washington, D.C.
© 1996 by Georgetown University Press. All rights reserved.
Printed in the United States of America

10 9 8 7 6 5 4 3 2 1   1996

THIS VOLUME IS PRINTED ON ACID-FREE OFFSET BOOK PAPER

Library of Congress Cataloging-in-Publication Data

War and its discontents : pacifism and quietism in the Abrahamic
    traditions / edited by J. Patout Burns.
        p. cm.
      1. Nonviolence—Religious aspects—Comparative studies—
    Congresses.   2. Pacifism—Religious aspects—Comparative studies—
    Congresses.   3. War—Religious aspects—Comparative studies—
    Congresses.   4. Peace—Religious aspects—Comparative studies—
    Congresses.   5. Just war doctrine—Congresses.   I. Burns, J.
    Patout.
    BL65.V55W37   1996
    291.1'7873—dc20   95-42086
    ISBN 0-87840-603-4 (alk. paper)

Contents

Preface

In July 1990, Washington University in St. Louis established the Center for Interreligious Dialogue in its Faculty of Arts and Sciences. Rather than addressing religious questions debated by the faith traditions, the Center was charged with leading investigation into and discussion of common social issues. By bringing the resources of the religious traditions represented in its constituencies and in the larger American society to bear on these problems, the Center might identify common ground and help marshal forces to effect solutions.

The pressure of international events moved the Center to focus attention on the conflict in the Persian Gulf region. Congress debated the justice and wisdom of an armed response to Iraq's initiatives and President Bush formed an international coalition. Rembert Weakland, Roman Catholic Archbishop of Milwaukee, noted that the same religious communities, particularly Christian and Muslim, would be on both sides of the impending conflict. He called for an immediate interreligious dialogue on the ethics of warfare. Dr. John Borelli, an officer in the Secretariat for Interreligious Relations of the National Conference of Catholic Bishops, initiated planning with the Center at Washington University. In late November, the decision was made to organize a conference for January 1991 that would address the ethics of waging war in Judaism, Christianity, and Islam. Once the project was undertaken, Dr. Borelli proved invaluable in winning commitments to participate from key figures in the three religious communities. Scholars agreed to provide overviews of the teaching of each tradition and to lead the discussions. During the first week of hostilities in January 1991, these scholars met with representatives of the Jewish, Christian, and Muslim communities in St. Louis to address the restrictions that each tradition placed on the use of force once war has been declared. After intense private exchange, they laid out their conclusions in a two-hour presentation to the university community and the news media.

In these discussions of the ethics of warfare, the growing influence of the Christian pacifist tradition on the development of justifiable war theory was noted: Violence was becoming increasingly difficult to justify. Similarly, the emergence of Gandhian nonviolence as a means of effecting social change also functioned as a brake on the legitimation of coercive force. The evolution of military technology and the difficulty of containing conflict had, it seemed, raised the social and political cost of warfare.[1]

O'Ray Graber, then local secretary of the National Conference of Christians and Jews, suggested that the Center for Interreligious Dialogue investigate the pacifist tradition within Christianity and its resonances in Jewish and Muslim legal teaching. Thus a second conference, under the auspices of the United States Institute of Peace, was organized to explore the foundations for an ethic of pacifism or quietism in each of the Abrahamic traditions. During the spring and fall of 1992, a series of papers was presented on the Washington University campus, addressing the various positions operative in each tradition. The first of these was offered in conjunction with a conference held to honor the memory of Steven Schwarzchild, long-time Professor of Philosophy at Washington University and an advocate of pacifism within the Jewish tradition. In addition, a fourth speaker was invited to discuss the response of the government of the United States to religious pacifism, in the form of conscientious objection to military service. Each of these papers was sent to another expert for comment. Then in February 1993, the original speakers, the invited commentators, and representatives of the religious communities converged on the campus for two days of concentrated debate. A major snowstorm that disrupted travel and closed the campus turned what had been planned as a public conference into a more private colloquy. Each of the speakers and commentators was then asked to prepare a paper for publication in this volume.

The United States Institute of Peace itself organized a workshop in July 1993 to explore these issues further, with a particular focus on the conflict in Yugoslavia. Many of the participants in the two

---

1. For a report on these discussions, see J. Patout Burns, "The Ethics of Warfare: Muslim, Jewish and Christian Religious Traditions," *Journal of Religious Pluralism* 2 (1993):83–96.

Washington University conferences contributed to these interchanges as well. A report on this meeting, including summaries of the presentations and discussions, has been published by David Smock.[2]

An explanation of the distinction made between pacifism and quietism that was operative in the Washington University meeting seems in order. For present purposes, pacifism denotes the principled rejection of all use of coercive force; quietism refers to abstaining from violence when the conditions necessary for its legitimate exercise are not actually fulfilled. Thus, the justifiable war theory does not forbid all exercise of force but enjoins quietism in the absence of, for instance, a reasonable expectation of success or a reasonable proportion between the good to be achieved and the anticipated damage of war. Religious traditions add other requirements that must be fulfilled, particularly for offensive war or civil sedition, the most important of which is approval by an agency authorized to speak for God. While pacifism renounces the use of coercive force in all circumstances, quietism practices restraint under specified conditions.

The three Abrahamic faiths whose stances toward warfare are here examined arose in significantly different social settings. The adherents of Judaism and Islam both bore responsibility for political sovereignty and defense of their communities during the formative periods of these traditions. Thus in their founding documents, in their traditions, and in authoritative interpretations, these religious communities elaborated rules for warfare and specified the obligation of the faithful to participate in both the defense of the community and the expansion of the religious state. Teaching on warfare was further elaborated as each community's political identity was challenged by internal division and national sovereignty was lost for extended periods of time. New religious developments were necessary to guide the life of the faithful who found themselves deprived of military power, either in the dispersion or under foreign domination.

Christianity arose at a time when its mother tradition, Judaism, did not enjoy national sovereignty. During its formative period, it spread as an unrecognized and illegal religious community that was largely ignored but occasionally suppressed by Roman imperial power. The Christian church did not bear responsibility for civil order

---

2. *Perspectives on Pacifism: Christian, Jewish and Muslim Views on Nonviolence and International Conflict* (Washington, D.C.: United States Institute of Peace Press, 1995).

and national defense until the conversion of Constantine and its establishment as the preferred religion of the Empire under Theodosius
the Great at the end of the fourth century. In Byzantium, this imperial
form of Christianity continued until the fall of the Empire to Turkish
arms in the fifteenth century. The Western church, in contrast, found
itself presiding over the dissolution of the Empire during the fifth
century. As the surviving remnant of the Roman bureaucracy, its
bishops were required to participate in the formation of the new
kingdoms of Europe, to inspire European defense and counteroffen-
sive against the encroachments of an expanding Muslim civilization,
and finally to attempt to regulate hostilities among the principalities
and powers of an established Christendom. During this millennium,
the Roman church assumed many of the functions of a religious state,
including the responsibility for regulating war.

Thus the three religious traditions each developed criteria for
warfare, particularly for the defense and promotion of religious identity by resort to force. All three also set limits to coercion and championed a just peace as the only proper objective of violence. The question
posed for discussion in these studies is whether these religious traditions have also established a justification for pacifism or a requirement
of quietism. Do they define standards according to which the recourse
to arms, either for conquest or in defense of life and justice, would
be forbidden? Might they encourage, approve, or at least allow a
pacifist stance in the contemporary world order?

This volume contains a selection of the essays presented at both
the Washington University and United States Institute of Peace meetings on pacifism and quietism. Only two participants in the Washington University meeting declined to contribute. The editor solicited
additional papers from the Institute of Peace workshop in July 1993.
Some contributions have been elaborated to incorporate issues sig-
naled by the respondents and the editor; others are printed as they
were delivered.

Michael Broyde's paper and Everett Gendler's response were
presented at the Washington University conference. Yehuda Mirsky's
paper and Naomi Goodman's response are from the Institute of Peace
workshop. John Howard Yoder presented the case for Christian pacifism at the Washington University conference, where the response
was offered by John Langan. Walter Wink's paper was presented at
the Institute of Peace workshop. The Islamic tradition on quietism
was presented at both meetings by Abdulaziz Sachedina. The essay

contained here was then elaborated to take account of issues addressed in both conferences. Sachedina's, however, is the only Muslim voice in these discussions. Michael Nagler's response is limited to the issues raised at the Institute of Peace workshop. Edward Gaffney was asked, for the Washington University meeting, to discuss the way in which a secular state responds to religious objections to bearing arms. A lecture on the equivocations of modern pacifists by Peter Steinfels, delivered to the Washington University community during the conference, was not prepared for publication.

These lectures, discussions, and publication were underwritten by the United States Institute of Peace and by the Faculty of Arts and Sciences of Washington University, through its Center for Interreligious Dialogue. The organization of the lectures and the conferences was particularly assisted by Trudi Spigel and Nancy Galofre of the University's Special Events office, and by Doris Suits and Cathy Marler of the Classics Department. Namoi Gold, then a graduate student in Religious Studies, proved particularly adept and persevering in tracking stray citations and imposing a uniform mode of reference on the individual essays.

J. PATOUT BURNS

Fighting the War and the Peace: Battlefield Ethics, Peace Talks, Treaties, and Pacifism in the Jewish Tradition

MICHAEL J. BROYDE

Rabbi Jesse the Galilean states: "How meritorious is peace? Even in time of war Jewish law requires that one initiate discussions of peace."[1]

INTRODUCTION

Judaism is a system of law and ethics whose scope of regulation is designed to cover nearly every area of human action. Unlike many other religious legal systems, the mandate of Jewish law is limited only by the scope of human activity; no area of activity is free from direction, either legal, ethical, or both. Unlike many secular legal systems, Jewish law does not, however, set its boundaries at merely determining what is legal or illegal; Jewish law also regulates that which is ethical.[2] Frequently Jewish law will conclude that a certain activity is completely legal, but is not ethically correct.[3] This article reviews Jewish law's attitude to one of the areas of modern social behavior that "law" as an institution has shied away from regulating, and that "ethics" as a discipline has failed to regulate: war. In this area, as in many others, the legal and the ethical are freely combined in the Jewish tradition.

This article will start with a review of the legal or ethical issues that can justify the *starting* of war (*jus ad bellum*). This issue is crucial for any discussion of the ethics of the battlefield itself in the Jewish tradition. As developed below, there are numerous different theories as to why and when it is morally permissible to start a war that will kill people. What theory one adopts to justify the war, and what category of "war" any particular military activity is placed in, significantly affects what type of conduct is legally or morally permissible

1

on the battlefield (*jus in bello*). This article continues by addressing various ethical issues raised by military activity as they would be chronologically encountered as hostilities advance and then recede, including the issues raised by peace treaties and pacifism in the Jewish tradition.

This article demonstrates that the Jewish tradition has within it a moral license that permits war (and killing) which is different from the usual rules of individualized self-defense. However, the permissibility to "wage war" is quite limited in the Jewish tradition and the requirement that one always seek a just peace is part and parcel of the process one must use to wage a legitimate war. The love of peace and the pursuit of peace, as well as the eradication of evil, all coexist in the Jewish tradition, each in its place and to be used in its proper time.

GROUNDS FOR STARTING WAR

Jewish Law's View of Secular Nations at War

Jews have historically been a people living in the Diaspora and were (and still are) citizens of countries where Jewish law was not the ethical or legal touchstone of moral conduct by the government. As citizens of such countries it is necessary for Jews to develop a method for determining whether the country's military activity is permissible according to Jewish law.[4]

Two distinctly different rationales are extant to justify the use of military force. The first is the general rules of self-defense, which are as applicable to the defense of a group of people as they are to the defense of a single person. The Talmud[5] rules that a person is permitted to kill a pursuer to save his own life regardless of whether the person being pursued is a Jew or a Noachide. While there is some dispute among modern Jewish law authorities as to whether Jewish law *mandates* or merely *permits* a Noachide or bystander to take the life of one who is trying to kill another, nearly all authorities posit that such conduct is *at the least* permissible.

While Jewish law *compels* a Jew to take the life of a pursuer (Jewish or otherwise) who is trying to take the life of a Jew,[6] such is not obligatory for a Noachide. Rabbi Joseph Babad, writing in *Minchat Hinuch*, says that this is permissible but not mandatory for a Noachide.[7] The source quoted for this statement is the Talmud in Sanhedrin,[8] which derives from the verse in Genesis 9:6 ("One who sheds man's blood by man shall his blood be shed"), one of the dispensations to kill the pursuer. All commandments derived from this verse are binding equally on Jews and Noachides.[9] Tosaphot notes that this verse only makes the killing of the pursuer permissible but not obligatory.[10] Tosaphot claims that it is Deuteronomy 22:27 ("the betrothed damsel cried and there was none to save her") that makes this action obligatory rather than optional, and this verse only has legal effect on Jews.

Rabbi Shlomo Zevin argues with this position. He notes that the verses in Obadiah 1:11–13 chastise the kingdom of Edom for standing by silently while Israel was destroyed. Hence, he claims, it appears that all have an obligation to help.[11] He also argues that the Talmud in *T.B. Sanhedrin* 72b was referring to a house robber[12] and not to a pursuer. Other modern commentaries also disagree with Rabbi Babad and accept Rabbi Zevin's ruling.[13]

It is obvious that the laws of pursuit are as applicable to a group of individuals or to a nation as they are to a single person. Military action thus becomes permissible, or more likely obligatory, when it is defensive in nature, or undertaken to aid the victim of aggression. However, using the pursuer paradigm to analyze "war" leads one to conclude that all the restrictions related to this rationale apply also.[14] War, if it is to exist legally as a morally sanctioned event, must permit some forms of killing other than those allowed through the self-defense rationale; the modern institution of "war" cannot exist as derivative of the self-defense rules alone.

There are a number of recent authorities who explicitly state that the institution of "war" is legally recognized as a distinct moral license (independent of the laws of pursuer and self-defense) to terminate life according to Jewish law even for secular nations. Rabbi Naphtali Zevi Yehudah Berlin[15] argues that the very verse that prohibits murder, permits war. He claims that the words "from the hand of a man, your brother"[16] prohibit killing only when it is proper to behave in a brotherly manner, but *at times of war, killing that would otherwise be prohibited is permitted*. Indeed, such an opinion can also be found in the medieval Talmudic commentary of Tosaphot.[17]

Other authorities disagree. Rabbi Moshe Sofer[18] appears to adopt a middle position and argues that wars of aggression are never permitted to secular nations; however, he does appear to recognize the institution of "war" distinct from the pursuer rationale in the context of defensive wars. A number of other rabbinic authorities appear to accept this position also.[19]

A Jewish Nation Starting a War

The discussion in the commentaries concerning the issues involved in a Jewish nation starting a war is far more detailed and extensive than is that devoted to secular nations going to war.[20]

The Talmud[21] understands that a special category of permitted killing called "war" exists which is analytically different from other permitted forms of killing, like the killing of a pursuer or a house robber. The Talmud delimits two categories of permissible war: 1) obligatory; and 2) authorized.[22] It is crucial to determine which category of "war" any particular type of conflict is. As explained below, many of the restrictions placed by Jewish law on the type of conduct prohibited by war are frequently limited to authorized rather than obligatory wars.[23] Logic would dictate, and Jewish law accepts, that a specific divinely mandated conflict has certain ethical rules not found in any other type of military engagement.[24]

According to the Talmud,[25] obligatory wars are those wars started in direct fulfillment of a specific biblical commandment, such as the obligation to destroy the tribe of Amalek in biblical times. Authorized wars are wars undertaken to increase territory or "to diminish the heathens so that they shall not march," which is, as explained below, a category of military action given different parameters by different authorities.[26] Maimonides, in his codification of the law, writes that:

> The king must first wage only obligatory wars. What is an obligatory war? It is a war against the seven nations, the war against Amalek, and a war to deliver Israel from an enemy who has attacked them. Then he may wage authorized wars, which is a war against others in order to enlarge the borders of Israel and to increase his greatness and prestige.[27]

Surprisingly enough, the category of "to save Israel from an enemy . . . " is not found in the Talmud. In addition, the category of preemptive war[28] is not mentioned in Maimonides' formulation of the law even though it is found in the Talmud.[29]

What was Maimonides' understanding of the Talmud and how did he develop these categories? These questions are the key focus of a discussion on the laws of starting wars. The classical commentaries, both ancient and modern, grapple with the dividing line between "a war to deliver Israel from an enemy who has attacked them" and a war "to enlarge the borders of Israel and to increase his [the king's] greatness and prestige." Each of these approaches underlies different understandings of when a war is obligatory, authorized, or prohibited and the ethical duties associated with each category.

Ibn Tibbon's translation of Maimonides' commentary on the Mishnah suggests that Maimonides felt that an obligatory war does not start until one is actually attacked by an army; authorized wars include all defensive wars and all military actions commenced for any reason other than immediate self-defense.[30] According to this definition, the use of force prior to the initial use of force by the enemy other than for clearly defensive purposes can only be justified through the "pursuer" or self-defense rationale. All other military activity is prohibited.

Rabbi Joseph Kapach in his translation of the same commentary of Maimonides understands Maimonides to permit war against nations that have previously fought with Israel and that are still technically at war with the Jewish nation—even though no fighting is now going on. An offensive war cannot be justified even as an authorized war unless a prior state of belligerency existed.[31]

Rabbi Abraham diBoton, in his commentary on Maimonides (*Lechem Mishneh*),[32] posits that the phrase "to enhance the king's greatness and prestige" includes all of the categories of authorized war permitted in the Talmud. Once again, all wars other than purely defensive wars in which military activity is solely initiated by one's opponents are classified as authorized wars or illegal wars. Obligatory wars are limited to purely defensive wars.

Rabbi Abraham Isaiah Karlitz (*Chazon Ish*) claims that Maimonides' definition of an authorized war is referring to the use of force in a war of attrition situation.[33] In any circumstance in which prior "battle" has occurred and that battle was initiated by the enemy, the war that is being fought is an obligatory one.[34] According to this approach, the use of military force prior to the start of a war of attrition is prohibited (unless justified by the general rules of self-defense, in which case a "war" is not being fought according to Jewish law).

Summary

Wars by secular governments according to Jewish law can thus be divided into three categories:

1. *War to save the nation which is now, or soon to be, under attack.* This is not technically war but is permitted because of the law of "pursuer" and is subject to all the restrictions related to the law of pursuer and the rules of self-defense.
2. *War to aid an innocent third party who is under attack.* This too is not technically war, but most commentators mandate this, also under the "pursuer" rationale, but some rule this as merely permitted. In either case, it is subject to all the restrictions related to the "pursuer" rationale.
3. *Wars of self-defense or perhaps territorial expansion.* A number of commentators permit "war" as an institution even in situations where non-combatants might be killed; most commentaries limit this license to defensive wars.

So too, Jewish law divides wars by the Jewish government into three (different) categories:

1. Defending the people of Israel from attack by an aggressive neighbor. This is an obligatory war.
2. Fighting offensive wars against belligerent neighbors.[35]
3. Protecting individuals through the use of the laws of "pursuer" and self-defense from aggressive neighbors. This is not a "war" according to the Jewish tradition.[36]

Finally, it is crucial to realize that there are situations where war—in the Jewish tradition—is simply illegal. The killings that take place in such a war, if not directly based on immediate self-defense needs,[37] are murder, and participation in those wars is prohibited according to Jewish law.[38] How specifically one, as a citizen, is to respond to an improper war (by silence, protest, draft evasion, or disobedience, civil or otherwise) is a question beyond the scope of this paper: It is clear, however, that one may not actually serve in the army and kill the enemy unjustly.

BATTLEFIELD ETHICS

Type of War

The initial question that needs to be addressed when discussing battlefield ethics is whether the rules for these situations differ from all other applications of Jewish ethics, or is "battlefield ethics" merely a general application of the rules of Jewish ethics to the battlefield situation. This question is essentially a rephrasing of the question, "What is the moral license according to the Jewish tradition that permits war to be waged?" As explained above, Jewish tradition categorizes "armed conflict" into three different categories: obligatory war, permissible war, and societal applications of the "pursuer" rationale.[39] Each of these situations comes with different licenses. The easiest one to address is the final one: the pursuer rationale. Battlefield ethics based on the pursuer model are simply a generic application of the general field of Jewish ethics relating to stopping one who is an evil-doer from killing an innocent person. While it is beyond the scope of this article to completely explain that detailed field of Jewish ethics, the touchstone rules of self-defense according to Jewish law are fourfold. Even when self-defense is mandatory or permissible and one may kill a person or group of people who are seeking to kill one who is innocent, one may not:

1. Kill an innocent[40] third party to save a life;
2. Compel a person to risk his life to save the life of another;
3. Kill the pursuer after his evil act is over as a form of punishment;
4. Use more force than is minimally needed.[41]

Thus, the rules of this type of "armed conflict" would resemble the activities of a police force rather than the activities of an army. Only the most genteel of modern armies can function in accordance with these rules.

On the other hand, the situations of both obligatory war and authorized war are not merely global extrapolations of the principles of "self-defense" or "pursuer." There are ethical liberalities (and strictures) associated with the battlefield situation that have unique ethical and legal rules unrelated to other fields of Jewish law or ethics.[42] They permit the killing of fellow human beings in situations where that action—but for the permissibility of war—would be murder. In order to understand what precisely is the "license to kill," it is necessary to explain the preliminary steps needed according to Jewish law to actually fight a battle after war has been properly declared. It is through an understanding of these requirements that one grasps the limits on the license to kill one's opponents in military action according to

Jewish law. Indeed, nearly all the preliminary requirements for a permissible war are designed to remove noncombatants, civilians, and others who do not wish to fight from the battlefield.

Seeking Peace Prior to Starting War

Two basic texts form Jewish law's understanding of the duties society must undertake before a battle may be fought. The Bible states:

> When you approach a city to do battle with it you should call to it in peace. And if they respond in peace and they open the city to you, and all the people in the city shall pay taxes to you and be subservient. And if they do not make peace with you, you shall wage war with them and you may besiege them.[43]

Thus the Bible clearly sets out the obligation to seek peace as a prelude to any military activity; absent the seeking of peace, the use of force in a war violates Jewish law. Although unstated in the text, it is apparent that while one need not engage in negotiations over the legitimacy of one's goals, one must explain what one is seeking through this military action and what military goals are (and are not) sought.[44] Before this seeking of peace, battle is prohibited. Rabbi Jesse Hagalili is quoted as stating, "How meritorious is peace? Even in a time of war one must initiate all activities with a request for peace."[45] This procedural requirement is quite significant: It prevents the escalation of hostilities and allows both sides to plan rationally the cost of war and the virtues of peace.

Rabbi Shlomo Yitzchaki (Rashi), in his commentary on the Bible, indicates that the obligation to seek peace prior to firing the first shot is limited to authorized wars. However, in obligatory or compulsory wars there is no obligation to seek a peaceful solution. Indeed, such a position can be found in the Sifri, one of the oldest of the midrashic source books of Jewish law.[46] Maimonides, in his classic code of Jewish law, disagrees:

> One does not wage war with anyone in the world until one seeks peace with him. This is true both of authorized and obligatory wars, as it says [in the Bible] "when you approach a city to wage war, you must first call out for peace." If they respond

positively and accept the seven Noachide commandments, one may not kill any of them and they shall pay tribute. . . .[47]

Thus, according to Maimonides, the obligation to seek peace applies to all circumstances in which war is to be waged. Such an approach is also agreed to in principle by Nachmanides.[48]

It is clear, however, according to both schools of thought, that in authorized wars one must initially seek a negotiated settlement of the cause of the war (although, it is crucial to add, Jewish law does not require that each side compromise its claim so as to reach a peaceful solution).[49] Ancillary to this obligation is the need for the goal of the war to be communicated to one's opponents. One must detail to one's enemies the basic goals of the war and what constitutes a victory in this conflict.[50] This allows one's opponents to evaluate the costs of the war and to seek a rational peace. Peace must be genuinely sought before war may begin.

There is a fundamental secondary dispute present in this obligation. Maimonides requires that the peaceful surrender terms offered must include an acknowledgment of and agreement to follow the seven laws of Noah, which (Jewish law asserts) govern all members of the world and form the basic groundwork for moral behavior;[51] *part and parcel of the peace must be the imposition of ethical values on the defeated society*. Nachmanides does not list that requirement as being necessary for the "peaceful" cessation of hostilities.[52] He indicates that it is the military goals alone which determine whether peace terms are acceptable. According to Nachmanides, Jewish law would compel the "victor" to accept peace terms which included all of the victors' demands except the imposition of ethical values on the defeated society; Maimonides would reject that rule and permit war in these circumstances purely to impose ethical values on a nonethical society.[53]

Most likely, this disagreement is just one facet in the debate between Maimonides and most other authorities as to whether Jewish law requires the imposition of the Noachide code on secular society. Elsewhere in *Laws of Kings*,[54] Maimonides explains that in his opinion there is a general obligation on all (Jews and Gentiles) to compel enforcement of these basic ethical rules, even through force, in all circumstances.[55] Nachmanides disagrees with this conception of the obligation and seems to understand that the obligation to enforce the seven laws is limited to the Gentile rulers of the nation, and is of a totally different scope.[56]

The Civilian, the Siege or Blockade, and Standards of Conduct

The obligation to seek peace, as explained above, applies to battles between armies in which no civilian population is involved. Jewish law requires an additional series of overtures for peace and surrender in situations where the military activity involves attacking cities populated by civilians. Maimonides states:

> Joshua, before he entered the land of Israel sent three letters to its inhabitants. The first one said that those that wish to flee [the oncoming army] should flee. The second one said that those that wish to make peace should make peace. The third letter said that those that want to fight a war should prepare to fight a war.[57]

Nor was the general obligation to warn the civilian population enough to fulfill the obligation: Maimonides codifies a number of specific rules of military ethics, all based on Talmudic sources.

> When one surrounds a city to lay siege to it, it is prohibited to surround it from four sides; only three sides are permissible. One must leave a place for inhabitants to flee for all those who wish to abscond to save their lives.[58]

Nachmanides elaborates on this obligation in a way that clearly explains the moral obligation:

> God commanded us that when we lay siege to a city that we leave one of the sides without a siege so as to give them a place to flee to. *It is from this commandment that we learn to deal with compassion even with our enemies even at time of war*; in addition by giving our enemies a place to flee to, they will not charge at us with as much force.[59]

Nachmanides believes that this obligation is so basic as to require that it be one of the 613 basic biblical commandments in Jewish law. However, Nachmanides clearly limits this ethical obligation to authorized and not obligatory wars, and this is agreed to by most other authorities.[60]

Essentially, Jewish law completely rejects the notion of a "siege" as that term is understood by military tacticians and modern articulators of international law. Modern international law generally assumes that in a situation where "the commander of a besieged place expel[s] the noncombatants, in order to lessen the number of those who consume his stock of provisions, it is lawful, though an extreme measure, to drive them back so as to hasten the surrender."[61] Secular law and morals allow the use of civilians as pawns in the siege. *The Jewish tradition prohibited that and mandated that noncombatants who wished to flee must be allowed to flee the scene of the battle.* I would add, however, that I do not understand Maimonides' words literally. It is not surrounding the city on all four sides that is prohibited; rather, it is the preventing of the *outflow of civilians or soldiers* who are seeking to flee. Of course, Jewish law would allow one to stop the *inflow of supplies* to a besieged city through this fourth side.[62]

This approach solves another difficult problem according to Jewish law: the role of the "innocent" civilian in combat. Since the Jewish tradition accepts that civilians (and soldiers who are surrendering) are always entitled to flee from the scene of the battle, it would logically follow that all who remain voluntarily are classified as combatants, since the opportunity to leave is continuously present. Particularly in combination with Joshua's practice of sending letters of warning in advance of combat, this legal approach greatly limits the role of the doctrine of "innocent civilian" in the Jewish tradition. Essentially, the Jewish tradition feels that innocent civilians should do their very best to remove themselves from the battlefield and that those who remain are not so innocent. If one voluntarily stays in a city that is under siege, one has the status of a combatant.[63]

The unintentional and undesirable killing of involuntarily remaining innocent civilians seems to me to be the one "killing" activity permissible in Jewish law in war situations that would not be permissible in the pursuer/self-defense situations. Just as Jewish law permits one to send one's own soldiers into combat (without their consent), possibly to be killed, Jewish law would allow the unintentional killing of innocent civilians as a necessary (but undesired) by-product of the moral license of war.[64]

The Jewish tradition mandated a number of other rules so as to prevent certain types of tactics that violated the norms of ethical behavior even in war. Maimonides recounts that it is prohibited to remove fruit trees so as to induce suffering, famine, and unnecessary waste in the camp of the enemy and this is accepted as normative in Jewish law.[65] Maimonides, in his *Book of Commandments*,[66] explicitly links this to the deliberate intention to expose the enemy to undue suffering. Nachmanides adds that the removal of all trees is permissible if needed for the building of fortifications: It is only when it is done deliberately to induce suffering that it is prohibited. Nachmanides too, however, understands the Jewish tradition as requiring one to have mercy on one's enemy as one would have mercy on one's own and not to engage in unduly cruel activity.[67] Even the greatest of scourges—rape of the enemy female civilian population—was regulated under Jewish law.[68]

A Note on Nuclear War and Jewish Law

The use of nuclear weapons as weapons of mass destruction is very problematic in Jewish law. In a situation of mutually assured destruction if nuclear weapons were used, it is clear that the Jewish tradition would prohibit the actual use of such weapons if such weapons were to cause the large-scale destruction of human life on the earth as it currently exists. The Talmud[69] explicitly prohibits the waging of war in a situation where the casualty rate exceeds a sixth of the population. Lord Jakobovits, in an article written more than thirty years ago, summarized the Jewish law on this topic in his eloquent manner:

> In view of this vital limitation of the law of self-defense, it would appear that a defensive war likely to endanger the survival of the attacking and the defending nations alike, if not indeed the entire human race, can never be justified. On this assumption, then, that the choice posed by a threatened nuclear attack would be either complete destruction or surrender, only the second may be morally vindicated.[70]

However, one caveat is needed: It is permissible to threaten to adopt a military strategy that is in fact prohibited in order to deter a war. While one injustice cannot ever justify another injustice, sometimes threatening to do a wrong can prevent the initial wrong from occurring. *Just because one cannot pull the nuclear trigger does not mean that one cannot own a nuclear gun.*[71] It is important to understand the logical syllogism that permits this conduct. It is prohibited—because of the prohibition to lie—to threaten to use a weapon that one is prohibited from actually using. However, it can be clearly demonstrated that lying to save the life of an innocent person is permissible.[72] Thus, this lie becomes legally justifiable to save one's own life too. An example proves this point: If a person desired to kill an innocent person and one could not prevent this act by killing the potential murderer, one could threaten this person by saying, "If you kill this innocent person, I will kill your children." While, of course, one could not carry out that threat in response to the murder, the threat itself would be a permissible deterrence because lying to avoid a murder is permissible. Thus, this demonstrates that threatening to do that which one cannot actually do is permissible to save a life. The possession of nuclear weapons is simply an amplification of this logical analysis.

Overemphasis on the minor prohibition against telling an untruth at the expense of letting a person die is an example of an ethical valuation that is completely contrary to the Jewish ethical norm. In general, the underemphasis of the biblical ethical mandate "not to stand by while one's neighbor's blood is shed" is the hallmark of those who adopt a system of pacifistic ethics and explains why such an ethical direction is contrary to Jewish law. If one could save a life by telling a lie, such a lie would be mandatory in Jewish ethics.

The use of tactical nuclear weapons designed solely to be used on the field of battle,[73] in circumstances in which the complete destruction of the combatants would be permissible (such as after the proper warning had been given and peace seeking tried), would be acceptable.

Summary

There clearly is a license to wage certain kinds of war and to kill certain people in the Jewish tradition. However, in order to exercise this license, one must first seek peace; this peace must be sought prior to declaring war, prior to waging a battle, and prior to laying a siege. While war permits killing, it permits the intentional killing only of combatants. Innocent people must be given every opportunity to remove themselves from the field of combat.

FIGHTING ON THE SAME TEAM: ETHICS WITHIN THE ARMY

Judaism not only mandated a particular type of ethical behavior towards one's enemies, but compelled one to adopt certain rules of conduct towards one's own soldiers as well. The Bible explicitly addresses the question of who shall be compelled to fight in a war. It states:

> And when you approach the time for battle, the priest shall approach and speak to the people. He should say to them, "Listen Israel, today you are approaching war with your enemies; do not be faint in heart; do not be fearful and do not be alarmed; do not be frightened of them. Because God, your God, is going with you to battle your enemies and to save you." And the officers shall say to the people, "Who is the person who has built a house and not yet dedicated it? He should return to his house lest he die in battle and another dedicate it. Who is the person who has planted a vineyard and never used the fruit? He should leave and return lest he die in battle and another use the fruit. Who is the person who is engaged to a woman and has not married her? He should leave and return home lest he die in battle and another marry her." *And the officers should add to this saying, "Who is the person who is scared and frightened in his heart? He should leave and return lest his neighbor's heart grow weak as his has."*[74]

Two distinctly different exemptions are present in the Bible. The first is that of a person whose death will cause a clear incompleteness in an impending life-cycle event. The second is a person whose conduct may be deleterious to the morale of the army as a whole. While the position of Maimonides is unclear, Ravad immediately notes that these two categories of exemptions are different in purpose and application.[75] Ravad states that the exemptions relating to impending life-cycle events apply only to an authorized war; in an obligatory war all must fight. However, he states that it is possible that the exemption for one who is fearful would apply even to an obligatory war.[76]

The Talmud[77] explains this exemption in two different ways. Rabbi Akiva states that this refers to a person who is lacking the moral courage to do battle and to see combat and watch people perish. Rabbi Yosi asserts that it relates to a person whose personal actions have been sinful (and who is thus afraid that in wartime he will be punished for his sins).[78] Most authorities maintain that one who is fearful of war to such a degree that he qualifies for such an exemption is compelled to take this deferral—it is not optional;[79] Jewish law *prohibits* one who is of such character from fighting.[80] While one could claim that this type of exemption is a form of selective conscientious objection, such an understanding of the law would be in error. A person who "objects" is not given an exemption; certainly a person who is physically and psychologically capable—but who merely objects to this particular war—can be compelled to fight. It is only a form of psychological unfitness that earns one this type of exemption.

In addition to the question of who serves, Jewish law mandated certain ethical norms on the battlefield so as to ensure certain moral behavior. For example, the Bible requires, and this is quoted in the Talmud and codes, that basic sanitary rules be observed in military encampments.[81]

PEACE TREATIES

The book of Joshua (9:3–12) recounts the story of the first treaty the Jewish nation entered into as follows:

> The people of Givon [who live in Israel] heard what Joshua did to Jericho and to Ai [they were destroyed]. And they worked with trickery and they made themselves to look like ambassadors . . . . And they went to Joshua at Gilgal and said to him, and to all the people of Israel, "We have come from a far land; make a treaty with us." . . . And they said to Joshua, "We are your servants." He said to them, "Who are you and where do you come from?" They replied "From a very far away land. . . ." And Joshua [and the Jews] made peace with them and he signed a treaty with them which was sworn on [ratified by] the presidents of the tribes. And it was at the end of three days after the treaty was signed that the Jewish nation heard that the Givonites were neighbors and lived nearby. The people of Israel traveled and came to their cities on the third day. . . . And the Jews did not attack them since the presidents of the tribes had ratified [the treaty]—in the name of God, the God of Israel. The Jews complained to the presidents of the tribes. The presidents replied, "We swore [not to attack them] by the name of the God of Israel and thus we cannot touch them."

Even though the treaty was entered into under fraudulent pretenses, the Jewish people maintained that the treaty was morally binding on them. Indeed, Maimonides, basing himself almost exclusively on just this incident, codifies the rules of treaty as follows:

> It is prohibited to lie [or breach] in treaties and it is prohibited to make them [the defeated nation] suffer after they have settled and accepted the seven commandments.[82]

Rabbi David Ibn Zimra (Radvaz) in his commentary on Maimonides explains that "this is learned from the incident of the Givonim since breaking one's treaties is a profanation of God's name."[83] According to this rationale, the reason the Jewish nation felt compelled to honor its treaty with the Givonim—a treaty that at the very least was entered into under fraudulent circumstances—was that *others would not grasp the full circumstances under which the treaty was signed, and would have interpreted the breach of the treaty as a sign of moral laxity on the part of the Jewish people.* One could argue, based on this rationale, that in circumstances where the breach of a treaty would be considered reasonable by others, it would be permissible to break it.[84]

Rabbi Levi ben Gershon (Ralbag) understands the nature of the obligation to observe treaties differently; he claims that the reason the treaty with the Givonim had to be honored was that the Jewish nation "swore" to observe its obligation, and if it did not do so, the nations of the world would think that the Jewish people do not believe in a God and thus do not take their promises seriously.[85]

Rabbi David ben Kimchi (Radak) advances an even more radical understanding of the nature of the obligation. Among the possible reasons he advances to explain why the treaty was honored—even though it was a void treaty because it was entered into solely on the basis of the fraudulent assurances of the Givonim—was because others would not be aware that the treaty was really void and would (incorrectly) identify the Jewish nation as the breaker of the treaty. This fear, that the Jewish nation would be incorrectly identified as a treaty breaker, he states, is enough to require that the Jewish nation keep all treaties duly entered into.[86]

Each of these theories, whatever the obligation to keep treaties is based on, presupposes that treaties are basically binding according to Jewish law. It is only in the case of a visibly obvious breach of the treaty by one party that the second party may decline to honor the treaty. Thus, Jewish law accepts that when the war is over, the peace that is agreed to is binding. Indeed, even in a situation where there is some unnoticed fraud in its enactment or ratification, it is still binding.

PACIFISM AND QUIETISM

Individual Pacifism

Difficult as it is in our society today to take a stand against pacifism as a social or individual moral philosophy, it is clear that the Jewish tradition does not favor pacifism as a value superior to all other values or incorporate it as a basic moral doctrine within Judaism. Judaism clearly has accepted a practical form of pacifism as appropriate in the "right" circumstances. For example, the Talmud recounts that in response to the persecutions of the second century (C.E.), the Jewish people agreed (literally: took an oath) to adopt pacifism in the process of seeking political independence or autonomy for the Jewish state.[87] This action is explained by noting that frequently pacifism is the best response to total political defeat; only through the complete abjuring of the right to use force can survival be ensured. So too, the phenomenon of martyrdom, even the extreme example of killing one's own children rather than allowing them to be converted out of the faith,[88] represents a form of pacifism in the face of violence.[89] However, it is impossible to assert that a pacifistic response is based on a deeply rooted Jewish tradition to abstain from violence even in response to violence. It is true that there was a tradition rejecting a violent response to anti-Semitism and pogrom; yet it is equally clear that that tradition was based on the futility of such a response rather than on its moral impropriety. Even a casual survey of the Jewish law material on the appropriateness of a violent response to violence leads one to conclude that neither Jewish law nor rabbinic ethics frowned on violence in all circumstances as a response to violence.[90]

Three examples prove this point. Jewish law commands (compels) one to save the life of one who is being murdered even if it is necessary to do so at the expense of the life of the murderer; the Talmud commands that one should have no mercy on the murderer and should take his life if need be—indeed this is true even if the murderer could not be punished by a court for his crime after the fact (for example, if the murderer were a minor).[91] So too, Jewish law recounts that if one sees two individuals fighting in circumstances in which one could hurt the other, Jewish law allows the use of force to separate the two combatants. In circumstances where force is the only means to separate the combatants, force is mandatory.[92] As is noted by Rabbi Joshua Falk-Cohen (Sema) and others, this rule encompasses two different moral duties. The first is to help one who is being attacked; the second is to separate a person from sin; *the use of force to hurt a person is wrong, but Jewish law sanctions the use of force to prevent another from using force improperly*. A clearer rejection of the philosophy of pacifism is not possible. Indeed, one who examines even the ritual area of the law discovers that the use of violence in the service of that which is right is sanctioned. Thus, *Shulchan Aruch*[93] mandates the use of force on the Sabbath in response to the threat of invasion of the Jewish community. It is simply untenable to claim that as a matter of theoretical ethical duty Jewish law perceives pacifism as the ideal response to evil in all circumstances.[94] But it is crucial to emphasize that the Jewish tradition does not reject pacifism as a practical response to immorality or evil. Rather, tactical pacifism has a place as the clearly superior alternative to cooperating with evil or perhaps even actively trying to separate one from evil and failing.

There is one element of pacifism that is clearly found in the Jewish tradition: the minimization of violence. In nearly all situations where Jewish law allows violence to prevent an evil from occurring, it mandates that the minimal amount of violence be used to accomplish one's goal. Thus, if one can stop a murderer from committing his crime without the use of deadly force, deadly force is prohibited;[95] if one can separate combatants without using physical force, nonviolent means are certainly preferred.[96] Judaism accepted that it is best not to use violence, and looked upon violence as the last resort, but when no other action would suffice, violence was morally acceptable and typically mandatory.

Societal Pacifism

The question of societal, rather than individual, pacifism is a much more complex topic in Jewish law. As demonstrated elsewhere in this paper, Judaism does not require that society go to war in all circumstances in which war is permissible. The decision as to whether or not to wage war is a societal burden, a judgment made by those who are part of the society who will suffer the consequences of waging the war. In response to a belligerent action, in situations where war is authorized rather than obligatory, *society has the right to adopt a pacifistic stance and decline to wage war (or to wage some kind of limited war).* In that sense, a society could adopt a generally pacifistic response to aggression and decline to exercise its right to respond to every aggression. That form of societal pacifism is permitted according to Jewish law. Even in that situation, these considerations are limited to cases of authorized war.[97]

Rabbi Maurice Lamm in his excellent seminal essay on pacifism and selective conscientious objection in the Jewish tradition concludes by stating:[98]

> It must be affirmed that Judaism rejected total pacifism, but that it believed strongly in pragmatic pacifism as a higher morally more noteworthy religious position. Nonetheless, this selective pacifism is only a public, national decision, and not a personal one.

Rabbi Lamm's essay demonstrates what is obvious to all students of Jewish law and ethics: *Theological pacifism has no place in the Jewish tradition.*

An individual's "selective conscientious objection" can be justified in the Jewish tradition as a response to an *unjust* war. Frequently societies will embrace a military policy directly contrary to the Jewish tradition as to when a war is permissible. Jewish citizens in that society are faced with a dilemma as to their own conduct: Should they fight in an unjust war? Should they publicly oppose the war (and risk societal scorn and perhaps a rise in anti-Semitism), or should they simply find a way to avoid fighting? A number of solutions have been addressed to this question, which forces an individual to weigh the consequences to Jews in one's country with the biblical commandment not to kill and not to stand by when others are killed. A number of solutions to this dilemma have been advanced in Jewish law, and there is no reason why selective conscientious objection should not be acceptable in a society that allows one to declare such a status and avoid military service in that manner. Second, pragmatic pacifism is a moral value in the Jewish tradition, but in my opinion, it is only a value of significance in situations where active (physical) removal of the impropriety is not possible.

One may not, under any circumstances, kill an innocent person to save one's own life; however, one *may* (but need not) be silent in the face of the killing of an innocent person by another if that murderer will seriously punish or kill one in retaliation for protesting. Historically, Jews in the Diaspora have sometimes been persecuted when they were involved in political opposition to a governmental policy. While Jewish law prohibits murder no matter what the consequences, Jewish law does not require that one do whatever one can, no matter what the consequences, to save the life of another. Indeed, as has been noted elsewhere, the obligation to save the life of another is perhaps suspended in the face of very significant financial consequences.[99] Absent an anti-Semitic taint, certainly it is suspended in the face of significant physical duress.[100]

Quietism

Evaluated from the Jewish perspective, quietism[101] as a moral philosophy suffers from all the failures of pacifism and then some. While without a doubt some aspects of this philosophy can be found in modern Hasidic doctrine,[102] the abrogation of responsibility for one's physical actions, the lack of moral responsibility towards other individuals in the world, and the tendency in quietism towards sexual promiscuity[103] can only lead a reasonable person to conclude that it is not a doctrine of any significance in the Jewish ethic.[104] Much of the doctrinal basis of quietism presupposes the lack of religious value of the routine rituals of prayer and penitence, whereas such doctrines are essential to Judaism. As a complement to ritual, the doctrines as incorporated in Hasidism have some basis in Jewish ethics; in contrast or opposition to religious ritual, it has no place.

CONCLUSION

When one reviews the rules found within Jewish law for waging war, one grasps a crucial reality of Jewish military ethics. The moral license that "war" grants a person or a country varies from situation to situation and event to event. The Jewish tradition treats different permissible wars differently. The battle for vital economic needs carries with it much less moral license than the war waged to prevent an aggressive enemy from conquering an innocent nation. Jewish law recognized that some wars are completely immoral, that some wars are morally permissible but accompanied by a very limited license to kill, and that some wars are a basic battle for good with an enemy that is evil. Each of these situations comes with a different moral response and a different right to wage war. In sum, it is crucially important to examine the justice of every cause. However, violence in the service of justice is not to be abhorred within the Jewish tradition.

NOTES

1. Leviticus Rabba, Tzav §9.
2. For a brief review of the methodology, structure, and history of Jewish law, see David Feldman, "The Structure of Jewish Law," *Contemporary Jewish Ethics*, ed. Menachem Kellner (New York: Hebrew, 1978), pp. 21–38.
3. For an example of this type of discussion, see our manuscript in preparation, M. Broyde and M. Hecht, "The Return of Lost Property in the Jewish and Common Law: A Comparison."
4. Should the country's military activities be deemed a violation of Jewish law, Jewish law would prohibit one from vitally assisting the host country in its military activity and certainly would prohibit serving in its armed forces and killing soldiers who are members of the opposing army. For precisely such a determination in the context of the Vietnam War, see David Novak, "A Jewish View of War" in *Law and Theology in Judaism* 1 (1974): 125–35. I do *not* intend to directly relate any of the arguments advanced in this article to any particular military activity of any particular government.
5. *B.T. Sanhedrin* 74a–b.
6. *Shulchan Aruch, Choshen Mishput* 425.
7. Rabbi Joseph Babad, *Minchat Hinuch, Aseh* 296.
8. *B.T. Sanhedrin* 72b.
9. Since it was stated twice in the Bible, once before and once after the giving of the Bible to the Jews.
10. Commenting on *B.T. Sanhedrin* 72b.
11. See Rabbi Shlomo Yosef Zevin, *Le-Or ha-Halacha*, 2d ed. (Jerusalem: Beit Hillel, 1978), pp. 150–57.
12. Literally, *bah ba-machteret*; according to Jewish law, one who robs houses presumably will kill the owner of the house if interrupted. Thus the owner of the house may kill the robber during the burglary.
13. For a summary of the discourse on this point, see R. Yehuda Shaviv, *Betzer Eviezer* (Jerusalem: Zomet, 1990), pp. 96–99, who appears to conclude that most authorities are in agreement with Rabbi Zevin's ruling; see also R. Yitzchak Schmelks, *Bet Yitzchak, Yoreh De'ah* 1:162 and Novella of R. Chaim Soloveitchik on Maimonides, *Rotzach* 1:9. For an excellent article on this topic and on the general status of preemptive war in Jewish law, see Rabbi J. David Bleich, "Preemptive War in Jewish Law," *Contemporary Halakhic Problems* (New York: Ktav, 1977–89) 3:251.
14. What precisely these restrictions are will explained below, pp. 7–8.
15. *Ha'Emek Davar*, Gen. 9:5.
16. Literally *"m'yad ish echiv."*

17. Tosaphot *Shavuot* 35b, "Going to an authorized war." *Maharal Mi-Prague*, in his commentary on Genesis 32, also states that war is permitted under Noachide law. He claims that this is the justification for the actions of Shimon and Levi in the massacre of the people of Shechem. Furthermore, under this analysis even preemptive action, like the kind taken by Shimon and Levi, would be permitted. He at least implies that the killing of civilians who are not liable under the pursuer rationale is permissible; see also R. Shlomo Goren, "Combat Morality and the Halacha," *Crossroads* 1 (1988): 211; [published by Zomet in Jerusalem].

18. Rabbi Moshe Schreiber, *Chatam Sofer, Yoreh De'ah* 1:19.

19. See, e.g., Rabbi Abraham Kahana-Shapiro, *Devar Avraham* 1:11; Rabbi Menachem Zemba, *Zera Avraham* 24. The issue of selling weapons to Gentile nations is addressed in an essay of Rabbi J. David Bleich, "Arms Sales," in *Contemporary Halakhic Problems* 3:10–13. In this essay it is demonstrated that the consensus opinion within Jewish law permits the sale of arms to governments that typically use these weapons to protect themselves from bandits.

20. For reasons beyond the scope of this article, Jewish law did not historically develop a complete system of regulations relating to how Jewish law governs Gentiles. For many years this was perceived to be mainly a theoretical discussion, as Jewish law and ethics were not truly part of the Judeo-Christian ethic of Western culture; see, e.g., Rabbi Yecheil Michael Epstein, *Aruch ha-Shulchan he-'Atid*, who wrote two different works: *Aruch ha-Shulchan*, a standard code of Jewish law, and *Aruch ha-Shulchan he-'Atid*, a code of Jewish law for the future, which contained those areas of law not practical in his opinion; the laws of war are in the second work.

21. *B.T. Sotah* 44b.

22. The word *reshut* is sometimes translated as "permitted"; this is not correct, for reasons to be explained below. Rabbi J. Karo, in *Kesef Mishneh* (Kings 6:1), further divides the category of "obligatory" into two categories: "compulsory" and "commanded." Thus some modern commentaries divide the types of war into three. While this division is not incorrect, the legal differences between "commanded" and "compulsory" wars are not very significant, and it is for this reason that the Mishnah, Maimonides, and this article will continue to use that bifurcation rather than any other type of division. *Betzer Eveizer*, at 84, notes that the Talmud implicitly creates one other category of war, an illegal war. See note 4 above and note 39 below for a discussion of the ramifications of concluding that a war is illegal.

23. Or perhaps "compulsory" wars, according to those who accept a trifurcation of the categories; see note 22 above.

24. As explained above, Jewish ethics clearly distinguishes between the different categories of war. An obligatory war requires a different mode of ethical conduct from all other types of war. Particularly when discussing the obligation in the time of Joshua to conquer the land of Israel for the first time and the generic biblical obligation to destroy Amalek, Jewish law mandates a different set of ethical norms for these historical obligations. Thus Maimonides states: "It is a positive commandment to vanquish the seven nations [that used to occupy Israel] since it says 'you shall vanquish them.' Anyone who has one of the members of that nation subservient to him and does not kill him violates the negative commandment, since it says 'no life shall survive [from the seven nations].' *Their identity has since disappeared.*" So too, Maimonides, basing himself on a Talmudic source, states that in the wars against Amon and Moab, Jewish law forbids the Jewish people from initiating peace discussions with them, although if they initiate such discussions Jewish law allows one to reciprocate (*Laws of Kings* 6:6; similar sentiments can be found in *Yerayim Mitzvah* 250). Rabbi Joseph Karo, writing in the *Kesef Mishneh*, disagrees, stating that it is inappropriate to accept overtures of peace even when they are initiated by Amon and Moab. Unlike the Jewish law's rules concerning "regular" war, these rules are not based on normative ethical values, but were designed to be used solely in the initial period of the Jewish conquest of the land of Israel or solely in circumstances where God's direct divine commandment to the Jewish nation was clear. Thus, for example, Rabbi David Kimchi (Radak) notes that the primary sin of the Jews in the incident of the Givonim was that they had clear means of seeking God's counsel on what to do, and yet they chose not to seek his assistance; see, generally, Rabbi Eliezer Berkovits, *Not in Heaven: The Nature and Function of Halakha* (New York: Ktav, 1983), for a discussion of the role of the divine in Jewish law. Thus, "Jewish law" as used in this article refers to that time period when direct, visible divine interaction in the world ceases; it is methodologically improper to compare Jewish ethics in the presence of the active divine with any other system of ethics, since the active (acknowledged) presence of the divine changes the ground rules for ethical norms. Normative Jewish law confines itself to a discussion of what to do when the active divine presence is no longer in the world, and thus normative rules are in effect. This distinction, and the distinction between Old Testament Judaism and modern Jewish law, has been lost to some commentators; see, e.g., B. Roberts, "Note: Judaic Sources of and Views on the Laws of War," *Naval Law Review* 37 (1988): 221.

25. *B.T. Sotah* 44b.

26. The Talmud additionally recounts that there are three ritual requirements for an authorized war to commence. The first is the consent of the Sanhedrin (Parliament); see *B.T. Sanhedrin* 29b. The second is the presence of a king or ruler; see *B.T. Sanhedrin* 20a. The third is consultation with the *urim ve-tumim*, a mystical ornament worn by the High Priest (not in existence for more than 3,000 years); see *B.T. Sanhedrin* 16b. (For an explanation of what this garment is, see Maimonides, *Kelei Mikdash*, 8:1–6.) A number of commentators significantly limit each of these three Talmudic requirements. Maimonides does not list the requirement of *urim ve-tumim* at all in his code. He does, however, state elsewhere (see *Book of Commandments*, chap. 14) that the *urim ve-tumim* are needed. So too, *Aruch ha-Shulchan he-'Atid, Melachim* 74:7 states that the *Urim* are not needed and this is confirmed by R. Zevin, *Le-Or ha-Halacha*, p. 12. Nachmanides states (see Addendum to *Maimonides, Book of Commandments*, positive commandment 4) that a king is not actually needed. Rather war may be undertaken by "a king, judge, or whoever exercises jurisdiction over the people." Menachem ben Meiri argues that approval of the Sanhedrin is needed only if a significant minority of the nation does not approve of the war. However, he states that no approval is needed for popularly supported wars; see *B.T. Sanhedrin* 16a. The details of the ritual requirements for such a war are beyond the scope of this paper; see, generally, Bleich, note 13 above, and Zevin, note 11 above.

27. Maimonides, *Hilchot Melachim*, 5:1.

28. "War to diminish."

29. It is worth noting that Christian ethics developed a similar dichotomy between types of war: "Augustine and the other later Christian (Catholic and Protestant) writers recognized another type of war not recognized by Greek and Roman law. This was the concept of the Holy War. That is, a war in which God himself called His people to fight. In such a war, ruthlessness was the norm. . . . In just wars God's express will could not be so clearly discerned, so restraint was required." Roberts, "Judaic Sources," 221. However, the "failure" of Christian ethics occurred when this category was expanded beyond the small number of specified holy wars. "Later Christian writers maintained that the Church could 'take the part earlier played by God in commanding wars for the faith and directing Christians to battle against the Church's enemies. . . . ' It was argued that the Pope, as God's earthly representative, had the authority that, in the Old Testament, God wielded by His own hand. Hence, the justification and rationale for putting all heretics, pagans, and infidels to the sword. Christians were not only permitted to fight, they were commanded to by God's messenger, the Pope." Ibid. Jewish law never greatly expanded the category of compulsory war; Christian ethics might have had no choice, because it had no doctrine of authorized wars.

30. See Maimonides' commentary to the Mishnah, *B.T. Sotah* 8:7. Maimonides' commentary to the Mishnah was originally written in Arabic. This is the most common translation and is found in numerous reprints of the *Babylonian Talmud*.

31. See translation of J. Kapach, *Mishnah Sotah* 8:7. This is generally considered the better translation.

32. Commenting on Maimonides, Rabbi David Frankel, in *Korban Ha'Edah* (in his addendum, *Shiurei Korban*, to the Jerusalem Talmud, 8:10), has a slightly narrower definition, which is very similar to diBoton's. An authorized war may be undertaken: "against neighbors in the fear that with the passage of time they will wage war. Thus, Israel may attack them in order to destroy them." Thus, an authorized war is permitted as a preemptive attack against militaristic neighbors. However, war cannot occur without evidence of bellicose activity.

33. See Rabbi Abraham Isaiah Karlitz, *Chazon Ish, Mo'ed* 114:2. He writes, "they kill Israel intermittently, but do not engage in battle." Rabbi Menachem ben Meiri, in his commentary on the Talmud (*B.T. Sotah* 43b), states that an authorized war is any attack that is commenced in order to prevent an attack in the future. Once hostilities begin, all military activity falls under the rubric of obligatory.

34. Rabbi Yecheil Michael Epstein, *Aruch ha-Shulchan he-'Atid,* advances a unique explanation. He writes that the only difference between an authorized and an obligatory war is the status of those people exempt from being drafted—those people mentioned in Deuteronomy 20:5. In an obligatory war, even those people must fight. However, he writes, the king is obligated to defend Israel "even when there is only suspicion that they may attack us"; see *Laws of Kings,* 74:3–4. Thus the position he takes is that vis-à-vis the government there is only a slight difference between authorized and obligatory wars—the pool of draftable candidates.

35. See pages 4–5 for the various opinions on what is belligerent.

36. In addition, the varying types of wars are flexible, not rigid. Armed aggression can begin as being permissible because of "pursuer" and then, owing to a massive unwarranted counterattack by the enemy, can turn into an obligatory war; after the battlefield has stabilized, the war can become an authorized war.

37. See Rabbi Joseph Karo, *Beit Yosef, Choshen Mishpat* 425:6–7 (uncensored version, available in the Yeshiva University Library).

38. How one categorizes each individual conflict can sometimes be a judgment about which reasonable scholars of Jewish law might differ; that does not, however, mean that such decisions are purely a function of individual choice. As with all such matters in Jewish law, there is a manner and matter for resolving such disagreements. For further discussion of this issue, see *Shulchan Aruch, Yoreh De'ah* 242 and commentaries *ad locum.*

39. And prohibited wars. Perhaps the most pressing ethical dilemma is what to do when society is waging a prohibited war and severely penalizes (perhaps even executes) citizens who do not cooperate with the war effort. This question is beyond the scope of this paper, as the primary focus of such a paper would be the ethical liberalities one may take to protect one's own life, limb, or property in times of great duress; see, e.g., R. Mordecai Winkler, *Levushai Mordechai* 2:174 (permitting Sabbath violation to avoid fighting in unjust wars); but see also R. Meir Eisenstadt, *Imrai Eish, Yoreh De'ah* 52.

40. The question of who is "innocent" in this context is difficult to quantify precisely. One can be a pursuer in situations where the law does not label one a "murderer" in Jewish law; thus both a minor (*B.T. Sanhedrin* 74b) and, according to most authorities, an unintentional murderer may be killed to prevent the loss of life of another. So too, it would appear reasonable to conclude from Maimonides' rule that one who directs the murder, even though he does not directly participate in it, is a murderer and may be killed. So too, it appears that those who assist in the murder, even if they are not actually participating in it directly, are not "innocent"; see comments of *Maharal Mi-Prague* on Genesis 32. From this *Maharal* one could conclude that any who encourage this activity fall under the rubric of combatants. Thus, typically all soldiers would be defined as "combatants." It would appear difficult, however, to define "combatant" as opposed to "innocent" in all combat situations; each military activity requires its own assessment of what is needed to wage this war and what is not. (For example, sometimes the role of medical personnel is to repair injured troops so that they can return to the front as soon as possible, and sometimes medical personnel's role is to heal soldiers who are returning home so as to allow these soldiers a normal civilian life.)

41. These rules are generic rules of Jewish law derived from different Talmudic sources and methodologically unrelated to war as an institution. For a discussion of these rules generally and various applications of them, see Rabbi Joseph Karo, *Shulchan Aruch, Choshen Mishpat* 425 (and commentaries). In addition, Jacob ben Asher, *Tur, Choshen Mishpat* 425, contains many crucial insights into the law (however, the standard text of this section of the text has been heavily censored, and is not nearly as valuable a reference as the less widely available uncensored version).

42. See pp. 1–2.

43. Deut. 20:10.

44. See, e.g., Num. 21:21–24, where the Jewish people clearly promised to limit their goals in return for a peaceful passage through the lands belonging to Sichon.

45. Leviticus Rabba, Tzav §9.

46. Commenting on Deut. 20:10. One could distinguish in this context between obligatory wars and commanded wars in this regard, and limit the license only to wars that are obligatory. It would appear that such a position is also accepted by Ravad; see Rabbi Abraham ben David (Ravad), *Commentary on Laws of Kings* 6:1, and Meir Leibush Malbim, *Commentary on Deuteronomy* 20:10.

47. Maimonides, *Laws of Kings* 6:1.

48. See his commentary on Deut. 20:10.

49. I would, however, note that such is clearly permissible as a function of prudent planning. Thus, the Jewish nation offered to avoid an authorized war with Emor if that nation would agree to a lesser violation of its sovereignty; see Num. 21:21.

50. Of course, there is no obligation to do so with specificity as to battle plans; however, a clear assertion of the goals of the war is needed.

51. *Laws of Kings* 6:1. These seven commandments are: acknowledging God; prohibiting idol worship; prohibition of murder; prohibition of theft; prohibition of incest and adultery; prohibition of eating the flesh of still living animals; and the obligation to enforce these (and perhaps other) laws. For a discussion of these laws in context, see *Aruch ha-Shulchan he-'Atid, Laws of Kings* 78–80.

52. Nachmanides, *Commentary on Deuteronomy* 20:10. Of course, if after the surrender, a Jewish government were to rule that society, such a government would enforce these seven laws; however, it is not a condition of surrender according to Nachmanides.

53. Maimonides, *Laws of Kings* 6:4.

54. *Laws of Kings* 8:1–5.

55. See also *Laws of Kings* 14:14 for a similar sentiment by Maimonides.

56. For a general discussion of this, see R. Yehudah Gershuni, *Mishpatei Melucha*, 2d ed. (Jerusalem, 1982), 165–67. It is worth noting that a strong claim can be made that the *Tosaphot* agrees with Nachmanides in this area; See *Tosaphot, B.T. Avoda Zara* 26b.

57. *Laws of Kings* 6:5. Maimonides understands the Jerusalem Talmud's discussion of this topic to require three different letters. If one examines Shevit 6:1 closely, one could conclude that one can send only one letter with all three texts; see *Aruch ha-Shulchan, Laws of Kings* 75:6–7.

58. Maimonides, *Laws of Kings* 6:7.

59. Supplement of Nachmanides to *Maimonides' Book of Commandments,* Positive Commandment 4.

60. Ibid. See also R. Joseph Babad, *Minchat Hinuch* 527. Rabbi Gershuni indicates that the commandment is limited to compulsory wars, rather than obligatory wars. His insight would seem to be correct; *Mishpatei Melucha* at 165–67. It is only in a situation where total victory is the aim that such conduct is not obligatory.

61. Charles C. Hyde, *International Law* (Boston: Little, Brown, 1922), §656; for an additional article on this topic from the Jewish perspective, see Bradley Artson, "The Siege and the Civilian," *Judaism* 36 (1987): 54–65. A number of the points made by Rabbi Artson are incorporated in this article, although the theme of the purpose of the Jewish tradition in the two articles differs somewhat.

62. See R. Yecheil Epstein, *Aruch ha-Shulchan he-'Atid, Laws of Kings* 76:12.

63. Although I have seen no modern Jewish law authorities who state this, I would apply this rule in modern combat situations to all civilians who remain voluntarily in the locale of the war in a way that facilitates combat. For example, I doubt if anyone who voluntarily remained in Berlin during World War II would be classified as an innocent civilian according to Jewish law.

64. See Rabbi Saul Yisraeli, *Amud Hayemini* 16:5, and R. Joseph Babad, *Minchat Hinuch* 425, who discuss "death" in war in a way that perhaps indicates that this approach is correct. See also Bleich, "Preemptive War," note 13 above, at p. 277, who states: "To this writer's knowledge, there exists no discussion in classical rabbinical sources that takes cognizance of the likelihood of causing civilian casualties in the course of hostilities. . . ." In many ways this provides guidance into the ethical issues associated with a modern air- (and long-range artillery-) based war. Air warfare greatly expands the "kill zone" of combat and (at least in our current state of technology) tends inevitably to result in the deaths of civilians. The tactical aims of air warfare appear to be fourfold: to destroy specific enemy military targets; to destroy the economic base of the enemy's war-making capacity; to randomly terrorize civilian populations; and to retaliate for other atrocities by the enemy on one's own home base and thus to deter such conduct in the future. The first of these goals is within the ambit of that which is permissible, since civilian deaths are unintentional. The same would appear to be true of the second provided that the targets are genuine economically significant targets and are related to the economic base needed to wage the war and provided that civilian deaths are not directly desired. It would appear that the third goal is not legitimate absent the designation of "compulsory" or "obligatory" war. The final goal—retaliation designed to deter—raises a whole series of issues beyond the scope of this article and could perhaps provide some sort of justification for certain types of conduct in combat that would otherwise be prohibited, although its detailed analysis in Jewish law relates to circumstances in which retaliation or specific deterrence might permit what is normally prohibited; see Rabbi Moses Isserless (Rama), *Yoreh De'ah* 334:6 and Rabbi David Helevi (Taz) (*ad locum*) and *Minchat Hinuch* 338.

65. *Laws of Kings* 6:8; see *Betzer Eviezer*, at 120–21.

66. Negative Commandment 57.

67. In his supplement to *Maimonides' Book of Commandments*, Positive Commandment 6.

68. The rules related to sexuality in combat are unique in Jewish law because the Talmud (*Kiddushin* 21b) explicitly states that even that which is permissible was only allowed because of the moral weakness of men in combat. While the details of these regulations are beyond the scope of this paper (see Zevin, *Le-Or ha-Halacha*, pp. 52–54, for a detailed description of these various laws), it is clear that the Bible chose to permit (but discourage) rape in wartime in very narrow situations so as to inject some realistic notion of morality into what would otherwise be a completely immoral situation. The rules explicitly prohibited multiple rapes, encouraged the marrying of such women (in fact, nearly mandated it), and limited the time period when such rape was permitted to the immediate battlefield situation. A number of liberalities in ritual law were also allowed, reflecting the unique aspects of war. Why these particular laws did not apply in wartime, but others did, is a topic beyond the scope of this paper.

69. Shevuot 35b. *Tosaphot* notes that this applies even to a Jewish government fighting an authorized war; see generally, Rabbi J. David Bleich, "Nuclear War," *Tradition* 21 (1984): 84–88, reprinted in *Confronting Omnicide: Jewish Reflections on Weapons of Mass Destruction*, ed. Daniel Landes, (Northvale, N.J.: Jason Aronson, 1991), p. 209.

70. Immanuel Jakobovits, "Nuclear War," *Tradition* 4 (1962): 202, reprinted in *Confronting Omnicide*, p.199. See also Walter Wurzberger, "Nuclear Deterence and Nuclear War," ibid., p. 224, and "Judaic Sources of and Views on the Laws of War," *Naval Law Review* 37 (1988): 221.

71. Rabbi J. David Bleich, "Nuclear War." Although I find this statement logically persuasive, it is difficult to find a clear source in the Jewish tradition that permits one to threaten to do that which is prohibited to do; see, e.g., Rabbi Moses Isserless, *Shulchan Aruch Choshen Mishpat* 28:2.

72. See, e.g., Rabbi Aaron Zakai, *HaBayit ha-Yehudi* 7:3.

73. Assuming that such weapons exist and have the stated limited effect.

74. Deut. 20:2–9.

75. See *Laws of Kings* 7:1–4 and comments of Kessef Mishnah, Rabbi David ibn Zimoe (Radvaz), and Rabbi Abraham diBoton (Lechem Mishnah), *ad locum*, all of whom interpret Maimonides as agreeing with Ravad on this issue. Maimonides in his *Book of Commandments*, commandment 191, appears to adopt the position of Ravad in total.

76. Compare Lechem Mishnah commenting on *Laws of Kings* 7:1–4, and *Aruch ha-Shulchan, Laws of Kings* 76:3 for an analysis of Maimonides' position.

77. *B.T. Sotah* 44a.

78. There is some dispute over how a person would prove his acceptability for any one of these exemptions; see R. Yehudah Gershuni, *Mishpatei Melucha* 169, for a detailed discussion of this issue and Zevin, *Le-Or ha-Halacha*, pp. 31–32.

79. See commentaries on Maimonides, note 78 above.

80. Maimonides accepts the opinion of Rabbi Akiva as normative (*Laws of Kings* 7:3), while *Minchat Hinuch* (526) accepts the opinion of Rabbi Yossi. Most authorities accept Rabbi Akiva's opinion as normative; see *Aruch ha-Shulchan* 76:22, and also *Sha'agat Aryeh he-hadashot* 14:2 for more on this dispute.

81. See *Aruch ha-Shulchan Kings* 75:18.

82. As explained above, it seems to follow that those who argue with Maimonides' requirement of acceptance of the seven Noachide laws would disagree with its application here too; see, e.g., Rabbi Yehuda Gershuni, *Mishpatei Melucha* 173.

83. Such can also be implied from Maimonides' own comments on *Laws of Kings* 6:5.

84. In Judaism, the term *chilul hashem* (desecration of God's name) denotes a prohibition whose parameters are fixed not by objective legal determinations but by the moral values of the observers. This is a very atypical prohibition in the Jewish legal system.

85. Rabbi Levi ben Gershon (Ralbag) commenting on Joshua 9:12.

86. Radak, commenting on Joshua 9:12. This theory would have relevance to a duly entered into treaty that was breached by one side in a nonpublic manner and that the other side now wishes to abandon owing to the private breach of the other side. Radak would state that this is not allowed because most people would think that the second breaker was actually the first one and was not taking the treaty seriously.

87. *B.T. Ketubot* 111a.

88. See, e.g., Prof. H. Soloveitchik, "Religious Law and Change: The Medieval Ashkenazic Example," *AJS Review* 12 (1987): 205–23.

89. See, e.g., *Shulchan Aruch, Yoreh De'ah* 151 for a description of when such conduct is permissible.

90. See, e.g., *Shulchan Aruch, Choshen Mishpat* 421:11 and 425–26, which mandate violence as a response to violence. That is, of course, not to say that pacifism as a tactic is frowned on. Civil disobedience as a tactic to gain sympathy or as a military tactic to resort to in a time of weakness is quite permissible.

91. *B.T. Sanhedrin* 72a.

92. *Shulchan Aruch, Choshen Mishpat* 421:11.

93. *Shulchan Aruch, Orach Chaim* 329:6.

94. However, it is quite clear that there are many circumstances in which violent wrong unquestionably will occur regardless of the Jewish response. In that situation, certainly Jewish law prefers pacifism to assistance in the commission of a wrong. The Jewish response to intentional wrongdoing comes in three forms: 1) stopping the wrong; 2) rebuking the wrongdoer; and 3) declining to assist the wrongdoer. Level one is better than level two and level two is better than level three. For a detailed response on the hierarchical relationship among these three values, see Rabbi Moses Feinstein, *Iggrot Moshe Even Haezer* 4:61(2).

95. Rabbi Jacob ben Asher, *Tur, Choshen Mishpat* 425; Maimonides, *Laws of the Murderer* 1:13.

96. *Shulchan Aruch, Choshen Mishpat* 421:11.

97. Of course there are circumstances in which even obligatory wars need not be fought; however, these circumstances all relate to the inability to triumph rather than to a theological opposition to war.

98. Maurice Lamm, "After the War—Another Look at Pacifism and Selective Conscientious Objection," in *Contemporary Jewish Ethics*, pp. 221–38.

99. See Rabbi A. Cohen, "Privacy: A Jewish Perspective," *Journal of Halacha and Contemporary Society* 1 (1981):84.

100. See *Shulchan Aruch, Yoreh Deah* 157:1–2 and commentaries *ad locum*.

101. Quietism originated as a late-seventeenth-century devotional movement in the Catholic church whose main figure was Miguel Molinos, a priest (d. 1696). Quietism maintained that anyone "can achieve an entirely disinterested insight into God; this insight is permanent, internally undifferentiated and free from images and affects, and it involves á previous destruction of one's own will and consciousness. . . . This state of perfectly passive contemplation is not only the highest form of religious life, but makes other, more specific forms of worship . . . either useless or even harmful insofar as they divert the soul from union with God." See "Quietism" in *Encyclopedia of Religion* (New York: Macmillan, 1987) 12:153–55.

102. See Rebecca Shatz-Uffenheimer, *Hachasidot Kemisticah* (Jerusalem: Manges, 1980), chaps. 2–4 for a description of the various quietistic practices found in modern Hasidism.

103. "[S]exual permissiveness is thus justified. . . .," in "Quietism," *Encyclopedia of Religion*, p. 154.

104. That is not to say that each and every one of its values is without a place in the Jewish tradition. Certainly, as ably demonstrated in *Hachasidot Kimisticah* (see the English preface, pp. vi–vii, for a clear statement of this principle), there are certain overlaps in philosophy between early Hasidism and quietism. However, Hasidism never denied the legal or moral value of Jewish law as quietism denied the value of canon law. So too, Hasidism kept the essential framework of Jewish ritual observance; the same cannot be said of quietism.

The Pursuit of Peace:
A Singular Commandment

RABBI EVERETT GENDLER

> For thus says the Lord,
> Who created the heavens
> (God is God!),
> Who formed the earth and made it
> (God established it);
> God did not create it a chaos,
> God formed it to be inhabited:[1]

A habitable earth, one that can sustain life for all its creatures, including us humans, that divine intention for our planet proclaimed with such clarity by Isaiah, compels me to question at the outset an early assertion of Michael Broyde's learned paper: "War, if it is to exist legally as a morally sanctioned event, must permit some forms of killing other than those allowed through the self-defense rationale; the modern institution of 'war' cannot exist as derivative of the self-defense rules alone."[2] As I read his admirable assemblage of pertinent classical Jewish teachings relating to the issue of war, I am left with the impression that this dubious initial assumption has distorted his presentation.

May one take as a given that war as we have come to know it is "a morally sanctioned event"? Some of the very teachings cited by Professor Broyde call this into question. The Talmudic prohibition of war in a situation where the casualty rate exceeds a sixth of the population is, indeed, pertinent to our situation today, as Lord Jakobovits plainly asserts: "A defensive war likely to endanger the survival of the attacking and the defending nations alike, if not indeed the entire human race, can never be justified."[3]

Rabbi Jakobovits is referring to nuclear war as an option and clearly rejects it. But what of the preparation for such an eventuality?

Professor Broyde affirms the legitimacy of such preparation: "Just because one cannot pull the nuclear trigger does not mean that one cannot own a nuclear gun."[4] Yet he does concede that "it is difficult to find a clear source in the Jewish tradition that permits one to threaten to do that which is prohibited to do."[5] His doubts, I believe, are reinforced by a provision in the Mishnah and its elaboration by Maimonides: "(During their festivals) one should not sell them (Gentiles) bears, lions, or anything which may injure the many."[6]

"The reason is because they may injure the many."[7] Maimonides spells out more fully the implications of this dictum:

> It is forbidden to sell to idolaters any weapons of war. Neither may one sharpen their weapons nor make available to them knives, chains, barbed chains, bears, lions, or anything which might cause widespread injury. One may sell to them shields or shutters which are purely defensive.[8]

One notices that the nature of the weapons themselves, and *not* the purported intentions of their users, determines the prohibitions! In further treating this provision, Maimonides extends the principle to include indirect supplying of such material, and makes clear that the prohibition applies to Jewish brigands as well:

> That which is prohibited for sale to idolaters is also prohibited for sale to Jews who are suspected of then selling such material to idolaters. Likewise, it is forbidden to sell such weapons to Jewish brigands (*listim*).[9]

Also pertinent in evaluating the threat of nuclear deterrence is this Talmudic opinion: "Resh Lakish said: 'He who lifts his hand against his neighbor, even if he did not strike him, is called a wicked man.' "[10]

The modern institution of war as "a morally sanctioned event," dubious in the light of such classic Jewish teachings as these, is further called into question by the limitations on the destruction of the life-sustaining environment to which Professor Broyde refers. The full biblical prohibition is:

> When in your war against a city you have to besiege it a long time in order to capture it, you must not destroy its trees, wielding the ax against them. You may eat of them, but you must not cut

them down. Are trees of the field human to withdraw before you under siege? Only trees which you know do not yield food may be destroyed.[11]

The provisions that mandate consideration for the civilian population, cited by Professor Broyde,[12] further challenge the possibility of morally sanctioning war as we have come to know it, whether it be nuclear or "merely" conventional. Taken together, they challenge the individual conscience with considerable force. Individual conscience may *not* be left out of consideration, contrary to the conclusion of Rabbi Lamm's "excellent seminal essay" to which Professor Broyde refers.[13] Lamm asserts that "selective pacifism is only a public, national decision, and not a personal one." While there are some admirable elements in that essay to which I shall return later, the proposition that such decisions are to be left to the authorities is not only a seed alien to classical rabbinic Judaism but, to borrow Isaiah's telling image,[14] it yields bitter wild grapes rather than the sweet vine cultivated by the beloved.

Can one admit, post-World War II, post-Holocaust, post-Nuremberg, post-Vietnam, the refuge that *it* was a "public, national decision, and not a personal one?" Simply to ask the question is to answer it. Furthermore, classical Judaism long ago asserted quite the opposite: Individual conscience must be operative, and merely "following orders" does not excuse committing a prohibited act.

With respect to the latter, let me cite briefly from an essay on selective conscientious objection published twenty-five years ago.[15] There is on record a specific case in which constituted authority commands an act contrary to the most basic moral teaching of Judaism. In such a case, the Talmud and latter rabbinic tradition are at one in counseling refusal no matter what the personal consequence.

> In every other law of the Torah, if a man is commanded, "Transgress and suffer not death," he may transgress and not suffer death, excepting idolatry, incest, and shedding blood. Murder may not be practiced to save one's life. . . . Even as one who came before Raba and said to him, "The governor of my town has ordered me, 'Go, and kill so and so; if not, I will slay thee.' " Raba answered him, "Let him rather slay you than that you should commit murder: who knows that your blood is redder? Perhaps his blood is redder."[16]

Many instances could be cited of disobedience to established authority, whether Jewish or non-Jewish, where such authority violated the basic moral and religious convictions of Judaism. Abraham, Moses, Elijah, Jeremiah, Shimon bar Yochai, Jochanan ben Zakkai, etc. are the heroes of numerous tales and legends lauding their refusal to obey illicit authority and unjust laws.

It should be mentioned, finally, that a well-established principle of Talmudic law is: "There is no agent for a sinful act."[17] This is held to mean that a responsible adult cannot evade the legal consequences of the act committed by pleading that he was "merely following orders." More precisely, in the opinion of the Talmud he is guilty of following wrong orders: "If there is a conflict between the words of the Master (God) and the words of the student (man), whose are to be obeyed?"[18]

That this is the prevailing thrust of rabbinic thought rather than the exception is supported by the essay of Moshe Greenberg, the distinguished Professor of Bible at Hebrew University, which concludes his discussion of defying illegal orders with these words:

> But if, when all is done, he finds himself with an order he knows to be illegal, what is his duty? On the basis of the Talmudic material here assembled we can sum it up in three propositions:
>
> 1. He must refuse to carry out the order even if it means a fall in rank and status;
>
> 2. He must actively oppose the order and try to prevent its execution; otherwise he will be guilty before God;
>
> 3. If he voluntarily obeys the order, he is not only guilty before God, but legally culpable as well. He cannot exempt himself on the ground of being merely the king's agent, for there is no agency for wrongdoing—and, unlike Joab, he can no longer plead ignorance of the limitations on royal authority.[19]

As for the operation of individual conscience, the following citations from that same essay on selective conscientious objection make clear the dedication of rabbinic Judaism to the strict limitation of effects in any armed engagement. In these life-and-death confrontations, restraint, limitations, and scruples are explicitly affirmed as appropriate. This is so both in individual and collective confrontations:

> It has been taught by Rabbi Jonathan ben Saul: If one was pursuing his fellow to slay him, and the pursued could have saved

himself by maiming a limb of the pursuer, but instead killed his pursuer, the pursued is subject to execution on that account.[20]

Especially revealing are the classical rabbinic comments on the anticipation of war between Jacob and Esau, deriving from the following verse in Genesis 32:8: "Then Jacob was greatly afraid and was distressed." R. Judah b. R. Ilai said:

> Are not fear and distress identical? The meaning, however, is that "he was afraid" lest he should be slain, "and was distressed" lest he should slay. For Jacob thought: If he prevails against me, will not he slay me; while if I am stronger than he, will not I slay him? That is the meaning of "he was afraid"—lest he should be slain; "and was distressed" lest he should slay.[21]

Another rabbinic comment ascribes to Jacob the following sentiment: "If he overpowers me, that is bad, and if I overpower him, that is bad!"[22] There are two classical statements, referring to the same verse of Genesis, which affirm explicitly that murder (*shefichut damim*) is a category applicable to armed conflict:

> "And Jacob was greatly afraid and was distressed." One might think that Jacob was literally afraid of Esau, fearing that he might not be able to defeat him; but this was not the case. Why, then, was Jacob afraid of Esau? Because Jacob took seriously the prohibition against murder (*shefichut damim*). And so Jacob reasoned as follows: If I succeed and kill him, behold, I have transgressed the commandment "thou shalt not murder." And if he kills me, woe is my lot! Hence it is written: "And Jacob was greatly afraid and was distressed."[23]

Even more remarkable is the comment of Rabbi Shabetai Bass, compiler of *Sifte Hahamim*, the classic subcommentary on the commentary of Rashi. Bass takes explicit note of the Talmudic permission to defend oneself, yet suggests that murder is still an issue, even in a situation of armed combat:

> Yet one might argue that Jacob surely should have had no qualms about killing Esau, for it states explicitly, 'If one comes to slay thee, forestall it by slaying him.'[24] Nonetheless, Jacob did indeed have qualms, fearing that in the fray he might kill some of Esau's

men, who were not intent on killing Jacob (for only Esau had this intention) but merely fighting against Jacob's men. And even though Esau's men, and every person has the right to save the life of the pursued at the cost of the life of the pursuer, nonetheless that provision applies which states: 'If the pursued could have been saved by maiming a limb of the pursuer, but instead the rescuer killed the pursuer, the rescuer is liable to capital punishment on that account.' Hence Jacob rightly feared lest, in the confusion of battle, he kill some of Esau's men outright when he might instead have restrained them by merely inflicting injury upon their limbs.[25]

Thus Bass, whose subcommentary is a summary of "the best work of his fifteen predecessors who had commented on Rashi,"[26] relays the opinion that even in an actual combat situation, the principle does obtain that the least possible and least injurious force should be applied, even to combatants!

Rabbinic comments on Abram's participation in the War of the Kings[27] sustain the validity of this concern:

"After these things the word of the Lord came unto Abram in a vision, saying: 'Fear not, Abram. . . .' "[28] This relates to the verses from Proverbs: "Fortunate is the man who fears perpetually; But he who hardens his conscience shall fall into evil";[29] and "A wise man is fearful and turns away from evil, but a fool is overbearing and careless."[30] Who is the wise and fortunate man alluded to? Abraham. And of whom was he afraid? Of Shem, for he killed in battle Chedarlaomer, King of Elam, and his three sons, descendants of Shem . . . Thus Abram was afraid, saying: "I have killed the sons of a righteous man, and now he will curse me and I shall die."[31]

Even more telling is the further speculation in Midrash Tanhuma:

Still another reason for Abraham's fear after killing the kings in battle was his sudden realization: "Perhaps I violated the Divine commandment that the Holy One, Blessed be He, commanded all men, 'Thou shalt not shed human blood.'[32] Yet how many people I killed in battle!"[33]

For this reason, too, the Midrash imagines Abram needing divine reassurance. Among other explanations of the grounds for Abram's fear, R. Levi suggests the following: "Abraham was filled with misgivings, thinking to himself, 'Maybe there was a righteous or God-fearing man among those troops which I slew.' "[34]

There are, of course, other explanations advanced which take Abram's fear in the most self-concerned sense: He feared for his life when the avengers of the dead would pursue him. Yet the interjection of scruples about killing in the midst of conflict is highly significant for our considerations, and that Abram needed direct divine reassurance indicates that the bloodshed consequent upon warfare was not to be taken lightly. This and other material suggest that Professor Broyde's attempt to distinguish between the self-defense and the war rationale with respect to shedding innocent blood is not supported by a large body of classic Jewish teaching.

The provision in Deuteronomy 20:8, which provides exemption from combat for one who is "fearful and/or tenderhearted," has received comment from the rabbinic tradition also:

> R. Akiba says: "Fearful and tender-hearted" is to be understood literally, viz., He is unable to stand in the battle-ranks and see a drawn sword. R. Jose the Galilean says: "Fearful and faint-hearted" alludes to one who is afraid because of the transgressions he had committed.[35]

Lest Rabbi Akiba's interpretation be understood in purely medical or psychological terms, the Tosefta cites Akiba's position in these words:

> Why are both terms, 'fearful' and 'tender-hearted' specified? To indicate that even the most physically fit and courageous, if he be a *rachman* (compassionate, gentle), should be exempted.[36]

With respect to the final citation from Tosefta, this calls into question Professor Broyde's interpretation of the Talmudic characterization of Akiba's position as referring "to a person who is lacking the moral courage to do battle and see combat and watch people perish."[37] The term *rachman* is, after all, a highly honored term in rabbinic discourse, and is cited as one of the three distinguishing characteristics of the Jewish people.[38] *Rachman*, gently scrupulous and compassionate, when referring to "the mightiest of the mighty" (*gibor shebegiborim*) as in this citation, is surely not to be construed as "lacking the moral courage to do battle," an issue to which we shall soon turn further attention. Nor would anyone, I trust, argue that the Jewish people has been characterized by lack of moral courage throughout the centuries.

To Professor Broyde's credit, he does affirm in a footnote that "an individual's 'selective conscientious objection' can be justified in the Jewish tradition as a response to an *unjust* war."[39] Yet I am troubled by the relegation of this important principle to a footnote, and by a general thrust that, I perceive, continues to make a case for war even in this age when it has become so menacingly destructive of that which it would protect.

Nor should the tendency to legitimize public authority over individual conscience go unchallenged in an age when, in truth, the emphasis should be the reverse: that the individual conscience must scrutinize public demands, especially in matters of life and death. This is especially so in the United States, where the separation of church and state leaves room for and, indeed, invites the active involvement of the individual citizen's religious conscience. Thus laws of conscription include provisions for conscientious objection on religious grounds, and these provisions clearly include those whose religious basis for conscientious objection is Judaism. From this perspective, one would wonder about Professor Broyde's references both here and earlier[40] to Jews as living in "a host country." Is this to suggest that Jews are merely "guests" in the United States? How so? Who, then, are the purported "hosts"? The Jewish nationalistic overtones of such wording must not go unchallenged, even if a fuller discussion of the validity of Diaspora Jewish existence cannot be entertained in the context of this inquiry.

Returning to the core issue of Professor Broyde's essay as I see it, the question remains: How is it that so much of Professor Broyde's admirable learning is here dedicated to making a case for the possibility of modern war being "a morally sanctioned event?" What he and we confront, I suggest, is a shattered ends-means continuum, a paradigm no longer able to maintain equilibrium with disparate demands. On the one hand we have the divine mandate to be fully engaged on behalf of the life of this world, an engagement extending even unto its ultimate life-and-death boundary traditionally associated with violent struggle. On the other hand, there stands the divine mandate to limit strictly that violence so that it does not destroy the innocent nor those it was intended to save. Rabbi Lamm's essay, admired by Professor Broyde, states forcefully the first demand, but fails, as does Professor Broyde, to give sufficient weight to the second. The result of such a misemphasis is to leave us defenseless against the expansion of war at precisely the time when greatly increased destructiveness requires the forceful reassertion of such a limitation.

Although it confronts us with an urgency unprecedented in human history, the core of the problem is ancient:

> However mighty the man, once the arrow leaves his hand he cannot make it come back. However mighty the man, once frenzy and power take hold, even his father, even his mother, and even his nearest of kin he strikes as he moves in his wrath.[41]

Also ancient are early stirrings of alternative forms of struggle and resistance. Evidence of this is generously provided in Professor Reuven Kimelman's essay, "Nonviolence in the Talmud,"[42] together with a knowledgeable discussion of the judiciously chosen sources. While some are further statements of teachings, others describe specific incidents, and seem to me all the more compelling by virtue of their actuality.

Were there but space enough and time, I should like to focus on two further life episodes from the Tanaitic period. One, of course, would be the life and teachings of Yohanan ben Zakkai. His refusal to support the Zealots' armed revolt against the Romans, his defection from their control of Jerusalem, and his "constructive programs," including establishing the Academy at Yavneh, which entailed accommodation with the Romans, are generally acknowledged to have preserved Judaism. Precisely because of its scope and importance, which defy brief treatment, and because it is probably widely known to many readers, I shall omit this from my written response and instead draw your attention to another significant and dramatic instance of ancient nonviolent resistance in Jerusalem some thirty years earlier, when Caligula was emperor of Rome (37–41 C.E.).

Incited by Apion of Alexandria, Caligula became convinced that the Jews' refusal to install his statue in the Temple in Jerusalem was a sign of disrespect rather than fidelity to the biblical prohibition against graven images. Determined to rectify this presumed affront, he ordered his appointed president of Syria, Petronius, to invade Judea "with a great body of troops; and if they would admit of his statue willingly, to erect it in the temple of God; but if they were obstinate, to conquer them by war, and then to do it." When Petronius arrived at Ptolemais, he was met by tens of thousands of Jews bearing petitions that he "not compel them to transgress and violate the law of their forefathers." Josephus records their further words:

> But if thou art entirely resolved to bring this statue, and erect it, do thou first kill us, and then do what thou hast resolved on; for while we are alive we cannot permit such things as are forbidden us to be done by the authority of our legislator, and by our forefathers' determination that such prohibitions are instances of virtue.[43]

Petronius pleads that he is merely following orders, to which the Jews respond:

> "Since, therefore, thou art so disposed, O Petronius, that thou wilt not disobey Caius's epistles, neither will we transgress the commands of our law."

Meeting such resistance in Ptolemais, Petronius moved on to Tiberias to check the communal response there. There also the Jews expressed concern about waging war with the Romans, yet were determined to resist the edict. They replied in these terms:

> "We will not by any means make war with him, but still we will die before we see our laws transgressed." So they threw themselves down upon their faces, and stretched out their throats, and said they were ready to be slain; and this they did for forty days together, and in the mean time left off the tilling of the ground, and that while the season of the year required them to sow it. Thus they continued firm in their resolution, and proposed to themselves to die willingly, rather than to see the dedication of the statue.[44]

In Josephus' account, principal representatives of the Jewish community met further with Petronius and urged that he write Caligula of the undesirable consequences, both moral and material, from the implementation of the proposed policy:

. . . that the Jews had an insuperable aversion to the reception of the statue, and how they continued with him, and left off the tillage of their ground that they were not willing to go to war with him, because they were not able to do it, but were ready to die with pleasure, rather than suffer their laws to be transgressed: and how, upon the land's continuing unsown, robberies would go up, on the inability they would be under of paying their tributes; and that Caius might be thereby moved to pity, and not order any barbarous action to be done to them, nor think of destroying the nation . . . .[45]

The portrayal of Petronius' response together with its purported motivation is both remarkable in itself and strikingly modern in its ascription of effective political power to a mass nonviolent civil disobedience campaign:

. . . because of the great consequence of what they desired, and the earnestness wherewith they made their supplication,— partly on account of the firmness of the opposition made by the Jews, which he saw, while he thought it a horrible thing for him to be such a slave to the madness of Caius, as to slay so many ten thousand men, only because of their religious disposition towards God, and after that to pass his life in expectation of punishment: Petronius, I say, thought it much better to send to Caius, and let him know how intolerable it was to him to bear the anger he might have against him for not serving him sooner, in obedience to his epistle, for that perhaps he might persuade him; and that if this mad resolution continued, he might then begin war against them; nay, that in case he should turn his hatred against himself, it was fit for virtuous persons even to die for the sake of such vast multitudes of men.[46]

Calculation as well as conscience seems to have been a factor in the situation:

"Do you, therefore, every one of you, go your way about your own occupations, and fall to the cultivation of your grounds; I will myself send to Rome, and will not refuse to serve you in all things, both by myself and by my friends." When Petronius had said this, and had dismissed the assembly of the Jews, he desired the principal of them to take care of their husbandry, and to speak kindly to the people, and encourage them to have good hope of their affairs. Thus did he readily bring the multitude to be cheerful again.[47]

Considerations of space preclude any lengthy discussion of this striking instance of the actual application of nonviolence in a conflict with the Roman troops. Let it simply serve as the transition to a brief consideration of the possibilities of active nonviolence as the necessary element to expand and re-establish the means-ends continuum within Jewish tradition and perhaps others as well, without which our best-intended and most carefully calculated efforts are doomed.

For millennia, our scriptural traditions have offered us any number of teachings that have seemed both utterly appealing and utterly impractical, unrealistic. From Hebrew Scriptures let me cite but two: "For thus said the Lord God, the Holy One of Israel: 'In turning and stillness shall you be saved. In tranquillity and trust shall be your strength.' "[48] "Not by might nor by power but by My Spirit says the Lord of Hosts."[49] Until this century such passages must have sounded visionary but inapplicable to our world of creatureliness and conflict. And now? Post-Gandhi and post-King, they sound descriptive rather than visionary, operative rather than anticipatory. The pragmatic, political, strategic efficacy of Spirit, Spirit flexing its muscle, so to speak, Spirit with clout (you should pardon the expression) are present-day realities covered by daily newspapers and intensively analyzed by such frontline social science institutes as Gene Sharp's Albert Einstein Institution or Harvard's Program on Nonviolent Sanctions in Conflict and Defense.

The application of Spirit, *satyagraha*, soul-force is more visible now, I submit, than ever before, even as the bloody alternatives increasingly reveal their self-destructive impotence. Within only the past decade, consider the fall of Marcos in the Philippines, of Duvalier in Haiti, and the hardly to-be-believed shifts of power in all of Eastern Europe and the former Soviet Union. These transfers of power have not yielded instant redemption, comparatively bloodless though they were; but would greater measures of violence and bloodshed have provided more promising outcomes? Probably just the reverse.

Nor should we downgrade or dismiss these extraordinary accomplishments by saying, "But these were not war situations." First of all, how easily they might have become such, for they were intense conflict situations. Second, they are not alone as instances of the worldly efficacy of spirit. Although the terms of his analysis are more rational and scientific, Sharp's study of nonviolence through the centuries includes, within the past half-century, such previous experiences as these:

1. The Norwegian teachers' strike and active resistance against the Nazi occupiers in 1940. Despite severe treatment in a concentration camp north of the Arctic circle, the teachers managed to persist and administered a stunning defeat to Quisling and his Nazi supporters;[50]
2. Czech nonviolent resistance to the Warsaw Pact invasion of 1968. This resistance persisted for seven months and did manage to exact some concessions from the invading forces;[51]
3. The uprising in the Siberian forced labor camp, Vorkuta, in 1953. Limited achievements were gained;[52]
4. Numerous Danish acts of nonviolent resistance, including the remarkable successful rescue of the Danish Jews (95 percent of them) in October 1943;[53]
5. The little-known rescue of several thousand Jewish husbands of non-Jewish wives through an act of nonviolent defiance by the wives in Berlin, 1943![54]

How could this have succeeded in the heart of the capital of the Third Reich during the height of the extermination programs? What were the dynamics?

Please do not misunderstand. I am not speaking of messianic fulfillment: These are not cases of the lion and the lamb lying peacefully together. They are, indeed, struggles in an imperfect and conflict-ridden world, but struggles which, with this alternative means, may manage to preserve, not destroy, those ends on whose behalf the struggle is undertaken.

That such methods and achievements are more harmonious with the moral aspirations of Judaism, Christianity, and Islam than the waging of destructive war need hardly be argued. What must be asserted now, in the light of events this century, is that some fulfillment of these visions, however partial and halting, is not only a possibility but an actuality. From within Christianity and moving to the farthest ends of the planet, the Reverend Martin Luther King, Jr.'s, eloquence in words and efficacy in deeds are well known.

Less well known, yet also significant for a common religious approach to these issues, are the early-twentieth-century writings of Rabbi Aaron Samuel Tamaret, who wrote under the pen name of Ahad Harabanim Hamargishim. His essays offer a searing critique of violence from a deeply rooted and profoundly learned Jewish perspective. They also, in quite novel fashion, bring to sharp focus ways in which basic biblical and classical rabbinic teachings provide individual and social strategies for defense and social change.[55] Within Islam the example of Khan Abdul Ghaffar Khan also invites close attention. This respected chieftain of the warlike Pathans of the Northwest Frontier of India, himself an accomplished horseman and marksman, in the course of fifteen years (1926 to the late 1930s) organized a Muslim nonviolent freedom movement numbering over 100,000 people![56]

Admittedly we are without certainty in these matters. Yet as inheritors of religious resources from our respective traditions of the word, and heartened by such developments, we do have grounds for hoping, perhaps even trusting at this time of world crisis in the twice-repeated biblical promise: The Lord will not forsake His people; He will not abandon His heritage.[57]

NOTES

1. Isa. 45:18. This paper is presented in loving memory of Steven Schwarzschild, whose assuredly sharp critique of my response would truly have been a *yisur shel ahavat habriyot*, a chastisement stemming from love for God's creatures. May he rest in that true peace he so faithfully sought and pursued, cf. Psalm 34:14.
2. Supra, p. 3.
3. Supra, p. 12.
4. Supra, p. 12, emphasis omitted.
5. Supra, p. 28, n. 71.
6. Mishnah *Abodah Zarah* 1:7.
7. B.T. *Abodah Zarah* 16b.
8. Maimonides, *Code*, XI,v (*Roseah*) 12:12.
9. Ibid., 12:13–14.
10. B.T. *Sanhedrin* 58b.
11. Deut. 20:19–20.
12. Supra, pp. 10–12.
13. Supra, p. 19.
14. Isa. 5:2.

15. Everett E. Gendler, "War and the Jewish Tradition," in *A Conflict of Loyalties: The Case for Selective Conscientious Objection*, ed. James Finn (New York: Pegasus, 1968), pp. 78–102, at p. 98.

16. *B.T. Sanhedrin* 74a.

17. *B.T. Baba Mesia* 10b; *Qiddushin* 42b.

18. Ibid.

19. Moshe Greenberg, "Rabbinic Reflections on Defying Illegal Orders: Amasa, Abner and Joab," *Judaism* 19 (1970): 30–37; reprinted in *Contemporary Jewish Ethics*, ed. Menachem Marc Kellner (New York: Hebrew, 1978), pp. 211–20, at p. 218.

20. *B.T. Sanhedrin* 74a.

21. Genesis Rabba 76:2.

22. Lakach Tov. Cited in *Torah Shlemah*, ed. M. Kasher, 6:1266, n. 49.

23. Schechter Genizah Manuscript of an early edition of Midrash Tanhumah, cited in *Torah Shlemah*, ed. M. Kasher, 6:1266, n. 49.

24. *B.T. Sanhedrin* 72a; *Berakot* 58a, 62b.

25. *Sifte Hahamim* on Gen. 32:8.

26. Louis Ginzberg in *The Jewish Encyclopedia* (New York: Funk and Wagnalls, 1901–06), 2:584.

27. Gen. 14.

28. Gen. 15:1.

29. Prov. 28:14.

30. Prov. 14:16.

31. Tanhuma, ed. Buber, *Lek Leka*, 19.

32. Gen. 9:6.

33. Tanhuma, ed. Buber, *Lek Leka*, 19.

34. Genesis Rabba 44:4.

35. *B.T. Sotah* 44a.

36. *Tosefta Sotah* 7:22.

37. Supra, p. 14.

38. *Yebamot* 79a.

39. Supra, p. 19. [Moved into text in revision. Ed.]

40. Supra, pp. 21, n. 4; 19.

41. Mekilta, *Shirata*, on Exod. 15:3–4, ed. Lauterbach, II:32–33.

42. In *Roots of Jewish Nonviolence*, ed. Steven Schwarzschild (Nyack, N.Y.: Jewish Peace Fellowship, 1981), pp. 24–50.

43. *The Antiquities of the Jews*, 18.8.2. All citations are from the translation of William Whiston (Philadelphia: J. C. Winston, 1936).

44. *Antiquities*, 18.8.3.

45. *Antiquities*, 18.8.4.

46. *Antiquities*, 18.8.4.

47. *Antiquities*, 18.8.5–6.

48. Isa. 30:15.

49. Zech. 4:6.

50. Gene Sharp, *Social Power and Political Freedom* (Boston: Ponter Sargent, 1980), pp. 226–27, citing Sharp, "Tyranny Could Not Quell Them,"

Peace News (London, 1958). Norwegian sources include: Magnus Jensen, "Kampen om Skolen," in *Norges Krig*, ed. Sverre Steen (Oslo: Gyldendal Norsk, 1947–50), III: 73–105; and *Kirkenes Ferda, 1942*, ed. Sverre S. Amundsen (Oslo: J. W. Cappelens, 1946).

51. Sharp, 230–31.

52. Sharp, 224, citing the articles of Brigitte Gerland in *The Militant* (New York), 28 Feb. and 7 March, 1955.

53. Sharp, 80–81.

54. Sharp, 225, citing Heinz Ullstein's memoirs, *Spielplatz meines Lebens* (Munich: Kinkler, 1961), pp. 338–40. Nathan Stoltzfus's valuable article, "Dissent in Nazi Germany", *Atlantic Monthly*, September 1992, 86–94, is quite astonishing in this respect.

55. *Judaism Magazine* 12 (1963): 36–56; and 17 (1968): 203–10.

56. Joan Bondurant, *Conquest of Violence*, rev. ed. (Berkeley: University of California Press, 1971), pp. 131–44.

57. Ps. 94:14. Cf. 1 Sam. 12:22.

The Political Morality of Pacifism and Nonviolence: One Jewish View

YEHUDAH MIRSKY

In this essay, I propose to do three things. First, I will examine some of the fundamental questions of structure and method attending any inquiry into "Jewish" views of political morality. Then I will discuss some of the Jewish tradition's fundamental notions regarding the use of force in conflict among groups. Finally (and, I hope, suggestively), I will look at the issue of nonviolence from within the framework of lived Jewish experience over time, and as manifest in normative Jewish tradition.

This essay is subtitled "One Jewish View." I do not presume to offer the definitive Jewish position on this issue, not merely because of my own limitations, but, more to the point, because today one is hard-pressed to find any one commanding source of interpretive authority as regards the Jewish tradition's stance on an emergent issue, and because the tradition itself speaks in many voices. Nonetheless, I do believe that the positions set forth here are authentic, compelling, and true to the tradition on its own terms.[1]

Any attempt to offer a/the Jewish view of nonviolence, or of any issue of political morality, immediately raises a number of distinct though related questions about the nature of the enterprise at hand:

1. What does Jewish tradition direct Jews, specifically Jews, to do in given situations?
2. Is there a way of thinking "Jewishly" about this question? Is there a Jewish style of moral/prudential reasoning about this, one that could conceivably be of use to those outside the ambit of Jewish law and tradition?
3. Would the same norms (in this case, vis-à-vis pacifism and nonviolence) apply in both Israel and the Diaspora?

Needless to say, these questions range far and wide. Yet they must be addressed, however provisionally, for the discussion to proceed in any but anecdotal fashion.

An authentic Jewish politics meets two criteria. It preserves and protects the concrete interests of Jews as individuals and as a community, and it both reflects and enacts the values of Jewish tradition, as embodied in both texts and history, even as that tradition grapples with the radical newness of modern times.

This formulation meets different sorts of rival views, each of which has merit, and is ultimately deficient: first, strictly secular Zionism which not infrequently seems to denude Jewish politics of all religious meaning; second, the maverick neo-Orthodox thinker and critic Yeshayahu Leibowitz, who powerfully argued on theological grounds that it is simply idolatrous in any way to conflate the categories of religion and politics.[2] My answer to both of these views is that in the final analysis politics is inescapably informed by values. Jewish politics must be informed by Jewish values; it is adherence to those values that justifies the continuance of the Jewish community as an entity separate and distinct from the mass of Western society, as indeed any kind of separatist identity must ultimately be grounded in some moral claim. By "moral claim" I broadly mean nonchauvinist claims, whether of group mission or the dignity of cultural survival. Third, I also mean to counter the views of the ultra-Orthodox, who assert both that any and every question of Jewish interest can be answered by simply referring to the classic codes of Jewish law and the routine canons of Orthodox rabbinic decision making, and that, theologically speaking, historical experience counts for nothing. To that I say that as moderns we cannot but be aware of the historical circumstances that have shaped received norms, and that historical experiences, and especially the painful struggles of Jews to live and find a place for themselves in the world, are themselves acts of great significance, and perhaps part of a larger historical cunning which can disclose new meanings of well-worn religious ideas.

There is no one authentic Jewish politics as such; the tradition throughout reflects a dynamic tension between the celebration of Davidic leadership and a profound suspicion of all worldly power, even that of the divinely ordained king.[3] It is more accurate to speak of forms of Jewish political thinking that reflect greater or lesser authenticity, within certain inescapable parameters. This notion of authentic Jewish politics is nonetheless expansive, and would bring under its aegis both the religious peace movement and the religious nationalism of Gush Emmunim; similarly, though to a lesser extent, it also embraces Jewish socialist movements and revisionist Zionism. One may argue with any or all of these groupings on the grounds of prudence, interpretation, or sheer attractiveness, but they do offer authentic Jewish politics, by the aforementioned criteria.[4]

In looking for the sources of Jewish political thinking, the first difficulty that comes to mind is the obvious exclusion of Jews from political life for millennia. Yet, while Jews have not held sovereignty, they have not been utterly excluded from history. As Amos Funkenstein has argued, Jews do indeed possess a rich historiographical literature, with a difference: It is not political, but legal history.[5] Thus it is Jewish legal literature that provides ample, useful material for the study of Jewish politics.[6] Because the literary sources of the Jewish political tradition are more legal than philosophical, they, not surprisingly, yield a discourse that prefers the practical to the theoretical, the contextual to the abstract.

In attempting to formulate a Jewish perspective on pacifism and nonviolence, we would do well to begin with the former. Pacifism presents the clearer case of how Jewish tradition has viewed force; moreover, by working backwards from the extreme eschewal of force that pacifism represents we can more usefully move closer toward the middle ground of nonviolence where Jewish tradition, characteristically, finds itself.

It is my contention that a more authentic Jewish politics rejects pacifism not only in practice but in principle, for several reasons.[7]

First, Judaism's conception of humanity's place in the world is fundamentally activist, committed to the establishment of a just and godly social order here on earth, and through worldly means. The institutions of this world, of *olam ha-zeh*, including war and statecraft, are good or evil depending on the uses to which they are put. Clearly the Old Testament sees the use of force as a legitimate exercise in certain circumstances. Indeed, the Sixth Commandment, *lo tirtsach*, though usually translated as "Thou Shalt Not Kill" is more accurately rendered as "Thou Shalt Not Murder," implying, *ab initio*, a notion of the legitimate use of force that pervades the biblical corpus.[8] Might does not make right—"Not by might, nor by power, but by My Spirit, says the Lord of Hosts"[9]—but "there is a time for war" as there is "a time for peace."[10]

Turning to the Judaism we know, the Judaism of the rabbis, the ultimately tragic character of the human condition is not lost on them.

To the contrary, the rabbis depict ours as a broken world, badly in need of repair, but this tragic sense offers no release from the obligation to act.[11]

Second, pacifism is rejected because Judaism by its logic, nature, and structure is committed to the survival of a discrete worldly community. The exilic Jews of the Book of Esther take up arms to defend themselves, and the Talmud clearly establishes that "If someone comes to kill you, rise early and kill him first."[12]

The community, to be sure, is not to be conflated with the state. The two are, and indeed must be, thought of as two very different entities, if notions like the moral worth and dignity of the individual are to have any meaning, and if the seductive heresies of statist idolatry are to be avoided.

Yet, a Jewish community (and certainly a state whose *raison d'être* is quite literally the preservation of a community) must take the claims of survival seriously. The existence of the Jewish faith is inextricably bound up with the physical existence of the Jewish people.

Even so, the meaning of survival is not without its complexities. On the one hand, survival must have some purpose beyond itself; "survival for what?" At the same time, it is obscene to demand of Jews at the end of the twentieth century that they defend their survival by reference to some philosophically or aesthetically pleasing criterion or other.

It may be that Jewish survival, the inalienable right of Jews to live without fear of persecution or destruction, is a "deep metaphor" for the right of all people to live without fear of persecution or destruction.[13] Put somewhat differently, the right of Jews to survive is an articulation of the inner logic of the fact of their survival, a fact that would not have come to pass were it not for a monumental exercise of the will, both collective and individual, a will whose source is mysterious, which perhaps also means that it is divine.

Other theologians would ground Jewish survival not in the terms I am suggesting but in terms of the existence of the Jewish people as a discrete entity manifesting a "corporeal election"—the living, breathing Jewish people as a godly presence embedded in the world, shaping the religious life of humanity in dialogue, or dialectic, with the world's other religious traditions.[14] Be that as it may, to the extent that the existence of the Jewish people is a religious desideratum, the steps necessary to secure that survival receive some sort of religious sanction.

This is not to say that a pacific mankind is not ardently desired by Jewish tradition, in which Heraclitean celebration of conflict for its own sake is simply nowhere to be found. *Shalom*, "peace," is regarded by the tradition as one of the names of God; the pursuit of peace is regarded as the foundation of the social order and the highest calling of the individual; and war is seen as an expression of man's sinful nature. Yet these are aspirational, and not normative, prescriptive views.[15] The pacifistic ideal stands in judgment over us all, who are condemned to live in historical time, but it is not a useful reference point for Jewish political thought today. It fails to pass muster by the two criteria of Jewish political authenticity offered earlier: It simply cannot sustain the physical survival of the Jewish people, nor does it reflect and enact Jewish values—not only survival, but the imperative to combat evil and injustice in this world, in *olam ha-zeh*.

The thrust of the Judaic law of war is to accept war as more or less a given in the life of nations, but to hem it tightly with moral restrictions at every step of the way. As Reuven Kimelman has well put it: "The solution to the moral failings of nations lies not in the abolition of national entities, but rather in the moralization of national power . . . by subjecting nations to legal restraint [the Biblical prophets] seek to civilize them. In this manner the morally preferable can become the politically possible. . . . Jewish political theory, which bases itself on the Bible, sees a system of government which is both politically workable and morally acceptable."[16] Thus *halacha*, the corpus of traditional Jewish law, addresses itself to the gamut of war making, from *casus belli* to the conduct of war and even environmental damage in wartime.

With regard to *casus belli*, Jewish tradition, as is well known, differentiates between "mandatory wars" and "discretionary wars," the former waged to defend the Jewish people, conquer the Land of Israel (this having been done in the time of Joshua and thus rendered moot), and battle against Amalek, largely understood by tradition to be war against generalized forms of evil; the latter, for *raisons d'état* of national prestige, economic aggrandizement, and so on, and only with the permission of the Sanhedrin, and thus largely moot ever since. The only remaining category of legitimate war since the destruction of the Temple in 70 C.E. has been, and remains, war for the defense of the Jewish people.

The notion of legitimately defending the Jewish people from attack by force of arms persisted after the destruction of the Temple, through the Talmud, and well into the Middle Ages. The Talmud assumes that Jews may defend their persons from attack if they are able to do so; with regard to fighting on the Sabbath, the Talmud says that assaults on Jewish property are not to be repelled on the Sabbath unless a community is in a position of permanent or structural vulnerability (which, according to one view, encompasses every community in the Diaspora), in which case fighting back is permitted.[17] In other words, the exilic tradition affirms the use of defensive force if specific criteria are met.

The theological underpinnings of this notion of limited but legitimate force were interestingly formulated by Abraham Isaac Kook, first Chief Rabbi of Palestine, founder of religious Zionism, and one of the greatest Jewish thinkers of modern times.[18] One of the clearest expositions of his ideas on the subject appears in a letter written in 1904:

> With regard to the matter of wars, it was simply impossible at a time when all the surrounding neighbors were truly a pack of threatening wolves for Israel (i.e., the Jewish people)[19] alone to refrain from fighting, for then they all (i.e., the threatening neighbors) could gather together and—God forbid—eradicate the Remnant (i.e., the Jewish people); to the contrary, it was necessary to instill fear in the wild ones, even with some cruel measures, if only in the hope of bringing humanity to that which it should be, but not before its time. And bear in mind that in communal laws generally the Torah did not at all take upon itself to push the spirit of the people to extreme piety, for then piety would become a matter of rote and obligation, whereas the goal of the Torah is to establish enlightenment with the force of love and free will. This is the foundation for a number of the allowances the Torah law makes with regard to the conduct of war . . . yet, because of our sinfulness, we do not understand these matters in the requisite detail due to the absence of practical application resulting from the loss of national power, until God restores to us the glory of our sovereignty (literally 'crown'), speedily and in our days.[20]

Kook thus grounds the legitimacy of war strictly and solely in terms of the necessity of self-defense. He also works with an important distinction, not between public and private morality, but between public and private piety. The characterization of restraint as piety does not diminish piety's binding force. Indeed, commenting on this passage, one of Kook's most prominent latter-day disciples has noted that Kook clearly privileges the morality of piety over that of the law.[21] Indeed, he works to keep that distinction, to maintain a creative, dialectical tension that could preserve the power of the pietistic ideal, though as a matter of personal rectitude, not public policy. As we shall see, this distinction has played a significant role in nonviolent responses to persecution.

Which brings us to the subject of nonviolence, and particularly nonviolent resistance. One thing must not be forgotten about nonviolence, more precisely, the idea of nonviolence as it has most meaningfully crystallized in contemporary political thought and action—that it is first and foremost a form of struggle.[22] It does not shrink from recognizing the reality of evil or injustice nor the imperative to combat it. Where it differs from other forms of struggle with evil, and particularly armed struggle, is in its assertion of a bond between the two sides, and in its focusing attack on the structures of evil rather than on the individuals maintaining those structures. It should not be invoked as a justification or recipe for inaction in the face of pressing evil or injustice.[23]

Where the oppressor or evildoer seeks to vanquish or eradicate his victim pure and simple there is no call for nonviolence. Indeed, in that situation, nonviolence would do nothing but further empower the oppressor and force the oppressed to acquiesce in his or her own destruction, forfeiting human dignity in the process by ceding to the oppressor the validity of his aims. Nonviolent resistance aims to push the latent contradictions of an oppressive society to the surface. Hence it is inapplicable in societies whose violence and oppression are not contradictions but rather of their essence (the best examples of which are the totalitarian "republics of fear" that are the twentieth century's unique contribution to political taxonomy).[24] The "nonviolent moment," if you will, arises only in those situations where, to begin with, the oppressor does not seek annihilation but subjugation, not destruction but the act of submission.

The relationship between the oppressor and the oppressed in the "nonviolent moment" is thus profoundly dialectical, in which each defines himself or herself in terms of the other. The oppressor's self-definition resides in the oppressed's acquiescence in political subordination, socioeconomic injustice, and ideological hegemony. The self-definition of the nonviolent oppressed resides by contrast in the oppressor's perhaps flawed but still shared humanity, a humanity that makes the oppressor a full-fledged human being to whom the nonviolent testimony of the oppressed is meaningful, even if it is not fully, or just barely, understood.[25]

In looking for expressions of the philosophy of nonviolence in Jewish tradition and experience one is initially and naturally inclined to examine those passages in the authoritative texts which bespeak a nonviolent attitude toward conflict. Indeed, Reuven Kimelman, in an immensely learned article published some twenty-five years ago, has gathered an impressive collection of texts and discussions scattered throughout Talmudic literature around the themes of responses to enmity, to injurious intentions, and to persecution.[26] The texts Kimelman marshals perceptively and often movingly explore the dynamics of conflict and the challenges it poses to the religious and moral integrity of the individual, and demonstrate, he says, "that alongside the normative legal tradition there existed, in the Talmudic period, a concomitant undercurrent which may be considered the standard of the *hasid* [who] was not one who stood on his legal rights, but always sought a solution which would find favor in the eyes of God . . . a self-sufferer who avoided the remotest possibility of doing harm . . . ."[27]

Yet, these powerful and compelling displays of personal piety arise largely in the context of interpersonal relations, and not public policy. I would submit that a richer understanding of Judaic attitudes toward nonviolence as a public matter, and in the sense in which we in the late twentieth century encounter the issue, may be gleaned not from the rabbinic literature of conflict resolution as such but rather from the body of literature that has grown around a tragic but central fact of Jewish existence: martyrdom.

The literature of martyrdom provides a prism through which we can explore the related themes of responding to violence, preserving the community, and synthesizing physical and spiritual resistance.

The experience of persecution and martyrdom inescapably colors Judaic thinking on nonviolence and indeed on all aspects of political life. The rabbinic discourse of martyrdom (generally referred to as *Kiddush Ha-Shem*, or "Sanctification of The Name") may be characterized as an attempt to reconcile the attitudes suggested by the two verses that set the parameters of the Talmud's discussion: Leviticus'

"And keep my decrees and laws, which a person should do so that one can live,"[28] and Deuteronomy's exhortation (which observant Jews recite three times a day), "And you shall love God your Lord, with all your heart, and all your soul and all your strength."[29] If the former seems to modify the force of commandment by affirming the value of life, the latter calls for a degree of devotion and willingness to sacrifice beside which the claims of mere comfort and survival pale into insignificance.

The themes sounded by these verses are both central to Judaism. On the one hand, Judaism is a life-affirming religion. Its precepts center (some say too much so) on life in this world. It discourages celibacy and mandates close attention to the particulars of corporeal life. It wholeheartedly affirms and mandates the life of a community rooted in time and space. At the same time, the living of life under the aegis of the law bespeaks a commitment that would endure even unto death.

Synthesizing Judaism's life-affirming character and its call to martyrdom *in extremis* was no academic exercise, as Jews throughout history have time and again been forced to choose between their faith and their physical safety. (The brave new evils of the twentieth century have rendered even this unenviable choice something of a luxury, as we shall see.) The rabbis met these challenges by a characteristic attention to particulars of the specific acts in question and of the oppressors' motivations.

In brief, the Talmudic law of martyrdom is as follows. If a Jew is told to violate a commandment under pain of death, he is, ordinarily, to submit and save his own life, with two large exceptions: If the demanded violation involves idolatry, murder, or sexual immorality, the Jew is to allow himself to be killed no matter what.[30] If group solidarity would be threatened by the transgression, the Jew may have to submit to death, even if the requested transgression is a minor one (and, in some views, even if it is not technically a transgression at all but a purely symbolic gesture), depending on the circumstances, such as the public nature of the act or whether this particular act is a discrete incident or part of a larger climate of persecution.[31]

This straightforward willingness to evaluate martyrdom through a calibrated series of trade-offs and prudential judgments reflects the view that "the concept of martyrdom carries no special mystique in Judaism, it has no sacrificial connotation, and consequently no import of vicarious atonement. It is merely a question of the conflict of duties: on rare occasions, the duty of preserving one's life may be outweighed by even greater duties."[32]

It bears noting that a limited but, in its way, very influential, school of Jewish thought, the Franco-German Pietists of the twelfth and thirteenth centuries, whose communities were ravaged by the fierce anti-Jewish violence accompanying the Crusades, elevated martyrdom into not only a high ideal but the paradigmatic religious act.[33] In their chief work, the *Sefer Hasidim* [Book of the Pious], one finds extraordinary statements like the following:

> If an opportunity comes your way to do God's will in some matter, and you hesitate out of embarrassment, or difficulty, or an evil inclination within you, consider: if you were in a time of persecution, you would suffer all the tortures and die for your Creator . . . all the more so, then, should you overcome your inclinations and do this minor thing.[34]

Indeed, the Pietists regularly incurred martyrdom even when they were not halachically obligated to do so, and at times engaged in the very questionable practice of mass suicide rather than face the temptation of forced transgression of the law. Over the centuries this sparked discussion among halachic authorities, who concluded that this was a matter of personal discretion, laudable under some—but by no means all or many—circumstances, and not a matter of public policy.

A significant jurisprudence of martyrdom developed over the centuries. The *Shulchan Aruch*, the authoritative sixteenth-century codification of Jewish law, devotes a whole section to the subject, and its numerous glossators and commentators, summarizing the vast medieval halachic literature on the subject, explore the various permutations of martyrdom and self-sacrifice in harrowing detail.[35] One point that emerges rather clearly is that martyrdom is not called for if the oppressive Gentile is requesting the forbidden act for his own enjoyment and not for the theological purpose of trying to get the Jew, *qua* Jew, to violate his religious integrity; in that case, where no principle is at stake, the principle of the sanctity of human life takes precedence.

Put in the terms of our earlier discussion, where the anti-Semite is acting out of his own enjoyment, the oppressor-oppressed dialectic, the "nonviolent moment," does not take hold, and to resist for its own sake is meaningful only as an act of personal piety, a demonstration of that particular Jew's commitment, and not as a stand that all members of the community need to take upon themselves, because the fundamental integrity of the community is not under attack. Where, however, the anti-Semite is acting out of principle, out of an affirmative desire to strike at the community's religious foundations, the dialectic has taken hold and one must resist, unto death, for the community's sake.

The overall picture then, is that when Jews are faced with persecution that cannot be met with force, their chief goal is to survive, but to survive as a community whose basic structures and values are intact. Thus they may bend normative religious obligations a great deal, but may not violate them utterly, in a manner that would vitiate the community's reasons for being. Indeed, maintaining the community's fundamental integrity was its own form of spiritual resistance.

In the twentieth century, the new dimensions of martyrdom inescapably color all subsequent discussions of violence and nonviolence. The Holocaust was of course an event of indescribable evil unparalleled in the history of mankind. The bureaucratization of society, the extraordinary power of the nation-state, romantic nationalism, a rich legacy of Christian anti-Semitism, and the oldest impulses of sadism and cruelty met in a horrible synthesis that resulted in the deaths of millions and the destruction of an entire civilization in the space of just a few years.

For purposes of this discussion, the salient fact about the Holocaust is that it simply did not matter to Hitler and his multitude of accomplices whether a Jew was religious or secular, private or public, deracinated or ethnocentric, or even the child of parents who had converted to Christianity. A Jew was a Jew was a Jew was a Jew, and each and every one had to be killed, wherever he or she was found, no matter what he or she was doing. In other words, the concepts and categories of martyrdom elaborated by the rabbis over the centuries counted for nothing. In the Nazi kingdom a Jew was neither faithful nor faithless, affiliated nor assimilated, only alive or dead.

The question then arises, did martyrdom, as idea and lived reality, as a concept that offered some meaning and guidance in the face of centuries of implacable violence, really perish in the indiscriminate murder of the Holocaust?

Yes and no. The sheer enormity and totality of the Holocaust concentrated the collective Jewish mind on the basic tasks of survival. Thus it was, by way of illustration, that anti-Zionism ceased to be a viable intellectual or political stance in the Jewish world. Yet, if you will, the sensibility of martyrdom, of doing the utmost to ensure physical survival while preserving undying communal beliefs and values, did manifest itself.

The enormities of which we are speaking are such that one can only be suggestive; as so many have said, silence is, beyond a certain point, the only honest response one can make to the Holocaust. These caveats notwithstanding, I suggest that we can discern the outlines of a response by examining the responses to Nazi persecution, and to the imperatives of physical and spiritual survival, of two Jewish scholars, both steeped, each in his own and very different way, in the tradition, one a spokesman for the most traditional strictures of Jewish law, the other a celebrated spokesman for a kind of Jewish antinomianism and for the peaceful resolution of conflicts: Ephraim Oshry and Martin Buber.

Oshry, the lesser known of the two, was a rabbi and Talmudic lecturer in Kovno (Kaunas), Lithuania. Along with Rabbi Avraham Kahane Shapira, he served as rabbi and halachic authority for the Kovno ghetto and managed to save and later publish the many halachic rulings (or responsa) he issued during the war years in response to queries from the religious inhabitants of the ghetto, who, not surprisingly, turned to their rabbinic authorities for guidance in the frightening new situations in which they found themselves.[36] A listing of just a handful of the queries recorded by Oshry attests to the seriousness with which these Jews took their commitment to abide by the halacha: May a slave laborer eat on Yom Kippur even if he is not yet in imminent danger of starvation? May one make a prayer shawl out of wool stolen from a German warehouse? May one pose as a non-Jew in order to escape the ghetto? May one study Torah with an intellectually-minded SS officer? May one commit suicide?

These harrowing responsa exhibit three salient characteristics: the seriousness with which these questions are put; the degree to which Oshry tries to situate his answers within the conventional parameters of Jewish legal discourse (citations to sources and authorities, reasoning by precedent, qualification and analogy, etc.); and the extent to which the primacy of survival colors his halachic decision making. Throughout, Oshry deploys his considerable legal acumen in order to arrive at halachic solutions that the people could, literally, live with.

In these responsa one can observe the Jewish principles of martyrdom and self-defense coming together. The Jews of the Kovno ghetto spiritually resisted the Nazis by clinging to their religion and culture as best they could, including seeking rabbinic sanction for the hard decisions of survival so as to preserve some moral structure in the face of genocide. At the same time, they used every means in order to survive, and Rabbi Oshry invoked the Talmudic doctrine of communal self-defense in sanctioning joining the partisan groups offering armed resistance.[37]

Yet risk taking as a form of personal piety was also maintained. Thus Rabbi Oshry, who, despite his stature, also ran the ghetto's only laundry, kept the laundry closed on Sabbath and holidays even though by doing so he incurred the wrath of the Germans, and was not commanded to do so by the strict terms of the halacha of martyrdom.[38] This self-sacrifice is especially striking in light of the leeway and discretion he generally accorded his questioners in the conduct of their daily struggles.

Oshry, of course, is a representative of the most law-minded elements of the Jewish tradition. The striking thing is the similarity of his approach, emphasizing the primacy of survival in the face of attempted annihilation, to that of Martin Buber, the greatest Jewish antinomian. Buber, we may recall, was the intellectual godfather of the short-lived Brit Shalom movement, which attempted to reconcile competing Jewish and Arab claims to Palestine by promoting the idea of a binational state, and of course the expositor of the spontaneous, relational ethic of I-Thou over and against rule-bound codes of ethics and morality. Yet in response to Gandhi's suggestion, made in an article published in November of 1938, that the Jews of Germany engage in passive resistance to the Nazi regime rather than attempt flight to Palestine, Buber, writing from his own perspective, perfectly articulated a Judaic expression of nonviolence. He replied to Gandhi in a long open letter, written after several months of soul-searching, that must stand as the definitive Jewish statement on nonviolence in our time:

> In the five years which I myself spent under the present [Nazi] regime, I observed many instances of genuine *Satyagraha* among the Jews. . . . Such actions, however, exerted apparently not the slightest influence on their opponents. . . . An effective stand may be taken in the form of non-violence against unfeeling human beings in the hope of gradually bringing them thereby to their senses; but a diabolic universal steam-roller cannot thus be withstood. . . . Testimony without acknowledgment,

ineffective, unobserved martyrdom, a martyrdom cast to the winds—that is the fate of innumerable Jews in Germany. God alone accepts their testimony. God "seals" it, as is said in our prayers. But no maxim for suitable behavior can be deduced therefrom. . . .

I would not deny . . . that although I should not have been among the crucifiers of Jesus, I should also not have been among his supporters. For I cannot help withstanding evil when I see it is about to destroy the good. I am forced to withstand the evil in the world just as the evil within myself. I can only strive not to have to do so by force. I do not want force. But if there is no other way of preventing the evil destroying the good, I trust I shall use force and give myself up into God's hands.[39]

Put in terms of our earlier discussion, in Buber's presentation, the experience of Nazi persecution did not present a "nonviolent moment"; the dialectical relationship of oppressor and oppressed simply vanished in the totality of the Nazi drive for eradication.

Oshry and Buber, each steeped in Jewish literature and life—though nearly diametrically opposed in their respective theologies—arrived at remarkably similar understandings of the meaning of resistance in an age of total annihilation, an age which, having once been initiated, can henceforth never be said to have passed.

To conclude with the questions posed at the outset:

1. What does Jewish tradition direct Jews, specifically Jews, to do in given situations?

The literature of martyrdom indicates that Jewish tradition directs the Jewish community to fight against evil with whatever means are at its disposal, to do the utmost to preserve human life, even in the face of subjugation and humiliation, but not at the cost of tearing away at the very fabric of the religious and social order.

2. Is there a way of thinking "Jewishly" about this question? Is there a Jewish style of moral/prudential reasoning about this, one that could conceivably be of use to those outside the ambit of Jewish law and tradition?

The Jewish style of reasoning on these issues is highly contextual and fact-specific, informed by a rich understanding of textual warrant and historical experience, repeatedly evaluating circumstances in the light of both abiding imperatives and changing circumstances. This is both cause and effect of this reasoning's having been developed in legal, rather than theoretical, texts and contexts.

Thus the Jewish style of moral reasoning on this issue—and others—may best be characterized as akin to prudential legal reasoning.[40] What differentiates it from mere prudence as such is its grounding in exegesis and faith, within a fluid but determinate tradition that attempts to synthesize innovation with fidelity through interpretation.[41]

3. Finally, do the same norms apply in Israel and the Diaspora?

The appropriate theological characterization of the Jewish state of Israel has, not surprisingly, been the subject of lively and heated debate, with opinions ranging from the ascription of near-Messianic status to Jewish statehood, to the denial of any religious significance to statehood, with a variety of intermediate positions ranging in between.[42] My own view tends toward the latter, that the Jewish state is not itself sacred, but that its citizens are as a group charged with the responsibility of trying to accomplish sacred ends, as best they can.[43]

By this reasoning, one would have to say that the same fundamental norms apply in both Israel and the Diaspora. The state is not absolutized or reified. It is an instrument of communal survival, and the individuals leading it are bound by norms. The sustained Jewish protest against the corruption of this world must be part of the state's ethos, even as it partakes of this world's imperfections.

NOTES

1. As a précis, I would note that in my approach to the tradition, seeing it as neither relic nor idol, I am indebted to Jaroslav Pelikan, *The Vindication of Tradition* (New Haven: Yale University Press, 1984); and in my willingness to assert my own position notwithstanding the perils of "normativity," I take a thoughtful, if impish cue from Clifford Geertz: "A number

of things, I think, are true." Clifford Geertz, *Local Knowledge: Further Essays in Interpretive Anthropology* (New York: Basic Books, 1983), p. 19.

2. Though Leibowitz, who passed away as this essay was going to press, was a controversial thinker, and indeed worshipped in what John Milton described as "a church with only one member," he is a vital and significant thinker who must be reckoned with. A number of his most important essays have recently appeared in English under the title *Judaism, Human Values and the Jewish State* (Cambridge: Harvard University Press, 1992), which I have discussed in *The New Leader*, September 7, 1992, pp. 18–20.

3. See Gerald Blidstein, "The Monarchic Imperative in Rabbinic Perspective," *AJS Review* 7 (1982): 15–39.

4. Michael Walzer has expressed a similar idea in the more strictly Israeli context: "Israel's common Jewishness should be . . . a distillation of Jewish history and values in which all (or almost all) Jews can recognize themselves. What content the distillation will have, how rich it will be, depends on the creativity of Israeli Jews, on the continuing work of poets, philosophers, artists, historians and novelists. Bialik's poems, studied by school children, suggest one possibility; the appropriation of the Amalek story by right-wing politicians suggests another." Michael Walzer, *What Kind of State is a Jewish State?* (Jerusalem: Shalom Hartman Institute, 1989), pp. 13–14.

5. Amos Funkenstein, *Tadmit V'Todaah Historit B'yahadut Uv'svivatah Ha-Tarbutit* [Perceptions of Jewish History from Antiquity to the Present] (Tel Aviv: Am Oved, 1991), p. 27. An English edition of these essays, *Perceptions of Jewish History*, has recently been published (Berkeley: University of California Press, 1993). This assertion of a Jewish past lived in historical time need not conflict with the more strictly theological perspective of the Jewish people ontologically standing outside of history, expressed most powerfully by Franz Rosenzweig; see Paul Mendes-Flohr, "Franz Rosenzweig and the Crisis of Historicism," in *The Philosophy of Franz Rosenzweig*, ed. Paul Mendes-Flohr (Hanover, N.H.: University Press of New England, 1988), pp. 138–61.

6. The comments of Bernard Susser and Eliezer Don-Yehiya are worth quoting at length: "Speaking for at least the great span stretching from Talmudic times to the eighteenth century, most Jewish political theorizing was the handmaiden of quotidian life and pressing realities. Notably, the greater part of political discourse comes in direct response to actual and specific questions posed to celebrated legal scholars. On this level of responsa and legal debate, concern with the ideal state or the philosophical status of the state, or forms of government as a principle etc. [sic] is almost entirely absent. Instead, we encounter questions relating to the obligation of the Jewish community to the regimes under which they lived as well as questions regarding the internal organization and authority of the Jewish community. In the latter class are found such staples of Western political theory as the source and nature of the majority's political authority and the protection of the minority as well as individual rights . . . this constitutes as much an articulation of political culture and tradition as of political theory—somewhat comparable to reconstructing the American Public Philosophy [sic] from Supreme Court decisions." Bernard Susser and Eliezer Don-Yehiya, "Prolegomena to Jewish Polit-

ical Theory" in *Kinship and Consent: The Jewish Political Tradition and its Contemporary Uses*, ed. Daniel J. Elazar (Ramat Gan: Turtledove, 1981), pp. 91–111, at 94.

7. I do not mean to delegitimize categorically a pacifist stance that one may try to formulate on the basis of Jewish tradition, and certainly not to trivialize or dismiss the moral imperatives that would impel and underlie that stance. I do think, however, that any such stance would be very, very hard to square with the theory and practice of Judaism as it has been articulated in texts and lived in historical experience.

8. Had the verse meant to rule out all killing of any kind, it would have said, *lo taharog*. I am indebted for this observation to my colleague Dr. Harvey Sicherman. See also the commentary of Rashbam to Ex. 19:13.

9. Zech. 4:6.

10. Eccles. 3:8.

11. This was memorably put by the Talmud, *B.T. Eruvin* 13b: "Our Rabbis taught: For two and a half years the schools of Shammai and Hillel debated whether man would have been better off never to have been created at all. In the end, they concluded that man would have been better off never to have been created. But seeing as he has, he should scrutinize his deeds." Similarly, we read in the Mishnaic tractate *Pirkei Avot* 2: 17 [Commonly referred to as *Ethics of the Fathers*]: "It is not up to you to finish the work, nor are you free to desist from it." For a general discussion of the concept of repairing the world, *tikkun olam*, as developed in rabbinic literature, see Menachem Lorberbaum, "Maimonides' Conception of Tikkun Olam," in *Tarbits*, 1995.

12. *B.T. Berachot* 58a; *Yoma* 85b; *Sanhedrin* 72a, etc.

13. In speaking of "deep metaphors" I am attempting to adapt the notion put forth by the so-called "Lurianic" school of Jewish mysticism, named for the divine Isaac Luria of the sixteenth century, whose theological response to the catastrophic Spanish expulsion of 1492 was the notion that the exile of the Jewish people both represented and enacted God's exile from the world, and His alienation from dimensions of Himself. This characterization of Lurianism, offered by the magisterial Gershom Scholem, has come in for some serious criticism; see Moshe Idel, *Kabbalah: New Perspectives* (New Haven: Yale University Press, 1988), pp. 264–67. Nonetheless, the suggestive theological uses of Scholem's understanding of Luria need not be dismissed. As this essay was going to press, I came across adumbrations of this idea in some of Rav Kook's writings. See his *Arpilei Tohar*, (Jerusalem 1983) pp. 56–57, and *Orot*, standard ed., p. 138.

14. For a powerfully argued presentation of this idea, see Michael Wyschogrod, *The Body of Faith: God in the People of Israel* (San Francisco: Harper & Row, 1989).

15. See Avi Ravitzky, "Peace," in *Contemporary Jewish Religious Thought*, ed. Arthur A. Cohen and Paul Mendes-Flohr (New York: Free Press, 1987), pp. 685–702; a Hebrew version, with extensive footnotes absent in the English, can be found in the same author's *Al Da'at Ha-Makom: Mehkarim B'hagut Yehudit Uv'Toldoteha* [Studies in the History of Jewish Philosophy] (Jerusalem: Keter, 1991), pp. 13–34. For wide-ranging theological and historical analyses, which,

taken together, reinforce this view, see *Violence and Defense in the Jewish Experience*, ed. Salo W. Baron and George S. Wise (Philadelphia: Jewish Publication Society, 1977).

16. See Reuven Kimelman, "The Ethics of Power: Government and War from the Sources of Judaism" in *Authority, Power and Leadership in the Jewish Polity: Cases and Issues*, ed. Daniel J. Elazar (Lanham, Md.: University Press of America, 1991), pp. 247–94, 252. Kimelman's article provides a thorough discussion of the basic sources and issues. As to whether Jews may participate in wars waged by non-Jewish states for *raison d'état*, see Shlomo Zevin, *Le-Or ha-Halacha* [In Light of the Halacha] (Jerusalem: Beit Hillel, 1978), pp. 58–59. On the conceptual underpinning of war for the defense of the Jewish people, see Joseph B. Soloveitchik, *B'sod Hayahid V'hayahad* [In Aloneness, In Togetherness] (Jerusalem: Orot, 1976), pp. 392–93. It bears noting that a wide literature on the halachically proper conduct of war has been written in Israel; for a representative sample of the pre-1967 writings on the subject, see Yehudah Shaviv, ed., *Ha-Torah v'Ha-Medinah* [Torah and the State], Vol. I (Jeruslaem: Sinai, 1992), and for the post-1967 discussions, see the hefty volumes of *T'Humnin* (12 vols., 1979–94), published by the Institute for Zionism, Statehood and Torah in Alon Shvut.

17. See *B.T. Eruvin* 45a, *J.T. Terumot* 8:4; Maimonides' Code, *Mishneh Torah, Hilchot Shabbat* [Laws of Sabbath], 3:23; *Shulchan Aruch, Orach Chaim*, 429 (7).

18. A good selection of Kook's writings has appeared in English as part of the series "Classics of Western Spirituality," in *Abraham Isaac Kook*, translated and edited by Ben-Zion Bokser (New York: Paulist Press, 1978).

19. It is clear that by "Israel" Kook means the Jewish people, since this was written nearly forty-five years before the creation of the state, and the term *Israel* refers to the Jewish people throughout rabbinic literature.

20. Abraham Isaac Kook, *Ig'rot Ha-R'iyah* [Collected Letters] (Jerusalem: Mossad Harav Kook, 1962), 1:100.

21. See the comments by Yehudah Amital in *The World of Rav Kook's Thought*, ed. Benjamin Ish-Shalom and Shalom Rosenberg (n.p.: Avi Chai, 1991) p. 433. It bears noting that Amital, a Holocaust survivor and highly regarded rabbinic authority, though earlier in his career a premier theoretician of Gush Emmunim, has since emerged as a leading figure in the religious peace movement in Israel.

22. I can do no better than to quote the Rev. Dr. Martin Luther King, Jr.: "The nonviolent resisters can summarize their message in the following simple terms: We will take direct action against injustice without waiting for other agencies to act. We will not obey unjust laws or submit to unjust practices. We will do this peacefully, openly, cheerfully because our aim is to persuade. We adopt the means of nonviolence because our end is a community at peace with itself. We will try to persuade with our words, but if our words fail, we will try to persuade with our acts. We will always be willing to talk and seek fair compromise, but we are ready to suffer when necessary and even risk our lives to become witnesses to the truth as we see it." Dr. King repeated this formulation verbatim at least three different times that I am aware of, at various stages in his career, in 1958, 1960, and 1962. See *A Testament of Hope: The Essential Writings of Martin Luther King, Jr.*, ed. James M. Washington (San Francisco: Harper & Row, 1986), pp. 110, 149, 484–85.

23. Reinhold Niebuhr, explaining how he, a self-described "strong anti-pacifist," could support the civil rights movement's strategy of nonviolent resistance, said in 1963: "King's doctrine of nonviolent resistance is not pacifism. Pacifism of the really classical kind is where you are concerned about your own purity and not responsibility. And the great ethical divide is between people who want to be pure and those who want to be responsible. And I think King has shown this difference." Quoted in Taylor Branch, *Parting the Waters: America in the King Years, 1954–63* (New York: Simon & Schuster, 1988), p. 896.

24. The term *republic of fear* is borrowed from Kanan Makiya's *The Republic of Fear: The Politics of Modern Iraq* (Berkeley: University of California Press, 1989). Makiya, writing then under the pseudonym Samir al-Kkhalil, draws a chilling portrait of Saddam Hussein's Iraq, and offers a penetrating account of the logic of totalitarianism and of the role of terror in perpetuating it.

25. See Cornel West, "The Religious Foundations of the Thought of Martin Luther King, Jr." in *We Shall Overcome: Martin Luther King, Jr. and the Black Freedom Struggle*, ed. Peter J. Albert and Ronald Hoffman (New York: Pantheon, 1990), pp. 113–29, 126: "[T]he Gandhian method of love-motivated (*agapic*) nonviolent resistance provided King with both a response to Marx and an answer to Nietzsche. It gave him the means to apply the love ethic of Jesus Christ in the social sphere, as a moral and practical method—a way of life and a way of struggle—by which oppressed people could fight for freedom without inflicting violence on their oppressor or humiliating their opponent, thus preserving the possibility of transforming the moral disposition of their adversary."

26. Reuven Kimelman, "Non-Violence in the Talmud," *Judaism* 17 (1968): 316–34.

27. Kimelman, "Non-Violence," pp. 333–34.

28. Lev. 18:5.

29. Deut. 6:5.

30. The halacha does not as a rule require martyrdom of women forced to engage in sexual acts, out of recognition of their social and biological vulnerabilities.

31. The *locus classicus* of the Talmudic discussion is *B.T. Sanhedrin* 74a-b. See also Maimonides' Code, *Mishneh Torah, Hilchot Yesodei ha-Torah* [Laws of the Foundation of Torah], chap. 5. The earliest post-Talmudic sources leave open the possibility that God-fearing non-Jews may themselves at times be commanded to submit to martyrdom. See *Sheiltot d'Rav Ahai Gaon, Parshat Vaera*, ed. S. Mirsky (Jerusalem: Sura, 1964), 3:40.

32. Hyam Maccoby, "Sanctification of the Name" in *Contemporary Jewish Religious Thought*, p. 853.

33. Generally referred to as "The Hasidim of Ashkenaz," this group is not to be confused with the Hasidim of today, whose socioreligious origins lie in eighteenth-century eastern Europe. On the medieval Jewish Pietists of

Germany, see, generally, Gershom Scholem, *Major Trends in Jewish Mysticism* (New York: Schocken, 1946), chap. 3; Haym Soloveitchik, "Three Themes in the *Sefer Hasidim*," *AJS Review* 1 (1976): 318–57.

34. *Sefer Hasidim* [The Book of the Pious], ed. Reuven Margaliot (Jerusalem: Mossad Harav Kook, 1957), sec. 155, p. 157.

35. *Shulchan Aruch, Yoreh De'ah*, 157.

36. Ephraim Oshry, *Sh'elot U'teshuvot Mi'maamakim* [Responsa from the Depths], 5 vols. (New York: n.p., 1959–79). For a discussion of Oshry's work in English, see Irving J. Rosenbaum, *The Holocaust and Halakhah* (New York: Ktav, 1976).

37. Oshry, *Sh'elot U'teshuvot Mi'maamakim*, 4:73–79.

38. Ibid., 5:129–34.

39. The Gandhi-Buber exchange may be found in full in *A Land of Two Peoples: Martin Buber on Jews and Arabs*, ed. Paul R. Mendes-Flohr (New York: Oxford University Press, 1983), pp. 106–26.

40. For a depiction of this style of reasoning in a different context, see Anthony Kronman, "Alexander Bickel's Philosophy of Prudence," *Yale Law Journal* 94 (1985): 1567–616.

41. For a thorough discussion of the ways in which Judaic law resonates with, while significantly differing from, current issues of jurisprudence, see Suzanne Last Stone, "In Pursuit of the Counter-Text: The Turn to the Jewish Legal Model in Contemporary American Legal Theory," *Harvard Law Review* 106 (1993): 813–94, and Perry Dane, "The Oral Law and the Jurisprudence of a Textless Text," *S'vara* 2 (1991): 11–24.

42. For thorough surveys, see Yoseph Gorny, *The State of Israel in Jewish Public Thought: The Quest for Collective Identity* (New York: New York University Press, 1984), and Aviezer Ravitzky, *Haketz Hamiguleh u-Medinat Hayehudim* [Messianism, Zionism and Jewish Religious Radicalism] (Tel Aviv: Am Oved, 1993). On the evolution of Zionist attitudes toward political violence, see Anita Shapira, *Land and Power: The Zionist Resort to Force, 1881–1948* (New York: Oxford University Press, 1992). I have discussed Shapira's analysis of what she terms Zionism's "defensive ethos" in *Jerusalem Report*, 3(17), Dec. 31, 1992, pp. 46–47. For a useful introduction to one very central—and often theologically overlooked—aspect of the question, see W. D. Davies, *The Territorial Dimension of Judaism* (Berkeley: University of California Press, 1982).

43. Rabbi Emanuel Rackman, noted authority on Jewish law and Chancellor of Bar-Ilan University, has suggestively characterized the theological standing of the Jewish state as being analogous to the "object needed for the performance of a commandment," which the Talmud says may be discarded after use, as distinct from a "holy object," which may not be discarded under any circumstances. (Private conversation with the author.) The distinction between the two sorts of objects is found in *B.T. Megillah* 26b.

Pacifism and Nonviolence:
Another Jewish View

NAOMI GOODMAN

The paper of Yehuda Mirsky, to which I am responding, begins with a series of provocative questions. The first two, on the Jewish tradition and whether there are ways of thinking "Jewishly" about nonviolence that would be relevant and helpful to non-Jews, seem to me interrelated and so must be considered together.

The Jewish tradition is quite specific on this point. Violence is justified only if and when it is the means of self-defense. In short, violence is the last resort. Rabbi David Shapiro, in his major study of "Jewish Attitudes to War and Peace," writes:

> That the rights of humanity have to be protected everywhere through the concerned efforts of all who believe in justice, even by the use of force *if no other viable alternative exists,* has been the conviction of Judaism at all times[1] (emphasis added).

Always, the question is: What are the viable alternatives and have they been seriously tried?

As Jews, we have a peace tradition and a war tradition. Putting the word *peace* first is not the customary practice for these concepts, but peace first expresses the most fundamental Judaic attitude. Peace has always been the ideal, the messianic, the hoped for and prayed for; the goal to which we are taught to aspire, to teach our children, and to lend every effort, "to seek peace and pursue it."[2] Note that "the law does not require you to run after, or pursue, the commandments, but only to fulfill them, when the appropriate occasion comes . . . but peace you must seek in your own place and run after it to another."[3] Further, "there is nothing that comes before the saving of life except idolatry, incest and bloodshed only."[4]

The belief in shalom derives from the purest and highest in Jewish morality. The peace expressed by shalom encompasses far more than the absence of war. Shalom means wholeness, righteousness, justice, grace, and truth. Certainly, the modern theological concept that peace is not possible without justice is based on the Hebrew Scriptures. Shalom embraces the totality of human life, including environmental concerns, protection of animals, opposition to all killing. Shalom is the name of God.

The Jewish acceptance of wars of defense stems from nationalism, often extreme and chauvinistic, during the period of the kingdoms, as written in the Scriptures. But it also arises from the subsequent history of virulent anti-Semitism and more recently from the results of our bloody century, including the establishment of Israel. Jewish writings on the morality of warfare stress various "humane" procedures such as refraining from destroying fruit trees when besieging a city—better than the scorched earth practices prevalent in antiquity and carried out without remorse by many nations in our own times, although there is no way to make war humane.

Judaism's principles on these themes were codified first in the Hebrew Scriptures and have since been interpreted and reinterpreted both in the *Halakah*, the rabbinic interpretation of the laws, and in the *Aggadah*, all the nonlegal rabbinic commentary. Such explication is a continuing process that goes on to this very day.

Although an absolute, principled nonviolence was rarely demanded by the founders and interpreters of Judaism, quite another view can also be drawn from Jewish tradition. Above all, the tradition celebrates the belief that peace is the highest priority in Jewish life, which Steven Schwarzschild endorsed: "If one were to describe in one word the essence of Jewish morality, then the word would have to be 'peace.' "[5]

While self-defense was permitted in biblical and rabbinical Judaism, as the law evolved, acts of retribution, revenge, and violence were hedged with all sorts of restrictions. Each life was sacred: the person who preserves the life of one human being, it is as though they have preserved the whole world; while the person who destroys one human being is regarded as if they have destroyed the whole world.[6] This reluctance to hurt others pervades much of later Jewish writing, especially in the Talmud.

Indeed, Jewish history does not glorify the man of war. "Let not the mighty man glory in his might"[7] agrees with the peace positions of many prophets such as Isaiah, Micah, and Habakkuk. David was not permitted to build the Temple, because he was a warrior; that task was given to his son Solomon, as a man of peace.[8] Victory belongs to God, not to human beings. Jewish heroes are not the warriors but, rather, the prophets and sages. We celebrate Hanukkah not for the military victory but for the miracle of the oil, which was only enough for one day but kept the *Ner Tamid*, the Eternal Light, burning in front of the Ark for eight days until new oil could be brought. The story of the Maccabees is not in the Scriptures. The rabbinic deemphasis of the Maccabees has to do with their warfare and with the later experiences when they became oppressors and caused civil strife.

There has been much misunderstanding regarding the Hebrew position of "an eye for an eye," which has been misinterpreted as encouraging vengeance. But "an eye for an eye" established that the recompense for an evil deed could not be greater than the act itself: One could not demand a life for injury to an eye; only this limited and legal recompense was permitted. This law prevented the escalation of blood feuds, and thus prevented violence. " 'Vengeance is mine' saith the Lord" has meant that vengeance is not an appropriate response for human beings.

Having established an alternative interpretation of the Jewish peace tradition, a tradition of great value to other religions and one that influenced the other monotheistic religions, I would like to consider certain specific points in approximately the order in which they occur. Yehuda Mirsky's paper concentrates on politics, but peace and nonviolence are more than political concepts in that they are moral and religious as well. He notes correctly that Jewish legal history provides the material with which to study Jewish politics. Jewish legal history also gives us the means to study Jewish peace principles. I would dispute the assertion that Judaism rejects pacifism not only in practice but in principle, and have given a little of the vast evidence for this position above. The use of pacific means to achieve ends and the use of nonviolent direct action are activist stands for achieving a just and godly social order, and have been endorsed in theory and practice by Jewish authorities. These positions are not evasions, cop-outs, attitudes of the unworldly ignoring reality, but moral positions that have proved their validity.

Mirsky's paper considers the translation of the commandment usually rendered "Thou shalt not kill," and maintains, as do others, that the true translation is, "Thou shalt not murder." Killing, according to most definitions, is putting to death, slaying, while murder is the unlawful killing of one human being by another. Here we are involved in further definitions: Some rabbis maintain that there is no such thing as legal killing in Judaism. They cite the fact that, although the law permitted capital punishment for murderers, this law was surrounded with so many restrictions that such punishment rarely took place. There had to be two witnesses to the deed, who were required to warn the person involved of the nature of the projected crime and of its legal consequences. No circumstantial evidence was allowed. A Jewish court of sages that executed one person in seven years was called a murderous court. "One in seventy years," says Rabbi Elazar ben Azariah.[9]

After discussing the Israeli view, which can be debated, Yehuda Mirsky goes on to consider nonviolence. Of course, I would agree that the advocates of active nonviolence are well aware of struggle and conflict, but it must be emphasized that they have a different approach to handling and solving such conflict than do those who advocate force. Reinhold Niebuhr, who is quoted on pacifism, is in error when he equates pacifism with personal purity and evasion of responsibility.[10] Pacifism and active nonviolence are understood by their proponents as being closely related, if not synonymous. Unfortunately, pacifism is confused with passivity by some; the formerly common use of the term *passive resistance* for nonviolent resistance has made pacifism seem negative to its detractors. The pacifist, as the advocate of nonviolent resistance, is responsible and concerned, but believes that there are other, better methods of settling conflict than depending on force. This is perhaps a slight diversion from the topic of Jewish response, but the point was made. I can only add that Jewish pacifists do not condone evil or ignore it, and, like other pacifists, are concerned with larger issues of responsibility, of effecting change, and believe, with many Jewish theologians and scholars, that the ends and the means are one.

Those Israeli doves who seek peace, together with their supporters among worldwide Jewry, are concerned with the safety and security of Israel and believe that they are working to ensure peace for Israel so that it will have a future. They come from many backgrounds, but they are all convinced that Israel's survival is not dependent on a greater area, that land should be traded for peace, and that justice for the displaced Palestinian people is both necessary morally and wise politically.

Yehuda Mirsky quoted Reuven Kimelman's excellent essay "Nonviolence in the Talmud," which I recommend highly. I would like to quote from Rabbi Shapiro's study again:

> The prophets and sages of Israel believed that man must be educated for peace. Though they lived in a world that was rampant with violence . . . they sought out ways and means whereby

the combative and competitive aspects of human nature could be diverted into more constructive channels. . . . The Jewish doctrine of *Imitatio Dei*, which is the religious grounding of man's ethical life, signifies just this—that man is to be the preserver of life.[11]

Just as war is not glorified in Jewish tradition, neither is martyrdom. We both agree that Judaism is a life-affirming religion. I would add that martyrdom is neither to be desired nor sought, and does not carry the rewards it does in some other religions. The Masada mass suicides have been less celebrated in rabbinic literature than they are in contemporary Israel. Since the survival of the community is paramount, life must be preserved.

The recommended approach is spiritual resistance, which has been one of the reasons for the survival of the Jewish people. This view was summed up by Rabbi Leo Baeck in Thereseinstadt in 1944 when he told a group of his fellow prisoners that our prophets

turned against the sort of politics that creates its own moral code, they objected to any justification of right by victory. . . . True history is the history of the spirit, the human spirit, which at times may seem powerless, but ultimately is yet superior and survives because even if it has not got the might, it still possesses the power, the power that can never cease.[12]

As the discussion of the Holocaust continues, Buber's famous letter to Gandhi is quoted, but his advocacy of a binational state for Jews and Palestinians is slighted as "short-lived." Surely a concept cannot be measured by such a criterion; many influential Jewish thinkers were in favor of a binational solution: Hans Kohn, Arthur Ruppin, Judah Magnes, Ernst Simon, Henrietta Szold, among many others at that time and today. This approach might have prevented much bloodshed and was as essential a part of Buber's thinking as was his sad recognition that nonviolence could not help in the situation of the Holocaust. In terms of the Holocaust, the point is that nothing that Jews or other victims did could help. As Eli Wiesel has written:

Those who fought—and there were fighters in all the ghettos, in all the camps—did so not in order to win—they knew they could not win in a world that opposed and hated them—but to bear witness for history. . . . In every ghetto and every camp there were some men and women who fought with weapons, while others fought with words.[13]

The third question considered, whether the same norms in pacifism and nonviolence apply in Israel as in the Diaspora, provides a point of partial agreement. Yehuda Mirsky and I both feel that the same standards must apply, but we differ strongly in defining those standards and beliefs. Thus, the conclusions of his paper seem to point in the direction of moral restraint, nonviolence, and not a call to arms, but it defines these qualities in a different way from Jewish advocates of active nonviolence. The paper praises the ethos of defense and restraint that eventually came to characterize Zionism's use of force. This statement, made without qualification, is highly debatable and seems to me inaccurate. The conclusion goes on to mention the Palestinian problem for the first time, but we must add that the suggestion that nonviolence on the part of the Palestinians would have helped their cause is disingenuous, to say the least.[14] It is worth noting that the Palestinians have employed many of the tactics of active nonviolence, including general or partial work stoppages, boycotts, closing of their places of business, efforts not to buy Israeli products, and so on. Weapons have been used to a greater extent by the occupying forces. Those Israelis who do not glorify the land but who regard peace, rather than a greater Israel, as the way to preserve their endangered community are following the principles of Jewish nonviolence. From the army officers in the Council for Peace and Security who advocate a Palestinian state as safer than the present unrest; to the soldiers in *Yesh G'vul* (There Is a Limit) who will not serve beyond the green line that marks the Occupied Territories; to the religious Zionists in *Oz veShalom/Netivot Shalom*; to those who work in Arab-Jewish cooperative ventures exemplified in such projects as Interns for Peace, *Neve Shalom*, and *Givat Haviva*; to the broad coalition of Peace Now and the numerous women's groups advocating peace—these are Israelis who believe that "the person who turns an enemy into a friend"[15] has accomplished the work of God—and protected the Jewish community.[16]

NOTES

1. Rabbi David Shapiro, "The Jewish Attitude Towards War and Peace," in *Studies in Jewish Thought* (New York: Yeshiva University Press, 1975), 1:90.

2. Ps. 34:15.

3. Numbers Rabbah, Hukkat XIX, 27.

4. Keth l9a.

5. Rabbi Steven Schwarzschild, "Shalom," in *Confrontation* 21 (1981): 166–76; reprinted in *Holy Land* 7 (1987): 171–80. Quoted from Hermann Cohen, *Religion of Reason out of the Sources of Judaism*, trans. Simon Kaplan (New York: Frederick Ungar, 1972), p. 459.

6. Mishnah Sanhedrin IV, 5.

7. Jer. 9:22.

8. 1 Chron. 22.

9. Mishnah Makkot 1:10.

10. Supra, p. 65, n. 23.

11. Shapiro, "Jewish Attitude," pp. 56–57. Reuven Kimelman's essay "Nonviolence in the Talmud" is from *Roots of Jewish Nonviolence* (Nyack, N.Y.: Jewish Peace Fellowship, 1981), pp. 24–50.

12. Albert H. Friedlander, *Leo Baeck: Teacher of Theresienstadt* (New York: Overlook Press, 1968), p. 216.

13. Eli Wiesel, "The Jew and War," in *A Jew Today* (New York: Random House, 1978), p. 180.

14. Mirsky's comment was removed in revision. Ed.

15. Abot d'Rabbi Nathan 23.

16. Further material on this topic is available in *The Challenge of Shalom: The Jewish Tradition of Peace and Justice*, ed. Murray Polner and Naomi Goodman (Philadelphia: New Society, 1994).

On Not Being in Charge

JOHN H. YODER

THE SHAPE OF THE QUESTION

If you begin thinking, as in our culture we usually do, with the assumption that it is our moral responsibility to administer the course of human events, then the position I have been asked to describe may be designated as "quietism." If the assumptions are further specified to provide that we normally have a duty to enforce upon others, by military means, our conception of the desirable direction of events, then the position I describe may be called "pacifism." Yet both these characterizations presuppose a framing of the moral question that is already tilted. Therefore the more functional or formal phrase in my title, "not being in charge," is more fitting.

The dominant frame of reference for the institutional and moral thought of our culture is the legacy of the transitions symbolized, and to some extent caused, by Constantine.[1] Since then the public order, especially the civil order or "the state," is understood to be the primary bearer of the meaningful movement of history, so that social ethics is about how we would want those structures to move, and why. Despite the many structural changes in detail since the Middle Ages, including such major matters as royalty's yielding to democracy and the separation of church and state, the basic logic in most people's minds, including the unself-conscious assumptions of those who do not examine the matter, has not changed.[2] We assume that we both can and should "take responsibility" for the macro course of events, and then from that objective we derive the justification for the practical measures it takes to get there, such as getting elected to office, organizing and deploying military might, and whatever else it takes. That set of assumptions is so omnipresent that for many it is inconceivable that it might be doubted.

My task then is to make doubt at that point conceivable. In a prefatory way I shall remind you that doubting those assumptions might be justified on general logical and empirical grounds; but the substance of my assignment will be to narrate the experiences of some people from the underside of history, in order to concretize how reasonable the view from below can seem under certain circumstances, which in fact are not rare but typical.

THE LIMITS OF THE IMPERATIVE TO BE RESPONSIBLE

First, by way of preface: Logically and empirically it cannot be the case that "Thou shalt take responsibility for governing the world" is a univocal moral obligation. In the quadrennial civil ritual the United States experienced in the fall of 1992, at least half the persons offering to take on that responsibility as elected officials were not chosen. Many of the voters were not offered a candidate representing their values, and, thanks to low voter turnout, many of the persons elected probably were chosen by a minority of the electorate. Most of those elected and believing themselves mandated to do something have found that pre-existing structures in both the legislative and the executive agencies of state management keep them from doing what they believe in. This does not keep me from believing with Winston Churchill that parliamentary democracy is the worst form of government, except for all the others.[3] Yet this awareness should (and for a growing number of people does) undercut the naive notions of *vox populi* and "responsibility to serve" that dominate the public rhetoric. All civil government is oligarchy; all of it is a few people (to use the language of Jesus) "lording it" over the rest of us. The value of democracy is the relatively greater capacity that victims and third parties nonetheless have to speak critically.[4] But then those persons, sometimes heroic individuals and sometimes committed communities, who are committed to value systems that have no chance of being elected are not being "sectarian" or "withdrawing" when they do not join the electoral fray as if their dignity depended on it.[5]

A second logical observation: Some argue (and some take for granted as not even needing argument) that the price of "involvement" in public life and discourse is that one must filter out, or reserve to the private realm, or "compromise" the particular identifying value commitments of a faith community in favor of common-denominator moral language. Yet if in order to "be involved" you commit yourself to values less clear or less imperative than your own, which are more acceptable because the "public" out there already holds them, then your involvement adds nothing to the mix but numbers. Joining the majority on grounds that others already are committed to, being in favor of policies that others already support, winds up paradoxically having the same effect as abstention; it lets the values of the others be decisive.

These two prefatory comments are not meant to be probative; they seek only to open some space for the alternative narrative to which I now turn. I shall select several episodes from a much broader history, speaking schematically and not in chronological order.

THE SOCIAL CRITICISM OF THE FIRST REFORMATION

The movement Czech Protestants call "the First Reformation" faced its first crisis when the perfidy of Emperor Sigismund and the Council of Constance made a martyr of the nation's chief theologian, Jan Hus. The protest that resulted went off in three directions. One of them, nationalistic and noble, which came to be called "utraquist" or "calixtine," because the issue of communion in both kinds became its symbol, negotiated for a degree of ecclesiastical autonomy, with some success for a while. Another, the apocalyptic "Taborites," chose the path of revolutionary violence, with some success for a much shorter while. The third path, guided intellectually, noninstitutionally, by the lay theologian Peter Cheltschitsky, unfolded the first deeply thought-through critique of the Constantinian synthesis.[6] Having no military power base, Peter's movement grew slowly from below, thanks only to the power of his ideas and the way the other two "take-charge" strategies had failed. In 1467, his pupils formed the *Unitas Fratrum*, strictly speaking the first Protestant church.

Retrieving the Gospel image of the church as a net holding together 153 fish,[7] Cheltschitsky explained the sad shape of Christendom as being the result of two sea monsters that had broken the net, thereby making it impossible to discern the true church. The two monsters[8] were the Emperor and the Pope, jointly responsible for the betrayal of the Gospel.[9] Behind this metaphor Cheltschitsky was able to discern and denounce the Constantinian shift as a betrayal of Gospel substance.[10] Peter was nonviolent on both gospel and practical grounds. After both the noble Utraquists and the crazy Taborites had been beaten by the weapons they had chosen, namely militarily, nonviolence was not a hard position to take. Perhaps more crucial was Peter's social doctrine, prefiguring that of the Levelers. The three-level stratification of society into nobility, clergy, and the rest of us is to be rejected by appealing to both Genesis and Jesus. The ordinary Christian life is to be restructured around the Sermon on the Mount, which as taught by Jesus has the same moral status as the decalogue and the two great commandments.[11]

The implication of this revisionist reading of the fourth century is not that Constantine should not have become Christian, but that on becoming Christian, if he really had chosen to do so,[12] the Emperor should have, like anyone else, taken on the Christian life, subject to the same repentance and disciplines as other converts. This undercuts the same notion I identified among modern "pluralists," namely that in order to participate in the civil world one must forsake a specifically[13] Christian allegiance.

THE POLITY OF THE JEWISH DISPERSION

Peter's identifying the fourth century as historical hinge sends us back in time to our second specimen, whose specificity we may discern more easily now than if we had begun with it. It is the "not in charge" stance of Jewry, from Jeremiah into the Middle Ages, of which the early Christians were a derivative and minor strand. As I said at the outset, this position may not inaccurately be called "pacifist" or "quietist," but both characterizations would be skewed.

It is one of the marks of our culture's anti-Judaic heritage that the pacifism of the early Christians is routinely understood as having taken off from scratch from a few words or a few deeds of Jesus,[14] when as a matter of fact it was a part of the common Jewish legacy that Jesus and the apostles shared with their nonmessianic contemporaries like Johanan ben Zakkai.

There were exceptions to the "pacifism" of "not being in charge" that marked Jewish experience since Jeremiah, but they were exceptions and they failed. God did not prosper them. One set of exceptions were those people who concentrated on rebuilding and managing the Temple at Jerusalem, with the political and financial backing of the empires, first of the East and then of Rome. From Ezra and Nehemiah to the Sanhedrin of the time of Jesus, this restorative elite, called "Sadducees" in the Gospels, did the best it could to defend Jewish values, but ultimately it failed.

The other set of exceptions were the Maccabees and the so-called Zealots;[15] they too ultimately failed, but not before triggering the Roman Empire's devastating response. The "Judaism" that survived after the last Zealot defeat in 135 C.E. assumed the same stance that Jewry everywhere else but in Palestine had already been taking since

Jeremiah, namely "seeking the peace of the city where they had been sent."[16]

The Jewish settlers in Babylon (and in all the other cities to which they were scattered of which we know less) did not accept "not being in charge" as a lesser-evil strategy of mere survival, nor as a mere tactic, but as their mission.[17] That experience created the culturally unique traits which define "Judaism" and thereby Christianity in turn:

- The phenomenon of the synagogue—a decentralized, self-sustaining, nonsacerdotal community life form capable of operating on its own wherever there are ten households.
- The phenomenon of Torah—a text around the reading and exposition of which the community is defined. This text is at once narrative and legal.
- The phenomenon of the rabbinate—a nonsacerdotal, nonhierarchical, nonviolent leadership elite whose power is not civil but intellectual, validated by their identification with the Torah.

Each of these marks was sociologically innovative. Each was indispensable to defining Jewish identity outside of Palestine and to making it viable. Each had its Palestinian counterparts, but the home of each was in the Diaspora. Each of them guaranteed that while "quietist" and "pacifist" in the senses defined above, this community would be neither silent nor powerless. Cumulatively, they made of Jewry an effective missionary people all across the Middle East, not ending their outreach completely even when the Christians, with the same ethos and polity, took over that role.

I have first defined this "Jewish quietism since Jeremiah" in sociological terms; it is marked by the synagogue, the Torah, and the rabbinate. Of course I could have added *kashrut* and circumcision. Yet if you had asked those Jews to explain themselves, their answers would have been theological.[18]

1. They would have said that since God is sovereign over history, there is no need for them to seize (or subvert) political sovereignty in order for God's will to be done.[19] God's capacity to bring about the fulfilment of his righteous goals is not dependent upon us, and certainly not dependent on our need-

ing to make exceptions to his law in order to make things
come out the way he wills them.

2. They would have said that establishing the ultimate righteous
   social order among nations will be the mission of the *Meschiach*
   and should be left to him; to do his work for him would be
   presumptuous, if not blasphemous. This is what the main-
   stream critics of Zionism said a century ago, and what the
   neturei karta community says of the State of Israel even today.[20]

3. They would have said that the efforts of the Maccabees, the
   Zealots, and Bar Kochba to restore a national kingship had
   not been blessed by God, and that three failures should have
   been enough to teach that lesson.[21] The Maccabees and the
   Zealots have a larger place in the Christian memories of those
   centuries than they do in the thought of the rabbis.[22]

4. They would have said that if an all-righteous God wanted to
   chastise us for our sins, our self-defense would interfere with
   that purpose. The notion that God's own people are especially
   subject to having their sins punished by virtue of the special
   privileges of their election may have become more weighty
   in the Jewish thought of a later age than it was in the canonical
   period, but it is already present in the prophets. As soon as
   that attitude toward one's own sufferings is possible, the
   injustices suffered by God's people take on a different meaning, and seeking to prevent them becomes impious.

5. They would have said that the death of the righteous "sancti-
   fies the Name," that is, makes a doxological contribution on
   the moral scales of history which our avoidance of suffering
   (even if unjust) would obviate. We cannot be clear that "Your
   name be sanctified" in the Our Father already meant that,
   but clearly that phrase soon became the technical label for
   martyrdom as a positive contribution to the achievement of
   God's purposes.

Each of these explanatory sentences ought to be a chapter; yet
even in this brevity, the Jewishness of the case against "taking charge"
of the course of history is evident. From Jeremiah until Theodor Herzl
this was the dominant Jewish vision.

There is wide recognition that the Christians of the first two
centuries were pacifist, or at least that their most articulate teachers
of whom we have record were. The historians debate whether this

was univocally the case, and ethicists debate whether, if it was, it should be normative for later Christians. Yet in all of that voluminous debate, neither party takes account of the fact that the ethos of the early Christians was a direct prolongation and fulfilment of the ethos of Jewry.[23]

Both sides of the debate about the question "Were the early Christians pacifist?" have tended to proceed legalistically, as if the Christian movement had taken off from scratch with only a few words of Jesus to guide it, so that a fine-grained debate about whether those few words had to mean just this or that would have been the primary tool of moral discernment.

It is rather the case that Jesus' impact in the first century added more and deeper authentically Jewish reasons, or reinforced and further validated the already expressed Jewish reasons,[24] for the already established ethos of not being in charge and not considering any local state structure to be the primary bearer of the movement of history. To this same stance the second generation of witnesses after Jesus, the "apostles," added another layer of reasons, still utterly Jewish in form and substance, having to do with the Messiahship of Jesus, his Lordship, and the presence of the Spirit.[25] Much later, some nonmessianic Jews formally rejected these ideas about Jesus, or about the Spirit; nonetheless they were at the time unimpeachably Jewish ideas, and they made clear why a "quietist" stance in the Roman/Mediterranean world made good sense. Until the messianity of Jesus was replaced by that of Constantine,[26] it was the only ethos that made sense.[27]

Thus when Cheltschitsky reached past the Constantinian shift to "original Christianity," what he found back there to stand on was not a simple moral rigor about not shedding blood[28] but a robust alternative holistic social system, capable of surviving and prospering against the stream of the polytheistic cultures and state religions of the respective empires that the Jews and the Christians underwent and outlived. Not withdrawal for the sake of moral purity or immaterial spirituality, but resistance for the sake of justice and the honor of God, had set the tone for the nonconformity of the Jews after Jeremiah and the Christians before Constantine. It was when the Christians were still in a minority in the third century, benefiting from the respect of many of their neighbors, that their weight led some rulers to seek alliance with them and others to seek to destroy them. Both the phenomenon of occasional persecution and the event of its ultimately ending bear witness to the cultural and even political power of a morally committed minority.

When Jews in Babylonia "sought the peace of that city to which God had sent them,"[29] this did not mean merely that they hoped and prayed to be granted social tranquillity and saved from persecution. Jewish minorities, within a few generations of their arrival, almost everywhere they went, came to be valued as specialists in cross-cultural communication. Sometimes that meant leadership in trade, sometimes in literacy or language, sometimes in diplomacy. Sometimes they pioneered with schools, sometimes with medicine, sometimes with banking. The models of Joseph, Esther, and Daniel from the ancient story and legend found contemporary counterparts from Babylon to Salamanca to Worms. Not being in charge of the civil order is sometimes a more strategic way to be important for its survival or its flourishing than to fight over or for the throne. In dramatic and traumatic cases the Jews were murdered or banished; more often, they were needed and appreciated despite (or thanks to) their nonconformity. This was the case in similar ways for the pre-Constantinian Christians.

DISSENT IN EARLY MODERNITY

Having noted in Cheltschitsky an early strong specimen of the post-medieval critique of the concept of Christendom, and having seen in Judaism and early Christianity its fulcrum, I should return now toward the present. I shall renounce any vision of stopping in every century along the way,[30] leaping first to the rise of the Puritan witness toward the end of the reign of Queen Elizabeth I.[31] Once it had become clear that the most optimistic hope, namely that all of the Church of England would be reformed according to the Puritan vision, would be disappointed, the Puritans' attention turned to the conditions for the survival of the radically Protestant testimony under conditions of nonestablishment. The *internal* vision of the church as developed by congregationalism over the preceding generation had been derived from the convictions of those thinkers about the marks of the faithful community; but here we look at the *external* implications of that testimony.

The moral imperative of freedom for assembly, for speech including preaching, and for the press is derived according to the Puritan witness from the sovereignty of God whose word, already accessible in the Scriptures, must be communicated in every time and place without let or hindrance. The demand that speech and assembly be freed thus becomes a claim upon the civil order, but its rootage is in divine revelation. John Milton, partly because of his other claims to fame, became the most noted spokesman of this demand for freedom, but the case had been worked out well before him. If the omnipotent and all-wise Creator determined that he could afford to give his creatures the freedom to sin—the theodicy that underlies Milton's *Paradise Lost*, transposed to the civil order in his *Aeropagitica*—then certainly the kings of England could afford to let their loyal subjects read, gather, and preach freely.

At a second point as well, the inner integrity of dissent could extrapolate into a constructive witness *ad extram*. As is said most simply in Paul's epistle to the Corinthians, the right way for believers to hold a meeting in the power of the Holy Spirit is to authorize everyone to speak. Scripture guides the church not primarily when its words are exposited by a linguist (and certainly not when their meaning is decreed by an absentee bishop) but rather when all believers gather and speak freely of its testimony.[32] Historians agree that in this reformation vision of the congregation as gathered and conversing freely we may find the model for the "town meeting" in congregationalist America.[33] A culture that calls for dialogue rather than zero-sum conflict has its roots in a faith understanding of the Holy Spirit as active in the assembly.

The call for civil liberties and the consent of the governed is the way the anti-Constantinian critique took shape in England. What would it do in the greater openness of the New World? For that we advance two generations to another radical Puritan, William Penn, who founded four of the original American colonies in the light of the Quaker vision of history,[34] after Roger Williams had begun something similar in Rhode Island.[35] In these two men it is evident that the religious position, which *usually* is not in a political position to determine the shape of a society as a whole because it does not have the power, would not be incapable of doing so in the odd case of its being entrusted with the chance to lead.

Penn did not fight to acquire his land, either from the crown or from the Indians. He was not a very good manager, did not choose very wisely the people to whom he delegated the care of his affairs, and could not prevent following generations from forsaking the Quaker faith.[36] The "experiment" could not succeed forever; yet the three generations from Penn's groundwork in 1681 to the Quakers' abandoning control of the Pennsylvania Assembly in 1756 are closer to a success story than most regimes, most dynasties can claim. Penn's establishment differed from the rest of the colonies (except for Rhode Island) in fundamental ways:

- in dealing honestly with the original occupants of the land, paying an agreed price for the land, making uncoerced treaties with them, and honoring those treaties as long as Quaker government lasted;
- in guaranteeing religious liberty, on theological and not merely pragmatic grounds, and encouraging free immigration of European dissenters;
- in humanizing civil justice and corrections;
- in moving more rapidly than other colonies toward one-man/one-vote democracy, including more rights for women than elsewhere;
- in creating the first public schools;
- in challenging slavery. Penn did not legally outlaw slavery, but when protest against slavery did arise, it was Friends and Mennonites who led it, on grounds dictated by their faith and not by their economic interests.

When Friends were outvoted by the nonpacifist Europeans with whom they had shared their commonwealth, during the buildup to the French and Indian War, their leadership in these realms did not cease; from then on they exercised it very effectively in the ordinary way, namely without being rulers.

My present concern is not to review the Pennsylvania experiment for its own sake but only to take note of it as a probative specimen on the systematic question. Those whose ethic *ordinarily* would disqualify them from "being in charge" of a civil society, *in the sense that* their ethic is expressly not designed after the Constantinian model with a view to enabling them to take charge violently, and *in the sense that* majorities would seldom elect them, and who could therefore be qualified as "quietist," can nonetheless, and do in fact, discharge social responsibilities when such are entrusted to them without demanding that they betray their truth-telling, nonviolent ethos. There is nothing intrinsically otherworldly about that ethos. It is not a priori inapplicable in the real world.

SOCIAL EFFECTIVENESS FROM BELOW

More often, the way in which "not in charge" minorities contribute to social process is backhanded. By denouncing the veneration of the national flag as idolatrous, the Jehovah's Witnesses in the United States enlarged the notion of religious liberty. By conscientiously declaring themselves unavailable for military service, the "objectors" widen the notion of religious liberty to include not only ideas but also behavior, not only cultic but also political behavior. By conscientiously claiming responsibility for their children's education, the Old Order Amish[37] break the stranglehold of homogeneous state education. Christian Scientists and charismatics who believe that God heals challenge the AMA medical care cartel. Noncooperation, when empowered by a level of conviction that is willing to suffer, is a more powerful way to move a society than is the ballot box; it can be used effectively by minorities.

Thus far I have been directing attention to the underside of history in a narrative mode. I have been demonstrating that people who are not in charge, and for whom therefore an ethic or an ethos of "responsibility" would be wrong or incoherent, are nonetheless socially important. I next need to indicate that most people who are in step with a different drumbeat in this practical way also hold to a different underlying cosmology. Their deviant behavior reflects a deviant reading of reality.

THE WORLDVIEW OF THE ELECT UNDERDOGS

The Paradox of the Power of Weakness

Sometimes this alternative vision of the shape of the world affirms that weakness is strong, that suffering is powerful, and that relinquishing control is the most responsible way to intervene in history. In very different ways this kind of argument has been represented by the Apostle Paul,[38] by contemplatives over the centuries, by movers and shakers like Gandhi and Martin Luther King, and by intellectuals like H. Richard Niebuhr.[39] It can follow as logical entailment from the notion that there is one true God who is at once all good and the ultimate historical actor. One of its oldest forms, though still alive, as already noted, is the Orthodox Jewish perspective of the *neturei karta*, which does not acknowledge the State of Israel because it was not established by the Messiah, but by human initiative.

The Power of Promise

In some settings the alternative vision is articulated in terms of hope. Hope sets aside our pragmatic notions of managing rationally the consequences of our actions, that is, of making our decisions on consequential grounds, by virtue of the promise that God will intervene to liberate and vindicate. The cultural mode and the literary genre that we call "apocalyptic" were once simply set aside by our contemporaries as useless, meaningless, or silly, whether they occurred in the Jewish and Christian Scriptures or in historical and social thought. Now they are being given more attention, as offering a way to make important statements about God's transcendence,[40] or about human sinfulness, or about the finiteness of the human project. These are dimensions that more ambitious visions of human dignity-as being "in charge" of history by virtue of one's own control of the levers of power-make people unable to perceive.[41]

Principalities and Powers

Yet another mode of articulation echoes the way in which the Apostle Paul spoke of the historical world as being the prey of "Principalities and Powers." These are creaturely structures whose role should be to serve human flourishing and God's glory, but which in their rebelliousness become our oppressors.[42] The fallenness of the world is not just the fallenness of individual sinners; the world as structure is awry. Those who seek to "take charge" of events by challenging the Powers at their own game, trying to manipulate events in terms of their own inherent dynamics, may be selling out morally and practically at the very point where they claim to be taking responsibility. By agreeing to play by the Powers' rules they grant the idolatrous claim to be in charge of history in JHWH's stead. A refusal to play the game by the agreed rules may be morally more basic than a courageous wrestling with things as they are.[43] Jesus defeated the Powers not by being better than they at their trade of domination but by refusing to meet them on that terrain, at the cost of his life.

Each of the above three paragraphs points to a theme which has made its way through history, and which would reward further attention in its own right. For my present purposes, what matters is not what further argument might be made, or what examples recounted for any one of them, or whether to these three a few more might be added.[44] What matters is what they have in common, namely that they testify to the possibility of a very intelligent, very realistic view of things, which makes good sense of living under God in a world we do not control, and in which moral discourse is guided by

rules other than those of generalizability and optimizing consequences.

Matthew's Jesus told his listeners not to worry about their material survival, not because he was summoning them to ascetic renunciation but because their heavenly Father knew their needs. "Seek first
the righteousness of the Kingdom, and the rest will be thrown in"[45]
is a recipe not for poverty but for plenty. It may be similar when we ask
how the value-laden subcommunity goes about caring about justice in
the wider society. It may be the case not only by happenstance but
by a deep inner logic, if God is God, that the subcommunity's fidelity
to its own vocation will "contribute to state policy" more strongly—
and certainly more authentically—than if it worried about compromis-
ing its principles in order to be effective.

NOTES

1. My fullest statement of the logic of this shift is in my essay "The
Constantinian Sources of Western Social Ethics," in *The Priestly Kingdom* (Notre
Dame, Ind.: University of Notre Dame Press, 1984), pp. 135ff.

2. I described this persistence of the Constantinian logic in ever new
forms in my essay "Christ, the Hope of the World," in *The Original Revolution*
(Scottdale, Pa.: Herald Press, 1972), pp. 141ff; reprinted in *The Royal Priesthood*
(Grand Rapids, Mich.: Eerdmans, 1994), pp. 181ff.

3. I have myself argued this point, on grounds that seem to me more
valid than the usual ones, in my "The Christian Case for Democracy" in
Priestly Kingdom, pp. 151ff.

4. *Priestly Kingdom*, pp. 151ff.

5. I have commented elsewhere on the inappropriateness of the code
word *ghetto* to describe the moral consistency of minority communities. The
ghetto in medieval and Renaissance Europe was not a place to which Jews
withdrew in order to keep kosher. It was a place in which the "catholic"
Christians penned them in order the better to dominate them.

6. Cf. Peter Brock, *Political and Social Doctrines of the Unity of Czech
Brethren* (The Hague: Mouton, 1957); Murray Wagner, *Petr Chelčický* (Scottdale,
Pa.: Herald Press, 1983). There had been less clear precursors of the same
posture in the Waldensian movement, and among radical Franciscans. In
important ways, Vaclav Havel is the successor of the distinctivness of the
Czech Reformation. I use here the German orthography for Peter's name
because it is phonetically more accessible to Western readers.

7. John 21:11. In the Gospel account the abundant catch is neither a
miracle nor a parable; yet preachers had long since made it the latter.

8. Stanislav Segert, "Two Whales of Petr Chelčický," *Communio Viatorum* XXXI (1988): 127–44. Neither Jonah's big fish nor Job's Leviathan can be

the source of the image of two sea monsters. The term Peter uses is found in Gen. 1:21 and Ezek. 29:3 and 32:2. Ezekiel applies the image to the king of Egypt.

9. The historiography of the time believed the legend of the *donatio* whereby Constantine and Pope Sylvester were supposed to have reciprocally ratified each other's monarchies.

10. That the Constantinian shift was epoch-making was no new idea. Picking on Constantine as symbol of that tectonic shift was not something the radicals thought up. That had been done by Eusebius already in Constantine's lifetime. What the radicals did was to evaluate the change as a loss rather than as a gain. Cf. my "Primitivism in the Radical Reformation: Strengths and Weaknesses," in Richard T. Hughes, *The Primitive Church in the Modern World* (Champagne: University of Illinois, 1995), pp. 74–97, and in my *Priestly Kingdom*, pp. 135ff.

11. Cf. Martin Lupáč, *Probacio preceptorum minorum*; edited by Amedeo Molnar, *Communio Viatorum* IX (1966): 55–62. The "minor precepts" were the six ". . . but I say to you . . . " words of Jesus in Matt. 5: They stand beside the "two great commandments" and the decalogue. We should remember that this discussion of what constitutes a binding commandment represents a time before the Lutheran polemic placed "law" in tension with "gospel." Geoffrey Nuttall is right in using the phrase "the Law of Christ" to describe the spirituality of late medieval pacifism in his *Christian Pacifism in History* (Oxford: Blackwell, 1958; reprinted Berkeley: World Without War Council, 1971), pp. 15–31.

12. Constantine's postponing baptism to his deathbed testifies to a possible awareness on his part that authentic conversion would demand a different life-style.

13. "Specific" means fitting one's species. To be specifically Christian need not be "distinctive," since distinctiveness depends on the other parties in the comparison. A position that is specifically Christian might be specific to others as well, for their own reasons. Especially in the post-Christian West, there are very few humane ideas, even when of clearly Jewish and Christian origins, that will be held only by believers.

14. Cf. note 28 below.

15. This is a "type" name, describing an attitude toward righteous violence, as the term is used in Luke; few of the people who took this stance used the name. Cf. my comments on its use in the revised edition of my *The Politics of Jesus* (Grand Rapids, Mich.: Eerdmans, 1994), pp. 56ff.

16. Jer. 29:4–7.

17. It would be inappropriate to designate their reasons as "theological," only because that term as modern Westerners use it is alien to the Jewish tradition.

18. In the previous note I avowed that this term is not the one they would have used. Yet something like it is needed to undercut the claim, made in the paper by M. Broyde in this volume, that the renunciation of violence was *merely* tactical, with no roots in spirituality or in an understanding of how God works in history.

19. This is the obverse of the Constantinian assumption that only the Christian king can move history as God wants.

20. Despite its near eclipse by political Zionism, the pre-Herzl vision of not being in charge before God intervenes still has its advocates: One thinks of the late Stephen Schwartzschild in whose shadow we met in the St. Louis colloquy; of the *Neturei Karta* in Jerusalem; of Michael Seltzer, *Zionism Reconsidered* (New York: Macmillan, 1970); and Daniel Boyarin and Jonathan Boyarin, "Diaspora: Generation and the Ground of Jewish Identity," in *Critical Inquiry* 19 (1993): 693–725. Without fully intending it, W. D. Davies, *The Territorial Dimension of Judaism* (Berkeley: University of California Press, 1982) supports the Boyarins' case.

21. It is not only that the Maccabees and the Zealots did not ultimately triumph. Their first successes led them to become oppressive and to fall out among themselves. They fell prey to what they claimed to defeat.

22. One need only note that the Books of Maccabees are not in the Hebrew canon of the Scriptures.

23. The neglect of attention to the Jewishness of Christianity is as striking in the pacifist-leaning works of Cadoux, Hornus, Bainton, and Brock as it is in the nonpacifist readings of Helgeland, Cunningham, Ryan, Swift, Johnson, etc. The literature has been most recently surveyed by David Hunter, "A Decade of Research on Early Christians and Military Service," *Religious Studies Review* 18 (1992): 87–94. The term *research* is something of a misnomer. Most of what Hunter reviews here is a revision of old and much-read material. Christians who are interested in learning from the dialogue with Judaism and the historians who follow the contested history of thought on the morality of war seem not to be doing their research in the same world.

24. Cf. my chapter "The Moral Axioms of the Sermon on the Mount," in *Original Revolution,* and my earlier projection of this part of the present paper's theme in a part of my Toronto paper, "War as a Moral Problem in the Early Church: The Historian's Hermeneutical Assumptions," in *The Pacifist Impulse in Historical Perspective,* ed. Harvey Dyck and Peter Brock (Toronto: University of Toronto Press, 1996), pp. 90–110.

25. Cf. my chapter "If Christ Is Truly Lord" in *Original Revolution,* pp. 52ff; reprinted as "Peace without Eschatology," in *Royal Priesthood,* pp. 144ff. Some interpreters make much of the delay of the Parousia as forcing on Christians of the second or third generation a revision of their worldview. There is no evidence that such a change made any difference for their attitude toward violence. The Jewishness of their pacifism was not contingent on a particular apocalyptic perspective.

26. By the fourth century, *christos* had become a proper name. Thus neither Constantine nor his biographer Eusebius would literally have used that title; yet functionally, "messianity" describes Eusebius' view of Constantine's place in salvation history. The *meschiach,* the "Anointed," is the man who by special divine intervention ("unction") has been empowered to inaugurate the next phase of God's saving history. That is what Eusebius said about Constantine and his age.

27. When not long after the middle of the second century some Christians did in some way participate in the Roman army (although we know about it only from the words of those who thought they should not), it was not because they had any theocratic visions of taking charge of history, or controlling the destiny of the empire. They probably did it because (in peacetime) the work was easy and the rewards generous, without troubling themselves with much moral analysis.

28. This is the Tolstoyan and Niebuhrian oversimplification. Since the advocate of legitimate violence considers himself to be a realist, he must project on the other option an idealistic purism.

29. Jeremiah 29:7. Originally and prototypically this "mission" applied to Babylon; but by implication it extended to all Jewry outside Palestine: in "all the peoples and places where I have sent you" (Jer. 29:14).

30. Donald Durnbaugh, *The Believers' Church* (New York: MacMillan, 1968; reprinted Scottdale, Pa.: Herald Press, 1985) does that. Durnbaugh has also used the image of "hop, skip, and jump" as a description of the way spiritual continuity occurs in nonestablished communities; this might well characterize my selective presentation here.

31. The account I summarize here is in no way original. Political thinkers like A. D. Lindsay, social historians like Christopher Hill, and church historians like Geoffrey Nuttall concur in its main outlines.

32. This view was held by the early Luther, by Zwingli, and by Martin Bucer, but most thoroughly carried out by the so-called Anabaptists. All of them called this practice "the Rule of Christ." It was implemented still more thoroughly by Friends a generation after Milton. It had appeared much earlier in the movement called "conciliarism," the late medieval vision for renewal, for which the model was not only 1 Cor. 14 but also Acts 15. I sketch its import for church and society today in my *Body Politics: Five Practices of the Christian Commmunity before the Watching World* (Nashville, Tenn.: Discipleship Resources Press, 1992), pp. 1–13.

33. I have further illustrated the paradigmatic role of the church's order elsewhere in my *Body Politics*. The link between 1 Cor. 14 and democracy is noted on pp. 67f.

34. Only Pennsylvania stayed in his hands and was named for him, but Penn was also involved in founding the colonies of East Jersey, West Jersey, and Delaware. In addition, there were large Quaker settlements in Nantucket, Long Island, Rhode Island, and North Carolina, where though involved in colony leadership they did not have charter status like Penn.

35. Williams received the charter for Rhode Island in 1644. His vision of the wrongness of religious persecution and his concern for humane relations with the Indians were like Penn's; but his Seeker style was less calculated to found a commonwealth.

36. The Penn heirs became Anglicans and thus could without embarrassment abandon the ethic of Friends. Other Friends continued to represent the same causes, no longer burdened with the status of Proprietors. They remained the strongest voices in the colony's Assembly for two more generations.

37. Many other faith communities have provided their own schools for their own children; the Amish made United States constitutional history by making their point from a position of weakness.

38. "God's weakness is stronger than human strength," 1 Cor. 1:25; "We have this treasure in earthen vessels, to make clear that this extraordinary power belongs to God," 2 Cor. 4:7; "The weapons of our conflict are not fleshly but mighty," 2 Cor. 10:4; "My power is made perfect in weakness," 2 Cor. 12:9.

39. Cf. his "The Grace of Doing Nothing," *Christian Century* 49 (1932): 378–80, "War as the Judgment of God," ibid. 59 (1942): 630–33, and "War as Crucifixion," ibid. 60 (1943): 513–15; all reprinted in *War in the Twentieth Century*, ed. Richard B. Miller (Louisville, Ky.: John Knox Press, 1992), pp. 6ff, 47ff, 63ff.

40. The many writings of John Collins, concerning the heritage present in Jesus' world, and of Adela Yarbro Collins, as concerns early Christian thought, have provided leadership in the interpretation of the apocalyptic genre.

41. I attempted to contribute to retrieving the apocalyptic mode as a part of moral discourse in my "Armaments and Eschatology," *Studies in Christian Ethics* 1/1 (1988): 43–61, and in "Ethics and Eschatology," *Ex Auditu* 6 (1990): 119–28.

42. The first popularly accessible sketch of this "Pauline theology of history" was my translation of Hendrik Berkhof's *Christ and the Powers* (Dutch original, Callenbach: Nijkerk, 1953; E.T. Scottdale: Herald Press, 1962, revised 1978). Since then it has been widely appropriated, most notably by William Stringfellow and Jacques Ellul. The textual basis of this vision in the New Testament has been thoroughly reworked by Walter Wink, beginning with *Naming the Powers* (Philadelphia: Fortress Press, 1984).

43. We become what we hate if we let hatred of the adversary set the terms of the clash.

44. In my *Politics of Jesus* I attended to such additional apostolic themes as imitation or participation (chap. 7), subordination (chap. 9), and justification (chap. 11).

45. Matt. 6:33.

Religious Pacifism and Quietism— A Taxonomic Approach and a Catholic Response

JOHN P. LANGAN, S.J.

The vigorous and provocative paper by Professor Yoder covers, it seems to me, a rather wide and interesting range of issues. As my own contribution, I would like to begin by offering a general taxonomy of the issues that are presented in the papers reflecting on the three Abrahamic traditions and to conclude by locating two Christian views within that taxonomy.

In laying out a taxonomy of views, there are two main strategies. The first is the one employed by Aristotle in the *Politics*, where he divides constitutions or polities according to the number of rulers (one, a few, many) and according to an evaluative distinction between good and bad forms. Aristotle ends up with six categories, about each of which he has a great deal to say. The alternative approach, which lays out many more possibilities and says comparatively little about each of them, can be found in St. Augustine's presentation of the views of the philosophers about the supreme good in *The City of God*, Book XIX, in which, following the Roman philosopher Marcus Varro, he distinguishes 288 possible views on this matter.

The course I will follow here is closer to Augustine, because I think his approach is more suitable for what is a preliminary survey of the territory rather than for the harvesting and orderly display of a vast amount of observation such as Aristotle offers us, but also because we are dealing with a series of issues that cross between different parts of our intellectual topography rather than remaining securely within the bounds of one discipline. The taxonomy presented will be incomplete and will not include many observations or clarifications that might succeed only in rendering it both invulnerable and tedious.

Let us begin by noting that the central topic here is the norms that are to govern a religious body and/or its members in their political activity in a larger social setting. Here we can somewhat arbitrarily but not unreasonably restrict the range of possibilities by observing that there have been and are five major possibilities for the religious identity of the state in the Western tradition. The religious group is confronted by a pagan state, a Jewish state, a Christian state, an Islamic state, or a secular state. In each of these cases, the state may have and may exercise its religious identity in a strong or weak form, that is, it may exert differing levels of pressure and coercion to persuade dissident citizens to conform to its religious identity (strong) or it may persist with a relatively low-key affirmation of its religious identity, tolerating considerable diversity (weak). The Roman Empire in its persecuting and tolerant phases provides us with a historical example of a pagan state alternating between strong and weak forms. Britain under Elizabeth I can be regarded as an example of a Christian state in a strong form; under Elizabeth II, it is a Christian state only in a weak and restricted form. Liberalism and Marxism give us examples of the secular state in weak and strong forms, respectively. The commitment to a weak form of secular state can itself be vigorous and explicit, as it is in the dual prohibition in the First Amendment against establishing a state religion and against restricting the free exercise of religion; it need not be the result of attenuated belief or indifference to religious values.

The three possibilities in our set that are of most interest to Christians are: 1) the pagan state, which often treated Christians as a subversive minority and which Christians were generally happy to see disappear; 2) the Christian state, which (usually but not always in monarchical form) most Christian communities felt called upon to establish after the decline of paganism as a force in the public life of the late Roman Empire but which often modelled itself on the behavior and the aspirations of the states of pagan antiquity; and 3) the secular state, which was usually set up in criticism of and in opposition to a Christian state but which in its weak form offered toleration, the exercise of religious freedom, and opportunities for citizen participation to Christians.

The Jewish state, established in Israel since 1948, has not presented major difficulties to Western Christians, though it has proved to be a source of some contention for those Jews who were committed to the secular state as the uniquely legitimate form of state in the modern world, as well as for those Jews who found it religiously insufficient because it was not established by the Messiah. It has been a serious problem for Muslims because its territory previously formed part of the Islamic world and because it includes Jerusalem, a holy site for Muslims as well as for Jews and Christians.

The Muslim state, especially in a strong form, strikes many Western Christians as an ominous and dangerous possibility. But Christian thought about these matters has not taken the problems and challenges of a Christian minority in an Islamic state as a central case for reflection and analysis, though some Christian states (notably France) have taken an active interest in protecting the status and the religious liberty of Christian minority groups in the Middle East (as well as in projecting their own imperial power). I should also record my own estimate that different proposals for an Islamic state will fall somewhere between the strong and weak forms of religious or ideological identity for states that I have proposed for consideration.

Religious identities in the Western monotheistic traditions bring with them moral obligations and moral commitments, among which a concern for justice in the dealings of human beings with each other and therefore in the activities of the state is of central importance. Both liberal and Marxist states have appealed to certain norms of justice to legitimate their activity, and Rome's apologists pointed to the benefits of Roman law and stability. The extent to which various regimes appropriate and act upon the concern for justice is quite variable; every religious tradition has to acknowledge recurring gaps between profession and practice, even among its most committed members and in its most vigorous periods. So it is always appropriate to ask whether a given regime is just or not and to understand this question as admitting a range of answers and requiring an exercise of judgment that is not merely the reporting of a simple fact.

But this question needs to be broken down further to fit a situation of religious and ideological pluralism or division. For there is both overlap and variation in the norms of justice espoused by the various traditions. So we can ask of a given regime whether it is just or unjust according to the norms of justice appropriate to its identity as a Christian or Islamic or Jewish or secular state, then whether it is just or unjust according to "our" standards (where "we" are people who may be in the same religious or ideological tradition or who may be in a quite different tradition), and finally whether it is just or unjust according to universal or transcendent norms of justice, which hold across or prior to or beyond the specific traditions. Recognizing the possibility of distinguishing these different questions about the justice and injustice of regimes allows for some dialogue even among those who hold, as Augustine did, that a state that fails to acknowledge the true God and to practice the true religion cannot be just, those who would make all particular moral judgments logically dependent on adherence to a specific tradition, and those who regard the justice of regimes as consisting essentially in their conformity to such universal norms as human rights or natural law.

If we are unable to settle the foundational and metaethical questions, we cannot determine whether a regime is just or unjust without qualification; but we can judge that it meets or fails to meet specific standards of justice; we can get a more nuanced reading of what its moral character is; and we can be in a position to make a specific moral critique of the regime's performance. So oppressed peoples in a colonial society can point to the injustice of a Western regime failing to observe liberal norms of justice; Jews can point to the inconsistency of anti-Semitism and bigotry with norms that are internal to the Christian tradition; Muslims can find a basis within Islamic norms for condemning criminal behavior by tyrannical governments. Marxists could find grounds within the Marxist canon for condemning the emergence of a "new class" seeking privilege and status and opposing democracy and for rejecting violations of socialist legality by the secret police. In this way people coming from different communities and traditions may be able to reach some common judgments about the justice or lack of it in a particular regime. This possibility takes us beyond the alternatives of either imposing the views of a particular community and tradition or preserving these views in a separate and restricted environment. It also raises the further possibility that there may be moral consensus for removing a regime that is gravely unjust, either because it violates the basic human rights of its own people or because it commits aggression against other peoples and regimes.

Often connected with the question of the justice of the regime, but not identical with it, is the question of who holds power within a regime or, in the terms used in Professor Yoder's title, who is in charge here. Partly, this is a matter of the classically recognized divisions of polity and constitution—monarchy, oligarchy, democracy—and of the different branches of political power: legislative, executive, and judicial. But answering the question in a contemporary setting requires us to attend to other forms of power and to recognize the interlocking character of many power relationships in modern societies. Different societies will link together in different ways the power exercised by the political leadership, the legal system, the military, police and internal security, religious leaders and communities, cultural elites, professional groups, the educational system, mass communications, and economic elites and institutions. These forms of power are all significant ways to get things done in society and to impede others from executing their projects. Those who exercise these forms of power in contemporary democracies are in some sense "in charge," but they are not likely to feel that they are free to command according to their own good pleasure.

The modern state endows the political leadership with a monopoly on the use of force even while it divides political power among separate branches. The complex nexus of lawmaking, law enforcement, and control of the military is at the heart of anything we would recognize as a state. The form that the nexus takes in liberal democracies is overturned in military dictatorships, and the nexus itself is overshadowed in totalitarian regimes when the political movement or party subordinates both the central organs of the state and the military to its own program for reshaping society in a comprehensive way. This ambition in its Marxist or fascist forms is so comprehensive that it has driven such regimes to move either to eradicate religion or to attempt to make it radically subordinate to the party and the party-controlled state.

Any religious body or community that aspires to shape itself as a free and independent community is bound to come into conflict with political totalitarianism (as well as with the strong forms of religious identity mentioned earlier). The precise terms and means of the conflict are not set in advance; but it is likely to be especially dramatic and vehement when totalitarianism is combined with nationalistic distrust of religious groups with a strongly transnational character (Judaism, Catholicism, and, perhaps in the future, Islam).

Liberal states separate religious institutions and leaders from the state and deny that the state needs to have a religious identity in order to be just or effective. (I admit that in this view the United Kingdom does not qualify as a liberal state). Liberal states repudiate the efforts of particular religious groups to control the core activities of the state and of other centers of power in the society, but they also leave religious groups free to regulate their own affairs and to propose ideals and criticisms applying to other centers of power.

Different societies and different regimes will structure the relationships among the various centers of power in different ways and will structure the centers themselves according to divergent principles of command and consent, of coercion and choice, and with different possibilities of participation for ordinary members of society and for professionals and specialists.

But the shape of the problem we are considering is not determined only by variables on the side of the state and of the broader society. It also depends on the beliefs, values, and practices of the religious group as well as on its status in relation to the broader society. Here I use the term *status* to point to two different considerations: the question of numbers and the question of historical and contemporary dominance. The religious group may be a majority or a minority; this need not be correlated with the religious identity of the state. For instance, Christians are the religious majority in the United States, which is a liberal society; Catholics are an overwhelming majority in Poland and Mexico, which until recently were secularistic states that failed to observe key principles of religious liberty. Practicing Anglicans are now a small minority in the United Kingdom, but they enjoy a privileged position as a result of their interconnections with politically dominant groups. Catholicism was able to enjoy a comparable position of dominance in French colonial regimes even while the government in Paris was actively anticlerical.

The status of a religious group, its prominence, its access to other centers of power, the internal cohesion and discipline of the religious group, the level of commitment of its members all shape expectations about what the religious group can reasonably do to alter political outcomes, to constrain the behavior of others, and to achieve the realization of its own preferences and ideals (as well as to protect and advance its interests). Attention will also have to be paid to the size, social organization, and theological position of other religious groups, which may be allies in potential coalitions or competitors for popular allegiance.

Within the belief and value systems of the religious body, there are several points that strike me as particularly salient for our theme. First, what is the predominant pattern of exemplary action within the tradition of the religious group? On what basis is this pattern established? Here one can compare the monarchy of David and Solomon, the cult of martyrdom in the Maccabean period and early Christianity, the exercise of authority by the Prophet, varying styles of papal leadership from Julius II to John Paul II, the various American efforts to establish holy commonwealths (Massachusetts, Pennsylvania, Utah).

Second, what scope does the religious tradition leave for human choice and action? What is our causal efficacy? What kind of responsibility does it entail? The Western monotheisms have emphasized the priority of divine action in their canonical texts and in many of their classic theological treatises. Theological determinism and occasionalist interpretations of human causality have flourished in Jewish, Christian, and Islamic traditions. They can also be paralleled in some forms of modern materialism and scientism.

Third, what rank among the various goods does the religious tradition give to the goods that can be realized or attained by political action either by individuals or groups? If these goods are not highly valued, we are probably dealing with a tradition that will tolerate or encourage passivity in the face of various social evils, which are held to be as nothing in comparison with more perfect, more interior, and less ambiguous gifts.

Fourth, does the religious group's tradition rule out the use of certain types of means in attaining these social and political goods and in opposing the corresponding evils? Here, of course, the central instance of a problematic or unacceptable means is the use of force. But it need not be the only one. Fraud and deception, patriarchal patterns of social domination and control, self-interested use of economic resources, collaboration with sinners and nonbelievers, and disobedience to civil law can all be rejected or tolerated or legitimized in roughly similar ways.

Fifth, what is the preferred procedure for resolving dilemmas in this area? Is it the leadership of the religious community? The text of scripture? The conscience of the individual? The votes of the members? The breath or the anointing of the Spirit?

Sixth, what kinds of considerations ought to guide the community's decision makers? Prudential and utilitarian calculations? Precedents from within the religious tradition? Intuitions of the faithful? Specific divine commands? Universally binding moral norms? As you can see, these last sets of questions take us into realms of metaphysical theology, church polity, religious and moral epistemology.

Somewhat like St. Augustine and the sorcerer's apprentice, I have created a monster set of categorizations relevant to our theme, a set that I cannot possibly manipulate or illuminate within the limits of this essay. Rather what I will try to do is to indicate where I could locate Yoder's views (as presented in his paper) on the schema I have constructed and, in parallel with this, to indicate where I would place what I take to be the characteristic or dominant views of modern Catholic social teaching. But before I do that, let me state what I take to be one conclusion from the taxonomy that I have laid out, which is that we are not dealing here with a simple, well-defined problem, but rather with many different overlapping problems. It is highly unlikely that there is one religiously correct solution to this cluster of problems even if we were to confine ourselves to one religious tradition. At the same time, the overlap among the problems means that comparative study of divergent solutions can be richly instructive.

If I understand Yoder's view correctly, he holds that for an authentic Christian community, the religious identity of the state is, and ought to be, a matter of profound indifference. I certainly agree with him that there is no valid religious or moral imperative calling Christians to seize power and thus to put themselves in charge, nor for that matter is there an imperative even within Catholicism calling for the preservation of the Constantinian state. Yoder makes it clear that he accepts representative democracy, not because it fully embodies moral values, but because it is in practice superior to the alternatives; but in practice it often becomes an oligarchy, it leaves many voters marginalized, and it generates a lot of morally misleading rhetoric. For Yoder's authentic Christian community the troubling cases with regard to the religious identity of the state are: 1) the Christian state, which purports to be guided by Christian values but which is inextricably bound up with the exercise of power and the use of force simply by reason of its being a state and which has given us abundant historical evidence that it often acts in un-Christian and scandalous ways; and 2) the liberal state, at least in those forms where it professes not to be at odds with Christian values and where it offers abundant opportunities for political participation to Christians. The other cases are less likely to be puzzling or corrupting for Christians, since the ruling groups and the dominant belief system will have comparatively few links with the Christian community. The issues are clearer, and the temptations less insidious, when the state is hostile and excludes the religious minority from participation in the dominant institutions of society. This, we should notice, is the limiting situation that historically confronted the Jewish community in the Diaspora. Such a situation can help to preserve the religious and cultural identity of the excluded community; but at the same time it constricts the freedom of that community, diminishes the equal respect due to its members, and deprives the larger society of a major source of generous and committed creativity. It may indeed be harder for Christians to make and to express accurate negative judgments about the justice/injustice of Christian and liberal states. One matter that Yoder's approach leaves unexplored is the connections (both positive and negative) between the powers normally concentrated in the state and the other forms of power that Christians, either ordinary Christians or members of Yoder's authenthic Christian community, may have and exercise in the economy and the culture.

Yoder, it seems clear, takes a skeptical view of the ability of human action to bring about justice in the political order and of the ability of human political actors to foresee the consequences of their own actions and to control the course of events. On this last point, his view aligns him with secular theorists of history such as Hegel and Burckhardt and pits him against some naive uses of Bonhoeffer and Teilhard de Chardin that flourished in the pop Christianity of the 1960s as well as against a cheerful, "take charge" sort of pragmatism. At the same time, his skepticism is far from comprehensive, as his treatment of the benefits of the Quaker experiment in establishing and ruling Pennsylvania makes clear. Yoder's treatment of the power of suffering, of contemplation, and of nonviolence presupposes both that some outcomes of political practices and decisions are preferable to others, that this difference can be generally understood and appreciated, and that it does matter to Christians, even those who are members of his authentic Christian community. So, as Yoder himself insists, the teaching of Jesus and the appropriation of it by his authentic Christian community are not to be dismissed as purely otherworldly or totally withdrawn from the larger society and irrelevant to its problems.

Yoder's authentic Christian community will judge the state, whatever be its explicit religious identity or lack thereof, in terms of its conformity to the principles, values, and example of Christ. It will feel called to oppose the state when it acts unjustly; this will happen routinely in totalitarian societies and in Christian and liberal societies when the state enters into war as well as on other occasions when the state's injustice is taken to be insupportable. Members of the community will not be devoid of power, even if they have no inclination to put themselves in charge (compare, for example, some Jewish Diaspora communities). Their involvement with other social institutions and centers of power will subject them to pressure from competing values and may well tempt them to compromise their Christian commitment. The standard-setting pattern of action in crisis situations will be nonviolent and resisting. The protection of some fundamental social goods will be entrusted to God, and morally unacceptable means will not be employed. The community and its members will decide these matters in accordance with its form of church polity but always aiming to follow the teaching of Christ in Scripture and respecting the consciences of the members. This is an approach that aims to protect the integrity of Christian commitment and witness.

How and why would a Catholic want to disagree? I will not focus on the views of this particular Catholic nor will I try to generalize about the views of almost a billion people and their ancestors in many different societies. Rather, I will indicate the main lines of the Catholic alternative to Yoder's approach as this is presented by contemporary Catholic social teaching, which is a body of thought rooted in the earlier stages of the Catholic tradition (especially Augustine, Aquinas, and the Spanish scholastics of the sixteenth century) but expressed primarily by the social encyclicals of the last hundred years and more recently by the Second Vatican Council and various national conferences of bishops.

More recent (since 1960) formulations of this teaching effectively accept the secular state as a normal part of the situation within which the members of the Christian community are to carry out their lives. The Catholic church continues to be concerned with preserving its own autonomy and affirming the freedom of the church (as it has been since the eleventh century). It has shown an intermittent readiness to confront both Christian and secular states, especially, of course, states with a strong secular identity when this is openly anticlerical or Marxist. At the same time it offers an extensive body of moral norms that are intended to guide the activities of states regardless of their religious identity (for example, requiring respect for human rights, demanding social justice). It regards political participation as a right that may not be denied to Catholics or to others and also as a good since it is a way in which the human person finds fulfillment as a free and responsible agent. The common good is to be achieved through the cooperation of persons who are all intrinsically and naturally social beings. Without renouncing the Christian and classical suspicion of pride and hubris, it inculcates a positive appreciation of human efficacy and ability to shape the future. It now expects its members to be collaborators with many different sorts of persons and to be actively involved in various institutions and centers of power. It therefore expects to be "in the loop," but not necessarily to be "in charge," at least in those societies where Catholics are a significant element in the population. As a result it has a variety of patterns of exemplary action ranging from the confrontational to the harmoniously celebratory. It is prepared to consider the possibility that the defense of the common good may indeed require the use of force both internally by the police and externally by the military. But it wants to assess this possibility in terms of the norms of just war theory along with an increasing sense of international interdependence and a vivid awareness of the destructiveness of modern forms of military technology. It acknowledges the place of individual conscience in responding to the dilemmas of national and international politics, but it also expects direction from church leadership in response to particularly flagrant acts of injustice by governments. It proposes to formulate moral norms in accordance with the values of Scripture but also in a way that is accessible to men and women of goodwill across the barriers of diverse traditions.

In this summary, there should be nothing that is surprising. But let me underline three things. First, the church's acceptance of a liberal and religiously neutral state and encouragement of a more active citizenry in effect authorize a diversity of Catholic responses to the problems we are looking at; these responses will be shaped by the laity to a greater extent than before. Second, the position I have sketched above will seem rather secular to a member of Yoder's authentic Christian community—especially in its warrants for moral judgments and its expectations about human agency, and its acceptance of moral ambiguity. Third, it retains some critical capacity and autonomy vis-à-vis the state and is capable of generating confrontation with both Christian and secular states. This has been particularly manifest in the church's comprehensive readiness to advocate human rights in a great variety of societies both when their governments were advocating an avowedly anti-Christian set of values and practices (Jaruzelski's Poland, the Islamic regime in the Sudan) and when the governments were relying on appeals to defend traditional Christian values (Pinochet's Chile, Franco's Spain in its last phase, Marcos's Philippines). This development reflects both the church's hard lessons in the tragic history of this century and its surrender of dreams and ambitions that were part of the Constantinian project. In this respect, it has moved belatedly to some of the conclusions reached earlier by the tradition of Christian protest and discipleship that Professor Yoder ably champions.

Beyond Just War and Pacifism

WALTER WINK

For over four centuries, the peace churches have kept alive the Gospel's witness against war.[1] During that period, roughly 140 million people have been killed in war, most of them in this century.[2] Two-thirds of these casualties were in "Christian" Europe.

Parallel to the escalation of violence, and, no doubt, in response to it, we are also seeing an increase in the use of nonviolence. In 1989 alone, thirteen nations experienced nonviolent revolutions, all but one of them (China) successful. These nonviolent struggles involved 1.7 billion people, almost a third of humanity (32 percent). If we add the other nonviolent revolutions waged in this century, the figure reaches 3.3 billion—a staggering 64 percent of humanity![3]

No one can say any longer that nonviolence "doesn't work." It has been working remarkably. It was only supposed to be effective against "genial" opponents like the British or the whites in the American South, but not against the brutal Communists. Now we have seen it succeed in one Communist nation after another. Given the near monopoly governments have on weaponry, and the enormous increase in firepower, nonviolence is virtually the only way left to an unarmed people. Paradoxically, it has been the exponential increase in violence in our century that has persuaded people to choose nonviolence.

These new international developments need to be met by new thinking on our part. Theology has been particularly slow to respond to the new possibilities. Many pacifists still base their opposition to violence and warfare on a misunderstanding of the teaching of Jesus, and many just war theorists do so as well.

The text in question is the famous passage in Matthew 5:38–41, where Jesus commands his followers not to resist evil, but to turn the other cheek, give the second garment, or walk the second mile. Many pacifists interpreted "resist not" as teaching nonresistance to evil—an odd conclusion, given the fact that Jesus himself resisted evil with every fiber of his being.[4]

Adapted and reprinted by permission from ENGAGING THE POWERS by Walter Wink, © 1992 Augsburg Fortress.

Augustine also agreed that the Gospel teaches nonresistance, and therefore declared that a Christian must under no circumstances attempt self-defense. However, he noted, if someone is attacking *my neighbor*, then the love commandment requires me to defend my neighbor, by force of arms if necessary.[5] With that deft stroke, Augustine opened the door to just war theory, the military defense of the Roman Empire, and the use of torture and capital punishment. Following his lead, Christians have ever since been declaring as "just" wars fought for nothing more than greed, revenge, or bravado.

JESUS ON NONVIOLENCE

But the Gospel does not teach nonresistance to evil. The Greek word translated as "resist" in Matt. 5:39 ("Do not resist one who is evil") is *antistenai*, meaning literally to stand (*stenai*) against (*anti*).[6] The translation, "resist," creates the impression that only two alternatives exist, resistance and nonresistance. Since Jesus clearly forbids resistance, nonresistance alone remains. What this has frequently meant in practice is passivity, withdrawal, submissiveness in the face of evil, an unwillingness to stand up for one's rights or the rights of others, and supine cowardice.

What the translators have overlooked is that *antistenai* is most often used in the Greek version of the Old Testament as a technical term for warfare (44 out of 71 times). "Stand against" referred to the practice of marching one's army up against the opponent's until the two fell upon each other in battle. The same usage characterizes Josephus' use of the word (15 out of 17 times). Ephesians 6:13 reflects precisely this imagery: "Therefore take up the whole armor of God, so that you may be able to withstand (*antistenai*) on that evil day, and having done everything, to stand firm (*stenai*)."[7] The image is not of a punch-drunk boxer somehow managing to stay on his feet, but of standing one's ground, keeping ranks, refusing to flee.

Jesus is not, therefore, telling us to capitulate to evil, but rather to refuse to oppose it on its own terms. He is urging us to avoid mirroring evil, to refuse to let the opponent dictate the methods of our opposition.[8] The correct translation would be the one still preserved in the earliest version of this saying: "Do not repay evil for evil."[9] The Scholars Bible brilliantly renders the phrase, "Don't react violently against the one who is evil."

The examples that follow confirm this reading. "If anyone strikes you on the right cheek, turn the other also."[10] Readers generally imagine this as a blow with the right fist. But such a blow would fall on the *left* cheek. To hit the right cheek with a fist would require the left hand. But the left hand was reserved only for unclean tasks; at Qumran, even to gesture with the left hand meant exclusion from the meeting and penance for ten days.[11] The only conceivable blow is a right-handed backhand.[12]

The backhand was not a blow to injure, but to insult, humiliate, degrade. It was not administered to an equal, but to an inferior. Masters backhanded slaves; husbands, wives; parents, children; Romans, Jews. The whole point of the blow was to force someone who was out of line back into his or her normal social station.[13]

Notice Jesus' audience: "If anyone strikes *you*." These are people used to being degraded. He is saying to them, "Refuse to accept this kind of treatment anymore. If they backhand you, turn the other cheek." By turning the cheek, the servant makes it impossible for the master to use the backhand again. The left cheek now offers a perfect target for a blow with the right fist; but only equals have fistfights,[14] and the last thing the master wishes to do is to establish this underling's equality. Logistically, the superior is deprived of any way to make his point. The servant has irrevocably conveyed the message: I am not a "thing," I am a human being, and nothing you do from now on can deprive me of that status. I refuse to be humiliated any longer. I am your equal. I am a child of God.

Such defiance is no way to avoid trouble. Meek acquiescence is what the master wants. Such "cheeky" behavior may call down a flogging or worse. But the defiance has had its effect. The Powers That Be have lost their power to make this person submit. And when large numbers begin behaving thus (and Jesus was addressing a crowd), you have the makings of a social revolution.[15]

How different this is from the usual view that this passage teaches us to turn the other cheek so our assailant can simply pummel us again! How often that interpretation has been fed to battered wives and children. And it was never what Jesus intended in the least. To such victims he advises, "Stand up for yourselves, take control of your responses, don't answer the oppressor in kind, but find a new, third way that is neither cowardly submission nor violent reprisal."

The other two examples Jesus gives are similar. "If a creditor takes you to court and sues you for your outer garment, give your undergarment as well."[16] He is not advising people to add to their disadvantage by renouncing justice altogether, as so many well-pro-

vided commentators have suggested. He is telling impoverished debtors, who have nothing left but the clothes on their backs, to use the
system against itself.[17]

The situation Jesus speaks to is all too familiar to his hearers:
The debtor has sunk ever deeper into poverty, the debt cannot be
repaid, and his creditor has summoned him to court (*krithenai*) to exact
repayment by legal means. Indebtedness was endemic in first-century
Palestine. Jesus' parables are full of debtors struggling to salvage their
lives. Heavy debt was not, however, a natural calamity that had
overtaken the incompetent. It was the direct consequence of Roman
imperial policy. Emperors had taxed the wealthy so stringently to
fund their wars that the rich began seeking nonliquid investments to
secure their wealth. Land was best, but it was ancestrally owned and
passed down over generations, and no peasant would voluntarily
relinquish it. Exorbitant interest, however, could be used to drive
landowners ever deeper into debt. And debt, coupled with the high
taxation required by Herod Antipas to pay Rome tribute, created the
economic leverage to pry Galilean peasants loose from their land. By
the time of Jesus we see this process already far advanced: large estates
owned by absentee landlords, managed by stewards, and worked by
tenant farmers, day laborers, and slaves. It is no accident that the
first act of the Jewish revolutionaries in 66 C.E. was to burn the Temple
treasury, where the record of debts was kept.[18] It is to this situation
that Jesus speaks. His hearers are the poor ("if any one would sue
you"). They share a rankling hatred for a system that subjects them
to humiliation by stripping them of their lands, their goods, finally
even their outer garments. Deuteronomy 24:10-13 provided that a
creditor could take as collateral for a loan a poor person's long outer
robe,[19] but it had to be returned each evening so that the poor man
would have something to sleep in.

So Jesus says to these poor, "Next time they take you to court
and require of you your outer garment, give the undergarment as
well." Strip naked, right there in the court! Nakedness in Israel
brought shame, curiously enough, not on the naked person but on
the one who viewed nakedness.[20] Imagine the poor debtor handing
over his outer cloak, and then, to everyone's consternation, taking
off his clothes and walking out of court stark naked! There stands the
creditor, covered with shame, the poor debtor's outer garment in the
one hand, his undergarment in the other. The tables have suddenly
been turned on the creditor. The debtor had no hope of winning the

case; the law was entirely in the creditor's favor. But the poor man has transcended this attempt to humiliate him. He has risen above shame. At the same time he has registered a stunning protest against the system that created his debt. He has said in effect, "You want my robe? Here, take everything! Now you've got all I have except my body. Is that what you'll take next?"

Imagine the debtor leaving the court, naked. His friends and neighbors, aghast, inquire what happened. He explains. They join his growing procession, which now resembles a victory parade. The entire system by which debtors are oppressed has been publicly unmasked. The creditor is revealed to be not a legitimate moneylender but a party to the reduction of an entire social class to landlessness, destitution, and abasement. This unmasking is not simply punitive, therefore; it offers the creditor a chance to see, perhaps for the first time in his life, what his practices cause, and to repent.

The Powers That Be literally stand on their dignity. Nothing depotentiates them faster than deft lampooning. By refusing to be awed by their power, the powerless are emboldened to seize the initiative, even where structural change is not immediately possible. This message, far from being a counsel to perfection unattainable in this life, is a practical, strategic measure for empowering the oppressed, and it is being lived out all over the world today by powerless people ready to take their history into their own hands.

Jesus provides here a hint of how to take on the entire system by unmasking its essential cruelty and burlesquing its pretensions to justice. Here is a poor man who will no longer be treated as a sponge to be squeezed dry by the rich. He accepts the laws as they stand, pushes them to absurdity, and reveals them for what they have become. He strips naked, walks out before his fellows, and leaves this creditor, and the whole economic edifice that he represents, stark naked.

Jesus' third example, the one about going the second mile, is drawn from the relatively enlightened practice of limiting to a single mile the amount of forced or impressed labor (*angareia*) that Roman soldiers could levy on subject peoples.[21] Such forced service was a constant feature in Palestine from Persian to late Roman times, and whoever was found on the street could be compelled into service. We are familiar with its use in the Passion narrative, where the soldiers "compel" (*angareuousin*) Simon of Cyrene to carry Jesus' cross.[22]

The frequency with which decrees were issued to curb misuse of the *angareia* indicates how lax discipline on this point was. Infractions were punishable at the discretion of the centurion. Penalties might have involved a monetary fine, a ration of barley instead of wheat, a flogging, or a mere rebuke, probably depending on the soldier's standing with the centurion. The point is, the soldier had no way of knowing in advance what the centurion's response would be.

It is in this context of Roman military occupation that Jesus speaks.[23] He does not counsel revolt. One does not "befriend" the soldier, draw him aside and drive a knife into his ribs. Jesus was surely aware of the futility of armed insurrection against Roman imperial might; he certainly did nothing to encourage those whose hatred of Rome was near to flaming into violence. But why carry his pack a second mile? Is this not to go to the opposite extreme of aiding and abetting the enemy?[24] Not at all. The question here, as in the two previous instances, is how the oppressed can recover the initiative and assert their human dignity in a situation that cannot for the time being be changed. The rules are Caesar's, but how one responds to the rules is God's, and Caesar has no power over that.

Imagine then the soldier's surprise when, at the next mile marker, he reluctantly reaches to assume his pack, and the civilian says, "Oh no, let me carry it another mile." Why would he want to do that? What is he up to? Normally, soldiers have to coerce people to carry their packs, but this Jew does so cheerfully, and *will not stop!* Is this a provocation? Is he insulting the legionnaire's strength? Being kind? Trying to get him disciplined for seeming to violate the rules of impressment? Will this civilian file a complaint? Create trouble?

From a situation of servile impressment, the oppressed have once more seized the initiative. They have taken back the power of choice. The soldier is thrown off balance by being deprived of the predictability of his victim's response. He has never dealt with such a problem before. Now he has been forced into making a decision for which nothing in his previous experience has prepared him. If he has enjoyed feeling superior to the vanquished, he will not enjoy it today. Imagine the situation of a Roman infantryman pleading with a Jew to give him back his pack! The humor of this scene may have escaped us, but it could scarcely have been lost on Jesus' hearers, who must have been regaled by the prospect of thus discomfiting their oppressors.

Jesus does not encourage Jews to walk a second mile in order to build up merit in heaven, or to exercise a supererogatory piety, or to kill the soldier with kindness. He is helping an oppressed people find a way to protest and neutralize an onerous practice despised throughout the empire. He is not giving a nonpolitical message of spiritual world-transcendence. He is formulating a worldly spirituality in which the people at the bottom of society or under the thumb of imperial power learn to recover their humanity.

One could easily misuse Jesus' advice vindictively; that is why it must not be separated from the command to love one's enemies integrally connected with it in both Matthew and Luke. But love is not averse to taking the law and using its oppressive momentum to throw the soldier into a region of uncertainty and anxiety where he has never been before.

To those whose lifelong pattern has been to cringe before their masters, Jesus offers a way to liberate themselves from servile actions and a servile mentality. And he asserts that they can do this *before* there is a revolution. There is no need to wait until Rome has been defeated, or peasants are landed and slaves freed. They can begin to behave with dignity and recovered humanity *now*, even under the unchanged conditions of the old order. Jesus' sense of divine immediacy has social implications. The reign of God is already breaking into the world, and it comes not as an imposition from on high but as the leaven slowly causing the dough to rise.[25] Jesus' teaching on nonviolence is thus of a piece with his proclamation of the dawning of the reign of God.

In the conditions of first-century Palestine, a political revolution against the Romans could only be catastrophic, as the events of 66–70 C.E. would prove. Jesus does not propose armed revolution. But he does lay the foundations for a social revolution, as Richard A. Horsley has pointed out. And a social revolution becomes political when it reaches a critical threshold of acceptance; this in fact did happen to the Roman empire as the Christian church subverted it from below.[26]

The logic of Jesus' examples in Matthew 5:39b–41 goes beyond both inaction and overreaction, capitulation and murderous counterviolence, to a new response, fired in the crucible of love, that promises to liberate the oppressed from evil even as it frees the oppressor from sin. "Do not react violently to evil, do not counter evil in kind, do not let evil dictate the terms of your opposition, do not let violence draw you into mimetic rivalry"—this is the revolutionary principle, recognized from earliest times, that Jesus articulates as the basis for nonviolently engaging the Powers.[27]

From a situation of powerlessness, Jesus in all three examples shows his hearers how to take command of the situation, using the momentum of the system to throw it, judo-like. This is not "nonresistance" to evil. It is active nonviolence. It is not passivity. It is proactive, aggressive, and courageous.

Jesus' teaching on nonviolence forms the charter for a way of being in the world that breaks the spiral of violence. Jesus here reveals a way to fight evil with all our power without being transformed into the very evil we fight. It is a way—the only way possible—of not becoming what we hate. "Do not counter evil in kind"—this insight is the distilled essence, stated with sublime simplicity, of the experience of those Jews who had, in Jesus' very lifetime, so courageously and effectively practiced nonviolent direct action against Rome.[28]

Jesus, in short, abhors both passivity and violence. He articulates, out of the history of his own people's struggles, a way by which evil can be opposed without being mirrored, the oppressor resisted without being emulated, and the enemy neutralized without being destroyed. Those who have lived the nonviolent way—Leo Tolstoy, Mohandas K. Gandhi, Martin Luther King, Jr., Abraham Heschel, Dorothy Day, César Chavez, Adolpho Pérez Esquivel—point us to a new way of confronting evil whose potential for personal and social transformation we are only beginning to grasp today.[29]

JUST WAR, OR JUST WAR?

The new reality Jesus proclaimed was nonviolent. That much is clear not just from the Sermon on the Mount but from his entire life and teaching and, above all, the way he faced his death. His was not merely a tactical or pragmatic nonviolence seized upon because nothing else would have "worked" against the Roman Empire's near monopoly on violence. Rather, he saw nonviolence as a direct corollary of the nature of God and of the new reality emerging in the world from God. In a verse quoted more than any other from the New Testament during the church's first four centuries, Jesus taught that God loves everyone, and values all, even those who make themselves God's enemies. We are therefore to do likewise.[30] The reign of God, the peaceable kingdom, is (despite the monarchical terms) an order in which the inequity, violence, and domination characteristic of oppressive societies are superseded. Thus nonviolence is not just a means to the kingdom of God; it is a quality of the kingdom itself. Those who live nonviolently are already manifesting the transformed reality of the divine order now, even under the conditions of the domination system.

For three centuries the church remained steadfastly nonviolent.[31] It saw the Roman Empire as the acute manifestation of the domination system and opposed it with the message of God's domination-free order. With the "conversion" of Constantine, however, the empire assumed from the church the role of God's providential agent in history. Once Christianity became the religion of the empire, its success was linked to the success of the empire, and preservation of the empire became the decisive criterion for ethical behavior. The church no longer saw the demonic as lodged in the empire, but in the empire's enemies.

Augustine (d. 430) made the accommodation of Christianity to its new status as a privileged religion in support of the state. As was stated earlier, Augustine believed that Christians had no right to defend themselves from violence. But he identified a problem that no earlier theologian had faced: what Augustine regarded as the loving obligation to use violence if necessary to defend the innocent against evil. Drawing on Stoic just war principles, he articulated the position that was to dominate church teaching from his time right up to the present.

Though most Christians, Catholic or Protestant, will, if questioned, claim that they support the use of violence in certain cases on the basis of just war thinking, they do nothing of the sort. Just war theory is a very rigorous and complex ethical discipline. It has never been taught to the average church member or even to most clergy. The vast majority of professional theologians would be at a loss to list the seven or more criteria used in just war decisions. What most people call "just war" is really something else. Some mean by it the entirely different idea of the *holy war* or *crusade*, which knows no limits and admits no ethical quandaries. Holy wars are total wars aimed at the utter subjugation or extermination of an enemy.[32] Others who believe they are advocates of just war are in reality supporting a *political war*, or a *war of national interests*.[33] These are military interventions made by nations into the affairs of other nations for purely pragmatic political and economic reasons. These wars have frequently been "justified" by religious sycophants, but they are driven purely by the necessities of power politics. And finally, others call "just" those wars that are pursued for the sake of *machismo or pride*, such as the personalization of the Gulf War by Saddam Hussein and George Bush.

Just war theory is quite distinct from these three types of war, though it is endlessly confused with them. Every war that Christians of the world's nations have engaged in has been either a holy war crusade, a war of national interests, or an affair of machismo. No authoritative Christian body has ever, prior to the commencement of fighting, decreed that one side or the other is justified in warfare on the basis of just war criteria. Instead, the sorry record reveals that Christian churches have usually simply endorsed the side on which they happened to find themselves. Significant parts of the population have even opposed a war, as in the case of the Mexican-American War, the U.S. Civil War, and the Vietnam War. But I know of no national church body (and very few significant Christian leaders) that, at the inception of hostilities, ever denounced a war of national interest fought by its own nation. (For the first time, in advance of a war, many prominent Christian leaders, the Pope included, declared that war in the Persian Gulf did *not* meet just war criteria.)[34]

Most Christians assume that any war that they *feel* is just, or merely necessary and unavoidable, *is* just. The just war criteria, however, are extraordinarily demanding. They presuppose that no Christian should be involved in a war unless it meets all or at least most of the criteria.[35] The burden of proof is *always* on those who resort to violence.

Just war theory assumes that initiating war is generally a crime and that only one party, usually not the aggressor, can be just.[36] Just war theory never assumes that survival is an overriding consideration for either the individual or the state. It anticipates situations where victory cannot be gained without the use of indefensible means, and renounces them, accepting defeat as an honorable outcome.[37]

Various writers present slightly different lists, but the essential conditions that must be met before a decision to go to war is considered justified (*jus ad bellum*) are these:

1. The war must have a *just cause*.
2. It must be waged by a *legitimate authority*.
3. It must be *formally declared*.
4. It must be fought with a *peaceful intention*.
5. It must be a *last resort*.
6. There must be reasonable *hope of success*.
7. The means used must possess *proportionality* to the end sought.

Three additional conditions must be met for the permissible conduct of war (*jus in bello*):

1. *Noncombatants* must be given immunity.
2. *Prisoners* must be treated humanely.
3. *International treaties and conventions* must be honored.

These general rules can be extremely difficult to apply in concrete situations.[38] What constitutes a legitimate authority—say, in a guerrilla insurgency aimed at overthrowing a dictator? How do we distinguish between an "offensive" and a "defensive" war or determine who really started it? Who are noncombatants in the age of democracies and total war? What happens when *both* sides believe they can construct a valid case for a just war? Do some criteria outweigh others? Must they all be met? Are they still applicable in the nuclear age, or in the face of the unparalleled firepower now available to assailants? Are the criteria too punctiliar, ignoring as they do the factors leading up to actual combat? And why should these criteria be regarded as authoritative?

Despite the casuistic cast of these criteria and the difficulty in applying them, I believe they are indispensable in the struggle to mitigate the violence of war. It is not the criteria themselves that are problematic, but the fact that they have been subordinated to the myth of redemptive violence: the belief that violence saves. In that mythic context, the just war criteria have normally been used simply to justify wars that are unjustifiable. Freed from that context, and subordinated to the church's vocation for nonviolence, these criteria can play a critical role in preventing wars and in reducing the level of violence in wars that cannot be averted.

Just war theorists have often bristled at the perfectionism of pacifists, whose concern for ethical means sometimes seems to obscure the demand for justice. Pacifists have often criticized just war theorists for functioning as a propaganda arm of the war machine, providing moral legitimacy for military interventions motivated by the needs of empire. Pacifists have seemed irresponsible. Just war theorists have appeared accommodating. Is there not a third way here as well, one that affirms the pacifist's nonviolence and the just war theorist's concern for moral accountability even in war? I believe that there is, but that it involves a prior commitment to nonviolence and a far more rigorous use of the just war criteria than has often been the case.[39]

Just war theory has taken seriously the possibility of making ethical judgments about the use of violence by or against a state. It assumes that we live in a morally coherent universe in which all human actions, even under duress, are susceptible to moral evaluation.[40] But it has been profoundly discredited because so many of the professional ethicists identified with just war theory supported the Vietnam War, even after its barbarity was evident for everyone to see. Paul Ramsey, John Courtney Murray, and Reinhold Niebuhr supported the Cold War and nuclear deterrence, further discrediting just war theory with the peace movement around the world.

What causes the gravest misgivings about just war theory and practice is that, for all its intellectual rigor, it often appears morally slack. To live a moral life means to form binding intentions and to act on them, even in the face of adverse circumstances.[41] Just war theory often seems more intent on finding a way around the binding intentions in the teaching of Jesus, and it tends to do so in the name of the bloodiest ideology of our time: nationalism. By their very nature, moral principles need to be highly resistant to the making of exceptions. Just war theory, by contrast, is notorious for the ease with which some of its proponents have made exceptions. Hence the impression that it is nothing more than casuistry in the service of the god Mars.

According to the criterion of noncombatant immunity, for example, civilians should be protected against direct attack. But this prohibits only "the deliberate human act of intentionally aiming at civilians, not their foreseeable destruction collateral to aiming at legitimate and important military targets," according to Paul Ramsey, one of the leading proponents of just war theory.[42] "There *is* no rule against *causing* the death of noncombatants, but only against intending to target them directly."[43] If guerrillas choose to hide among civilians, then it is legitimate to blow up civilians along with them. "No Christian and no moralist should assert that it violates the moral immunity of non-combatants from direct, deliberate attack to direct the violence of war upon vast Vietcong strongholds whose destruction unavoidably involves the collateral deaths of a great many civilians."[44] It was the incapacity of peasants in Vietnam to understand the "Christian" and "moral" rightness of their being napalmed and bombed that cost America their support in that war. But is the criterion flawed, or only its interpretation by Ramsey?

Ramsey believed that we may perform an act that we know will kill many civilians as long as we do not intend to kill them. This notion is ethically bankrupt. In practice it leads to the acceptance of civilian casualty rates so astronomical as to render the criterion of civilian *immunity* absurd. When this criterion was promulgated, the idea was that *no* civilians were to be killed. But if we include in civilian casualties those deaths made inevitable by war's disruption of farming, sanitation, and food distribution, we arrive at an average of 50 percent civilian deaths for all wars since 1700. Significantly, there has been virtually no fluctuation in the average of civilian casualties from 1700 until recently. This means that anyone planning war can be fairly certain that civilian casualties will be at least 50 percent, and, given modern firepower, more likely far higher. In the decade of the 1980s, the proportion of civilian deaths jumped to 74 percent, and in 1990 it appears to have been close to 90 percent. On this basis alone, very few wars in the last three centuries have not violated the criterion of civilian immunity.[45]

What these statistics fail to show is the enormous increase in *total* casualties in our century:

        1500s—1,600,000 killed
        1600s—6,100,000
        1700s—7,000,000
        1800s—19,400,000
        1900s—107,800,000[46]

At a constant 50 percent, civilian deaths increased over five centuries from 800,000 in the 1500s to 53,900,000 in the 1900s. As if that level of casualties were not enough to forever banish war beyond the pale of morality, some just war theorists justified nuclear deterrence, despite the certainty that civilian deaths would number in the tens or hundreds of millions. If one agrees that the killing of civilians is prohibited, by what distorted logic is one able to justify casualties of such magnitude? Even if we inflate the probable total casualties from war for *all* the centuries since domination states arose (ca. 3000 B.C.E.), *more people will have been killed in war in our century than in all the preceding 5,000 years combined.* And yet there are still Christian ethicists soberly pondering the question of justifying certain wars!

Now the Persian Gulf War has blurred the distinction between nuclear and conventional warfare, since tens of thousands of Iraqi soldiers were killed by nonnuclear bombing in only a matter of days. The distinction between civilian and military casualties also becomes indistinct, since conscription amounts to involuntary servitude. Those Kurdish and Shi'ite soldiers whom Saddam Hussein placed on the front lines in order to liquidate them as internal threats to his regime did not die willingly.

Or take the criterion of "last resort." Theoretically, just war theorists are committed to the use of every feasible nonviolent alternative before turning to war. In fact, I know of only one just war theorist— James F. Childress—who devotes any space at all to nonviolent alternatives.[47] The rest focus on what constitutes last resort. This focus has the effect, however, of shrinking the ethical field. "Last resort" becomes "timely resort," as in the writings of Ramsey; and we soon find ourselves discussing "preemptive strikes," the assassination of heads of state, and even Pentagon doublespeak like "anticipatory retaliation." In our war with Iraq, did we allow enough time for sanctions to work? Was that war truly a "last resort"?

The other just war criteria are as easily manipulated. A just war must be declared by a "legitimate authority," but the Vietnam War never was declared on the American side by the sole agency entrusted with that power: the American Congress. Yet this fact did not cause many just war theorists to declare that war unjust. No nuclear war could be "won" without a surprise attack; but that completely obviates the "formal declaration" required by traditional just war theory.[48]

War has to have a "just cause"; but how is the public really to know if the cause is just when the first casualty of war is truth? The Gulf of Tonkin incident off North Vietnam was apparently *staged* in order to gain congressional support for the war.

Again, the means used in a war must be *proportionate* to the end sought. But how can we know in advance what level of destruction will follow armed conflict? Even beyond casualties, ruined cities, a gutted economy, women raped or reduced to prostitution, children dying from malnutrition and intestinal diseases, how does one measure into the future the continuing hazard of exploding landmines and bombs, drug addiction, alcoholism, mental illness, physical crippling, suicide? How can this be weighed before or even during a war?[49]

Yet when all these objections to just war theory are analyzed, they come down to one point: Just war theory is objectionable only when it is captive to the myth of redemptive violence.

Perhaps charity requires a distinction between just war theory and some of its advocates, who during the Cold War period were wed to an interventionist credo. Perhaps, too, we should note the source of confusion built into the very phrase "just war," which implies that there *are* wars that are just, and that the church or its moral theologians have the ability and authority to discern which they are. Many would deny that *any* war can be just. This has caused some to jettison just war theory in its entirety. *But even they will be found using just war criteria to explain their rejection of the notion of a just war.* The fact is that just war criteria are indispensable in attempting to prevent or mitigate the hellishness of war.[50]

I propose that we terminate all talk of "just wars." Even as the word "pacifism" sounds too much like "passivity," "just war" sounds too much like "war is justifiable." The very term "just war" is saturated with illusions about the rightness of war that are no longer tenable. Those who regard all wars as criminal can scarcely avail themselves of these helpful criteria when they are forced to discuss them with nomenclature that is intrinsically inadequate.[51]

Christians can no more speak of just war than of just rape, or just child abuse, or just massacres (and all of these are inevitably drawn into the train of war). But we also cannot wish away a world of bewildering complexity, in which difficult decisions are forced on us by the violence of others, and where nonviolent solutions are not always forthcoming.

VIOLENCE REDUCTION CRITERIA

Instead, I suggest that we rename the just war criteria "violence-reduction criteria." That, after all, is what most of us are after. We are not seeking a rationale for legitimating particular wars, but ways of avoiding warfare before it starts, and of decreasing its horrors once it begins. Perhaps both just war theorists and advocates of nonviolence can find common ground for attempting to restrain bellicosity in the phrase "violence-reduction criteria."

After all, both nonviolence and just war theory agree on several key points:

1. Both acknowledge that nonviolence is preferable to violence.
2. Both agree that the innocent must be protected as much as possible.
3. Both reject any defense of a war motivated solely by a crusade mentality or national security interests or personal egocentricity.
4. Both wish to persuade states to reduce the levels of violence.

5. Both wish to hold war accountable to moral values, both before and during the conflict.[52]

Violence-reduction criteria might provide prudential moral leverage on political leaders for whom the language of the Gospel carries no conviction. Some nations have already taken steps to limit war and to allow moral resistance to it: by laws allowing conscientious objection to military service; recognition of the legitimacy of civil disobedience; establishing war-crime tribunals; and acknowledgment of the right of soldiers to refuse to carry out illegal orders.

What is being proposed here is nothing more than a return to the ancient position of the church, antedating Augustine's adaptation of Stoic just war theory. Early Christians, who opposed all wars, nevertheless made distinctions between wars, arguing that humane treatment of the enemy was superior to cruelty.[53]

BEYOND PACIFISM AND JUST WAR

Some pacifists, literally interpreting Matthew 5:38–41 as rejecting all resistance to evil, have refused to join in nonviolent direct actions or civil disobedience because they believed such actions constituted resistance to evil and were coercive. We now see that this position was based on false exegesis. The nonviolence Jesus teaches *is* coercive. But it is not lethal or injurious.[54]

But just war theorists have also justified their position on the same misreading of Matthew 5 as nonresistance. Of course we are to resist evil! But we are to do so nonviolently. Jesus was not counseling nonresistance, but nonviolence. And his kind of nonviolence was a good deal more aggressive than some pacifists might have liked. Jesus did not hesitate to use shame, condemnation, ridicule, and other forms of "tough love" (consider the cleansing of the temple episode!) in order to free both the oppressed from oppression and the oppressors from sin.

It appears that we are now in a position to move beyond the old arguments between pacifism and just war. Jesus is clearly against violence and domination in all their forms. As Gandhi observed, "The only people on earth who do not see Christ and His teachings as nonviolent are Christians."[55] It is now high time that Christians of every stripe recognize and embrace the nonviolence that is at the heart of the Gospel. Jesus teaches a new way that forswears both passivity and war. We must abandon the idea that there can be just wars. Perhaps then we might also retire the word "pacifist," with its hopeless entanglement with "passivity" and its inadequate foundation in Scripture. Instead of calling themselves pacifists, Christians should insist that they are simply Christians, committed to the coming of God's domination-free order.

From the "peace church" heritage, the position proposed here affirms nonviolence as a fundamental tenet of the Gospel of God's inbreaking new order. The church cannot then justify any violence or war as "good" or "just." And from the "just war" heritage, the just war criteria can be turned into "violence-reduction criteria" and used in an attempt to lessen the devastation of a given war from a position of principled nonviolence.[56]

Just war theory has been not so much mistaken as mis-married to the ideology of redemptive violence. Its pagan roots were never sufficiently purged of their origin in the domination system. Freed from their misuse as justifications for wars of national interest, or holy war crusades, or egotistical face-offs, these criteria can now be focused on preventing or mitigating the barbarities of war from a committed nonviolent perspective. Christians today can no longer regard war as an extension of policy, but must see it as a dangerous anachronism, destined for oblivion in the new, nonviolent order of God.

NOTES

1. The material in this paper is fully discussed in my book *Engaging the Powers* (Minneapolis: Fortress Press, 1992), where documentation in support of these arguments can be found. These notes direct the reader to the appropriate pages in the book (hereafter referred to as *Powers*) and offer information from the notes found there.

2. *Powers*, p. 221, citing Ruth Leger Sivard, *World Military and Social Expenditures, 1991* (Washington, D.C.: World Priorities, 1991), p. 20.

3. *Powers*, pp. 228, 389, n. 73.

4. *Powers*, p. 175.

5. *Powers*, pp. 212, 227, citing Augustine, *Sermon on the Mount* 1.19.56–68; *Reply to Faustus the Manichee* 22.76; *On Lying* 27; *Letter* 47.5. Reinhold Niebuhr exactly mirrored this view in *Christianity and Power Politics* (New York: Charles Scribner's Sons, 1940), p. 10, and *An Interpretation of Christian Ethics* (New York: Harper and Brothers, 1935), pp. 50, 62–83.

6. *Powers*, pp. 184–85.

7. *Powers*, p. 185.

8. *Powers*, p. 186.

9. Rom. 12:17; 1 Thes. 5:15; 1 Pet. 3:9.

10. Matt. 5:39.

11. The Dead Sea Scrolls, 1 QS 7.

12. *Powers*, pp. 175–76.

13. *Powers*, p. 176.

14. See the Mishnah, *Baba Kamma* 8:1–7.

15. *Powers*, pp. 176–77.

16. Matt. 5:40.

17. *Powers*, pp. 177–79.

18. *Powers*, p. 178, citing Josephus, *War* 2.427. On the loss of land through indebtedness, see Martin Goodman, *The Ruling Class of Judea* (New York: Cambridge University Press, 1987), pp. 55–58.

19. Matthew has this detail reversed; see Luke 6:29.

20. Gen. 9:20–29; *Powers*, p. 179. Nudity is abhorrent to the conventional because it violates the system of classification by which one can identify a person's place on the social map. Without clothes, the boundaries by which society is ordered and guarded are dissolved. Clothing signifies one's social location, gender, and status. See Jerome H. Neyrey, "A Symbolic Approach to Mark 7," *Forum* 4/3 (1988): 72. Therefore, to strip naked voluntarily before the creditor and magistrate, precisely in a context intended to shame the poor into repayment, is to deny the hierarchial system of classification in its entirety.

21. *Powers*, pp. 179–80. There is, so far as I can tell, no surviving Roman law limiting *angareia* to one mile, but scholars have almost universally inferred from the wording of the text (correctly I believe) that some such rule was in force.

22. Mark 15:21, parallel Matt. 27:32.

23. *Powers*, p. 181. Josephus gives an instance of a legion passing through Judea and the lengths to which Jewish leaders went to prevent it (*Antiquities* 18:120–24). But even in Jerusalem, Galilean pilgrims would have been treated to scenes similar to that enacted by the impressment of Simon of Cyrene to carry Jesus' cross.

24. *Powers*, pp. 181–82. Epictetus provides an example of passive submission to impressment that is the polar opposite of Jesus' advice in Matthew. "You ought to treat your whole body like a poor, loaded-down donkey . . . and if it be commandeered (*angareia*) and a soldier lay hold of it, let it go, do not resist (*antiteine*) or grumble. If you do, you will get a beating and loose your little donkey just the same." (Disc., 4.1.79). For the denigration of *angareia* to plain extortion by soldiers, see Ramsey MacMullen, *Soldier and Civilian* (Cambridge, Mass.: Harvard University Press, 1963), pp. 85–86; and M. Rostovtzeff, *The Social and Economic History of the Roman Empire*, 2d ed. (Oxford: Clarendon Press, 1957), 1:424 and 2:721–23 nn. 45–47.

25. Matt. 13:33, parallel Luke 13:20–21.

26. *Powers*, p. 183, citing Richard A. Horsley, *Jesus and the Spiral of Violence* (San Francisco: Harper & Row, 1987), pp. 318–26.

27. *Powers*, p. 186.

28. *Powers*, p. 189. See Josephus, *War* 2.169–74; *Ant.* 18.55–59; *War* 2.229–31; Philo, *Leg.* 299–305; and later, Josephus, *Ant.* 18.261–309, and Philo, *Leg.* 225–29; and Horsley's excellent discussion in *Spiral of Violence*, pp. 90–120.

29. I have attempted to apply Jesus' teaching on the "third way" to the situation in South Africa in *Violence and Nonviolence in South Africa* (Philadelphia: New Society Publishers, 1987).

30. Matt. 5:45; cf. Luke 6:35.

31. *Powers*, p. 209. C. J. Cadoux fills 160 pages with quotations from the New Testament and the early theologians expressing Christian disapproval of participation in war; see *The Early Christian Attitude toward War* (London: George Allen & Unwin, 1940).

32. *Powers*, p. 212. The Islamic *jihād* is not a "holy war" in our sense, in that it has sometimes acted as a brake on violence as well as a cause of it. The very term *jihād* was an attempt to restrict religous resort to war to a very limited set of cases (David Little, in a personal conversation).

33. *Powers*, p. 213, citing John Howard Yoder, *When War is Unjust* (Minneapolis: Augsburg, 1984), p. 21.

34. *Powers*, p. 213.

35. *Powers*, p. 214, citing Paul Ramsey, with Stanley Hauerwas, *Speak Up for Just War or Pacifism* (University Park: Pennsylvania State University Press, 1988), p. 71.

36. Bernard T. Adeney, *Just War, Political Realism, and Faith*, American Theological Library Association Monograph Series, 24 (Metuchen, N.J.: American Theological Library Association, 1988), p. 98.

37. Stanley Hauerwas, *Against the Nations* (Minneapolis: Winston Press, 1985), pp. 138–39. According to George Weigel, the just war tradition regards conflict as the political manifestation of original sin, and war as a legitimate but not inevitable means of resolving conflict. War is thus a just means for defending a legitimate political community and human rights, and not simply another expression of human fallenness; see *Tranquillitas Ordinis* (New York: Oxford University Press, 1987), p. 329. I argue just the opposite. War is a consequence of original sin, as is the violence system generally. War is the epitome of fallenness.

38. *Powers*, p. 215. Using the same just war criteria, James Turner Johnson argued that the Persian Gulf War was just, and Alan Geyer that it was unjust, in "Just War Tradition and the War in the Gulf," *Christian Century* 108 (February 6–13, 1991): 134–35. Their differences do not invalidate the criteria, but illustrate that their use is conditioned by one's starting assumptions.

39. *Powers*, p. 215.

40. *Powers*, p. 220, citing George Weigel, "Religion and Peace: An Argument Complexified," Conference on Conflict Resolution in the Post-Cold War Third World, United States Institute of Peace, Washington, D.C., October 3–5, 1990; see *Resolving Third World Conflict: Challenges for a New Era*, ed. Sheryl J. Brown and Kimber M. Schraub (Washington: United States Institute of Peace Press, 1992), pp. 171–92.

41. *Powers*, p. 220, citing Barrie Paskins and Michael Dockrill, *The Ethics of War* (London: Duckworth, 1979), p. 232.

42. *Powers*, p. 220, citing Paul Ramsey, *Speak Up*, p. 53.

43. *Powers*, p. 220, citing Ramsey, *Speak Up*, p. 102.

44. *Powers*, p. 220, citing Ramsey, *The Just War* (New York: Lanham, 1981), p. 503.

45. *Powers*, p. 221.

46. *Powers*, p. 221.

47. *Powers*, p. 222. See James F. Childress, *Moral Responsibility in Conflicts: Essays on Nonviolence, War and Conscience* (Baton Rouge: Louisiana State University Press, 1982).

48. *Powers*, p. 222.

49. *Powers*, p. 222. Augustine added another criterion that modern just war theorists have, mercifully, dropped: Every act of war must be conducted in love. The drift of Jesus' commandment seems to be loving our enemies *instead* of killing them, not loving them *as* we kill them. Augustine, however, grasped the implications of just war theory: Once killing is justified, it must somehow be integrated into the rest of the gospel of love and nonviolence.

50. *Powers*, p. 223.

51. *Powers*, p. 223.

52. *Powers*, pp. 223–24.

53. *Powers*, p. 226.

54. *Powers*, p. 227.

55. *Powers*, p. 216, citing Dale W. Brown, *Biblical Pacifism* (Elgin, Ill: Brethren Press, 1986), p. ix.

56. *Powers*, p. 228. Glen Stassen has also proposed a third way between just war theory and pacifism in *Just Peacemaking* (Louisville, Ky.: Westminster/ John Knox Press, 1992).

Justifications for Violence in Islam

ABDULAZIZ SACHEDINA

INTRODUCTORY REMARKS ABOUT COMPARATIVE STUDIES[1]

A note on the comparative approach is appropriate in a study which, like this one, attempts to identify common grounds on a particular issue that are shared by the Western monotheistic traditions of Judaism, Christianity, and Islam. Comparative studies in religion have been generally criticized for oversimplifying the complex and intricate variations and divergences within each tradition for the purpose of typifying them in broad terms. Whereas it is not difficult to catalogue broad categories like prophetic consciousness, the function of revelation and the religious-moral guidance based on it, and the salvation history shared by the Abrahamic faiths, special attention needs to be paid to the historical circumstances and social-political experiences of the respective communities that interacted with their religious orientation and shaped their attitudes, decisions, and actions.

To be sure, the three basic ingredients of the religiously inspired worldview are: (1) fundamental principles of the creed that provide authoritative perspectives for interpreting contradictions and tensions in human existence; (2) the dispositions that are evoked by these perspectives; and (3) the religious practices that reinforce both the creed and the disposition generated by it by means of special rituals and practices.[2] When these basic ingredients are examined and verified against the relevant literature produced by the group, they may reveal the intricate relationship between the tradition and its contextual formulations and reinterpretations within a specific time and space. This is what Max Weber calls the "internal structure of cultural values" by which a religious community justifies its adoption of a practical solution to the ontological anxieties caused by fear of death and an uncertain future.

It is possible to assert from the outset that in investigating the particular attitude regarding political quietism[3] and pacifism[4] in Western monotheistic traditions, the believers' opposition to or resignation in the face of all violent means of attaining a divinely ordained order would be settled in large measure by the way in which the religion maintained its relationship with power and legitimized the authority that exacted obedience to that power in the name of a sacred authority. In other words, Islamic views on activism or quietism, for instance, are part of a theory of statecraft that defines the state as a means to promoting the common good and as an instrument founded on the notions of an omnipotent, omniscient, and just God, of a humanity endowed with volition and cognition, and of relations between the divine and human will and act. There is little doubt that the beliefs, attitudes, and practices of the religious subject demonstrate the intricate developing relationship within the context of sociopolitical history between the authoritative and determinative teachings of a tradition and the emerging power to implement them as normative for the creation of the religious polity. Moreover, the beliefs and attitudes also determine the way in which the followers of that tradition deal with the questions of resistance and opposition to the abuse of power or submission to it. Furthermore, the ultimate outcome of this historical interplay between religion and power is also reflected in the way people have responded to the need to confront the obstacles to the realization of the idealized vision of a religious polity on earth. In other words, religious ideas have to interact with the realities that members of a given society must reckon with and must be continuously reevaluated to be relevant in current circumstances.

THE INTERPLAY BETWEEN RELIGION AND POWER IN ISLAM

Islam emerged in seventh-century Arabia in the midst of a serious socio-economic imbalance between the rich and the poor, and between extreme forms of individualism and tribal solidarity. Moreover, it arose in the very spirit of populism of the Abrahamic faiths, that is, as a moral challenge to humanity to rise above its personal grudges and petty interests and to respond to God by affirming belief in God's plan for the whole of humanity and by working for its ultimate realization. Abrahamic faiths taught doctrines and moral standards that were intelligible to the ordinary person. They emphasized concern for the ordinary moral needs and abilities of the common people to undertake to work for egalitarian justice in society. History required that all human beings support such an ideal and undertake the decisive responsibility to establish justice and equity on earth. This outlook may be summed up as "looking to justice in history through community." All the prophets had stressed just action as the most meritorious religious activity.[5]

Accordingly, as a religion with a set of beliefs, decisions, and practices, Islam embarked on creating its own public order that would translate the Islamic revelation into a specifically religious-moral social universe. In this sense, Islam inherently functioned as an "activist" ideology within a specific social-political order that it constantly evaluated, calling upon its adherents either to defend and preserve or to overthrow and transform. In addition, Islam as a religious ideology is both a critical assessment of human corporate existence and a divine blueprint that awaits implementation to realize God's will on earth to the fullest extent possible and, if necessary, through force.

Nevertheless, in view of its recognition of human volition and innate disposition in negotiating its spiritual destiny, Islam did not overlook the problem of disbelief and the tensions and inner stresses it caused in human beings. Rejection of truth and impairment of moral consciousness were problems that in large measure had to be resolved by means of appeal to the innate disposition (*fitra*) of human beings—the conscience—which was divinely guided and which possessed knowledge of good and evil, of godly existence, and of impiety. But there were times when this abnormal condition of human rejection of faith became a threat to the corporate well-being of the society and caused the spread of corruption on earth, a corruption that involved more than the damaging of the individual conscience. Unbelief came to signify not only a denial of truth but also a threat to the community of the faithful. Moreover, it came to be identified not only as a religious wrong, to be punished in the hereafter, but also as a moral wrong, to be corrected in the here and now—by use of force if necessary. Thus the Qur'anic command:

> O believers, fight the unbelievers who are near you, and let them find in you harshness; and know that God is with the godfearing.[6]

The successive revelation of the Qur'an points to a growing awareness in the Muslim community that it would have to engage in armed resistance to the threat posed by those who did not share its faith and the sociopolitical implications of that faith.

More immediately, the pre-Islamic Arab tribal culture had institutionalized military power on which depended the security of a tribe
and even its existence. Primacy among the tribes belonged to those
that were able to protect all their clients and to avenge all insults,
injuries, and deaths through their military strength. The Semitic system of retaliatory justice based on "a life for a life" in the circumstances
of desert life could not always ensure that crime would not be committed lightly and irresponsibly. In fact, a show of military prowess
through warlike expeditions in order to gain ascendancy among the
tribal groupings was quite common in pre-Islamic Arabia. Against
this background, the legitimate use of force prescribed by the Qur'an
was merely to provide appropriate moral restrictions on the use of
military power to resolve conflicts.[7]

Inasmuch as the Qur'an introduced the injunction legitimizing
the use of force through the instrumentality of *jihād*, it was responding
to the moral-religious and political conditions prevalent in seventh-
century Arabia. The following passage of the Qur'an illustrates the
moral restrictions and religious sanctions that were being introduced
to curb the violence prevalent in the tribal society:

> O believers, prescribed for you is retaliation, touching the slain;
> freeman for freeman, slave for slave, female for female. But if
> aught is pardoned a man by his brother, let the pursuing be
> honorable, and let the payment be with kindliness. That is a
> lightening granted you by your Lord, and a mercy; and for
> him who commits aggression after that—for him there awaits a
> painful chastisement.[8]

To be sure, the Qur'anic legitimation of *jihād* in the meaning of
fighting in the verse 2:193, where the commandment is declared in
no uncertain terms ("Fight them [that is, those who fight with you],
till there is no persecution and the religion be only for God"), is
concerned with the problem of eradicating unbelief that causes a
breakdown in the Islamic public order.[9]

> Fight in the way of God against those who fight against you,
> but begin not hostilities. Lo! God loveth not aggressors. And
> slay them wherever ye find them, and drive them out of the
> places whence they drove you out, for persecution is worse than
> slaughter.[10]

The permission to fight in this passage was a response to the problem posed by the powerful Meccan tribes. The Qur'an indicates that although unbelief is a religious problem, to be construed as one dimension of the work of God, unbelief can be, and in the case of the Meccans was, malicious—a willful act on the part of human beings who seek to deceive God or to deprive God of God's rights.

This was a prescriptive measure to arrest the harm caused to the people at large and to redress the wrongs suffered by the weak at the hands of those who perpetrated immoralities in order to defeat the divine purposes on earth. In other words, the "struggle" and the "striving" (primary signification of the word *jihād*) by means of force, as far as the religious attitude was concerned, underscored the divinely sanctioned endeavor as a response to actively hostile unbelief. It is not unbelievers as such who are the target of force, but unbelievers who demonstrate their hostility to Islam by, for example, persecution of the Muslims. In other words, it is not merely the negative attitude to religion per se that sanctions the use of force; it is the hostility to which it leads that makes it a prior moral offense and that requires a response with force.

The need for the use of force first became evident when the Muslims under the leadership of the Prophet established the first Islamic polity, in Medina. As willful disobedience, the unbelief of the Meccan tribes became a problem with moral as well as religious dimensions for the public order. The Qur'an indicates that various kinds of action were appropriate for the Prophet and the community to use in dealing with this situation. The important point to underscore here is that the more the Qur'an stresses the moral aspects of the problem of unbelief (for example, Meccan persecution of the Muslims, their expulsion of the innocent from their homes), the more the use of force is justified.

The use of force, then, as far as the Qur'an is concerned is defensive and limited to the violation of interpersonal human conduct. For the Qur'an it is crucial to emphasize its defensive strategy in dealing with the problem of human violence stemming from human rejection of faith. Nonetheless, in the historical development of the relationship between Islam and power, Muslim jurists regarded this explicitly Qur'anic principle of defensive warfare as abrogated. They maintained that fighting was obligatory for Muslims, even when the unbelievers had not begun hostilities.[11] This accommodation with the historical practice of *jihād* is not uncommon in the works of the jurists.

What happens when unbelief among the Peoples of the Book (Jews and Christians), who are otherwise tolerated as non-Muslim monotheists (*muwahhidūn*), takes the form of disregard for the moral standards prescribed by the Islamic public order? The Qur'an prescribes:

> Fight those who believe not in God and the Last Day and do not forbid what God and His Messenger have forbidden—such men as practice not the religion of truth, being those who have been given the Book, until they pay the tribute out of hand and have been humbled.[12]

There is no other place in the Qur'an than this verse where there remains room to interpret its directive to combat disbelief as going beyond the consistent defensive posture that must be adopted by the Muslim public order. Yet it is the moral clause in the verse ("do not forbid what God and His messenger have forbidden") that is within the jurisdiction of the community to assess for its negative impact and to respond to accordingly. Although the Muslim community, according to the Qur'an, was one among many divinely guided communities such as the Jewish and Christian, all equally sharing in their blessed Abrahamic origin, soon after the establishment of Muslim political power the Muslim community saw Islam as a political ideology that was first to rule over and then to supersede all other communities. Islam was to usher in the true and uncorrupted divine guidance to humankind, creating the worldwide society in which the Qur'an and the prophetic paradigm, the Sunna, would be the everyday norm of all the nations. Islam, Muslims believed, must guide the practical policies of a cosmopolitan world under its sphere of influence, the *dār al-islām*.

JIHĀD *AS A DEFENSIVE STRATEGY OR A MEANS OF "CALLING"?*

Long before the Muslim jurists undertook to provide a religious rationale for the historical practice of *jihād* by developing political-legal terminology like *dār al-islām* (the sphere of "submission" [to God]) and *dār al-ḥarb* (the sphere of war), the Qur'an had implicitly divided the world into *dār al-īmān* (the sphere of belief) and *dār al-kufr* (the sphere of disbelief). There is, however, a difference in the way the revealed law, the Shari'a, defined the two spheres and the way the

Qur'an projected the realm of "belief" and "disbelief." For Islamic law the division of the world into spheres of "submission to God" and "war" was in terms of the spatial-temporal as well as the religious hegemony of Islam; whereas for the Qur'an the spatial division was simply in terms of the spiritual and moral distinction between the spheres of "belief" and "disbelief."

Mecca was regarded as the sphere of "disbelief" so long as the people of Mecca had not accepted Islam. The "submission" of the people to the Islamic order brought about the conversion of Mecca to the sphere of "belief." The religious distinction is thus attached to the spiritual-moral condition of the people, and not necessarily to the land to which everyone should aspire to return as part of the divine promise. There are no prophetic promises in Islam resembling those in Judaism, for instance, that would inspire Muslims to undertake *jihād* so as to return from the "diaspora" to their "holy land" located somewhere in Arabia. Moreover, there are no divine guarantees that once the sphere of "belief" is established it will not revert to the sphere of "disbelief." Keeping the sphere of "belief" from turning into a corrupt and tyrannical sphere of "disbelief" is a human responsibility. Furthermore, there is no covenant between God and Muslims that certain parts of the earth will be immune from becoming corrupt and unjust. Ultimately, the human response to the divine challenge of becoming morally and spiritually attentive would decide the sacredness or otherwise of any part of the earth.

It was in such a conception of Islam as a political ideology for the entire world that the tension between the Qur'anic sanction of *jihād* as a defensive strategy in the face of persecution and *jihād* as a means of "calling" (*al-da'wa*) people to the divine path was discernible.[13] The tension is between the religious destiny of humanity, which must be negotiated between God and individuals without coercion from any human agency, including that of the Prophet, and the moral responsibility of living as a member of a society with well-defined rights and obligations. Muslim jurists and exegetes were engaged in legitimizing the *jihād* for purposes of "calling" persons to Islam—thus rendering the *jihād* a form of holy war. On the one hand, there was the problem of reconciling an evident discrepancy between the Qur'anic treatment of the *jihād* as a means of making "God's cause succeed"[14] and the manipulation of *jihād* by the de facto Muslim authorities to increase the "sphere of submission [to God]" by engaging in territorial expansion. There is, further, the tension between religious and moral justifications for the *jihād*, which although not explicitly distinguished in Islamic jurisprudence, are, at any rate, alluded to in the Qur'an.

Undoubtedly, tangible political circumstances forced the jurists to be pragmatic and realistic in their formulation of the justifications for undertaking *jihād*, especially if the de facto rulers were willing to uphold the supremacy of Islamic law in a Muslim public order. In the process of providing a religious legitimation for the territorial expansionism of the Muslim rulers, the jurists preferred on many occasions to overlook those passages of the Qur'an that point toward the moral justifications for *jihād* ("fight until there is no persecution"). Consequently, their rationalization of the *jihād* as the means by which the entire world might be converted to the "sphere of Islam" obscures the Qur'anic concept of the *jihād* as a defensive war fought to stop persecution.

The difficulty of keeping the moral and religious justifications for engaging in *jihād* separate in Islamic jurisprudence was inevitable because at no point did Muslim jurists ever undertake to distinctly define the ethical and religious foundations of Islamic legal thought. Moreover, because of the interdependence between religion and politics in the creation of an Islamic world order, Muslim legal authority was envisaged as a comprehensive power that exacted moral and civil obedience in the name of God. The promise of the creation of a just and equitable public order under the normative Shari'a that embodied the will of God was central to Islamic revelation and also to the social, political, and economic activity of the Muslim community. The connection between the divine will and the creation of such an order was fundamental to the jurists' regarding the *jihād* as an instrument in the fulfillment of an ideal Muslim society. Thus, it was not difficult to interpret the Qur'an in such a way that the relatively limited justification for *jihād* contained in the sacred text was broadened to associate *jihād* with the concept of justice and divine guidance and with the desire to secure the well-being of all humanity.

In the wake of the phenomenal conquests achieved by Muslims during the first/seventh century, the jurists began to apply the term *jihād* to military action and to efforts to expand the "sphere of Islam" through the extension of the boundaries of the Islamic polity. The juridical works produced during the second/eighth century provide the evidence that the treatment of the *jihād* in connection with the task of converting the "sphere of war" (*dār al-ḥarb*) to the sphere of Islam was, in effect, an ex post facto legitimation of the early conquests. In fact, the division of the world into two spheres, of "war" and "peace (*islām*)," was a legal construct based on the Muslim jurists' inference from the implicit Qur'anic division of the world into the spheres of "belief" (*īmān*) and "disbelief" (*kufr*).

That there is a relationship between the "call to faith" (*al-daʿwa*) and the undertaking of *jihād* is supported by the insistence of the Qur'an that it has been revealed for the purpose of making the entire world aware of the divine path, and of requiring humanity to obey God and the Prophet. But what are the means that the Prophet may use to exact this obedience? Does the Qur'an justify *jihād* in this connection?

The Qur'an gives the Prophet, in his capacity as leader of the Muslim community, the right to control "discord on earth" by means of *jihād*. This right points to the possibility—even the obligation—for the Prophet to resort to *jihād* when, in his judgment, such action is necessary to combat a breakdown of the public order. In particular, the Prophet may resort to the sword in response to a situation of general lawlessness that results from someone's "taking up arms (*yuḥāribūna*) against God and His messenger,"[15] that is, from a rebellion against the established Islamic order. The repeated injunction to eradicate "corruption on earth," taken together with the Qur'anic justification of a human institution that has the power to carry out "enjoining the good and forbidding the evil,"[16] represents a religiously sanctioned basic moral-civil requirement to protect the well-being of a human community.

In the light of the need to eradicate "corruption on earth" and to "command the good and forbid the evil," the Qur'an provides a sort of rationally derived moral basis for *jihād* in Islam. To be sure, the permission to use force in any form occurred, according to the jurists, during the Medina period of the Prophet's ministry (622 C.E.) when Muslims were given permission to fight back against the "folk who broke their solemn pledges":

> Will ye not fight a folk who broke their solemn pledges, and purposed to drive out the Messenger and did attack you first?[17] If they withdraw not from you, and offer you not peace, and refrain not their hand take them, and slay them wherever you come to them; against them We have given you a clear authority.[18]

It is not difficult to adduce strictly defensive warfare, justified on moral grounds (breach of contract, retaliation, self-defense, and so on), from this permission given to the Muslims to use force. That is, the permission is to respond to the rationally derived obligation to fight in retaliation for attacks upon Muslims. Hence, the Qur'an justifies defensive *jihād*, allowing Muslims to fight against and subdue hostile unbelievers who are dangerous to the community, and whose actions show them to be inimical to the success of God's cause. My categorization of the Qur'anic *jihād* as strictly a "defensive" *jihād* is based on the absolute absence of any reference in the Qur'an that would justify an "offensive" *jihād*, that is, a *jihād* undertaken to "convert" all humanity to Islam. As I shall demonstrate, the Muslim jurists, especially the Shi'ites, had great difficulty in justifying the "offensive" *jihād* without the presence of a legitimate, divinely designated authority of the infallible Imam who could protect against the shedding of innocent blood.

If the Qur'an had stopped at this duty of self-defense against hostile forces, then the possibility of offensive *jihād* would have been altogether out of the question. But it also requires the Prophet to strive to make "God's cause succeed." At this point, the *jihād* (the "struggle") becomes an offensive endeavor in connection with efforts to bring about the kind of world order that the Qur'an envisions.

The possibility of offensive *jihād* as a means in the creation of the Islamic world order gives rise to the tension between the tolerance advocated in matters relating to the religious destiny of human beings, on the one hand, and the active response encouraged and even required against unbelievers "until there is no persecution (*fitna*) and the religion be only for God,"[19] on the other. If this divine commandment is interpreted in the context provided by the general Qur'anic justification for engaging in *jihād* (as a response to aggression or moral wrong), it can be construed in terms of a moral-civil duty to fight "persecution," which, according to 2:191, "is worse than slaughter." On the other hand, if the verse is interpreted in terms of the development of Muslim political power, then it may be said to provide a warrant for wars of expansion. Undoubtedly, Sunni jurists, in legitimating the Muslim conquests, duly regarded them as the outcome of a Qur'anic *jihād*. However, Muslim political history clearly demonstrates that these conquests were undertaken with the explicit aim of expanding Islamic hegemony, not with the goal, as stated in the Qur'an, of ensuring that "the religion be only for God."[20] This verse clearly states that fighting cannot be started until the adversaries are first invited to come to the right path. If they accept the call, there will be no fighting; but if they reject it, then "know that God is your Master; the most excellent Master, and most excellent Helper."[21] This means that their rejection of responding to the call of religion is beyond human remedy. Only God can guide them to the right path.

Further evidence that the injunction to fight in this verse was morally restricted is provided by the fact that some Muslim commentators regarded it as abrogated by the more general command, in verse 9:29, that requires Muslims to fight against "those who believe not in God and the Last Day . . . ." However, this verse refers to an entirely different group of unbelievers. It speaks about the Peoples of the Book. And, as pointed out earlier, offensive *jihād* against Jews and Christians "until they pay *jizya* (poll tax)"[22] points more to the complex relationship among, and interdependence of religious and moral considerations in the treatment of, the "Peoples of the Book" than to their conversion to "God's religion," Islam.

To recapitulate, if *jihād* is understood as part of the human responsibility to strive for the success of God's cause, consistently maintained by the Qur'an,[23] then legitimizing the use of force against moral and political offenses cannot be regarded as contradicting the Qur'anic dictum of 2:256, "No compulsion is there in religion." The Qur'an justifies the use of force in the establishment of an order that protects the basic welfare of the Muslim community against "internal" and "external" enemies. The "internal" enemies include "tyrants" who, according to the Qur'an, "fight against God and His messenger, and hasten about the earth, to do corruption there."[24] "Fight" or "take up arms," as the Arabic verb *yuḥāribūna* suggests, is taken to mean "subverting a Muslim public order under God and His Messenger" leading to "chaos and lawlessness." Hence, "tyrants" are those engaged in seditious activity against the Muslim public order. The "external" enemies include the "leaders of unbelief" (that is, non-Muslim Arabs) who "break their oaths after their covenant and thrust at your religion"[25] and the Peoples of the Book (that is, Jews and Christians) who "do not forbid what God and His messenger have forbidden,"[26] thereby obstructing the struggle to make "God's cause succeed."

THE NEED FOR LEGITIMATE AUTHORITY TO SANCTION VIOLENCE IN THE NAME OF GOD.

The Prophet through the revelation, then, was not only representing divine goals on earth; he was also engaged in interpreting them to make them relevant in the given cultural context. Any armed struggle like *jihād* which, as the Qur'an admits, was by nature reprehensible to humanity in that it endangered its sense of security and well-being presupposed the existence of a divinely designated authority that could resolve the problems of the interpretability of supernaturally ordained obligations involving violence and the destruction of human life. *Jihād*, as the Muslim jurists correctly inferred, could not be waged without the divine authority being invested in the Prophet or his successor, who alone could justify the reasons and the ends for its undertaking. No bloodshed was warranted if the religious-moral goals were unclear or if there was no guarantee that it would eradicate the causes of corruption.

It is in connection with this last statement that Shiʿi jurists, by contrast with the Sunni scholars, argued that the presence of a divinely appointed leader (the imam) would be a necessary precondition of any offensive *jihād*. The Sunni jurists did not consider it a necessity that the leader of the Muslims be a divinely appointed imam. Rather, they argued that any de facto Muslim authority ought to advance the purposes of God in the *jihād*. This difference of opinion points to the fundamental differences between the two schools of thought in the matter of right authority. It also demonstrates their differing understandings of the political history of Islam and of the connections of the Qur'anic *jihād* with that history.

The Sunni jurists maintained that in the area of constitutional affairs the community should have a sovereign head in charge of all its affairs, including the declaration of *jihād*, and bound to give effect to the general purposes of God for Islamic society by ruling in accordance with the revealed law. This is known as the legal doctrine of "governance in accordance with the Shariʿa (*siyāsa sharʿiyya*)." The sovereign in the management of all the affairs of state should always be prepared to consult the community and to listen to the representations of the community. Neither side was to act independently of the other or to impose its own point of view. This was the tradition of the early Muslim caliphs following the Prophet's death. However, ways of ensuring such consultation and representation were not laid down in the juridical texts so as to avoid rigidity in the matter of "governance in accordance with the Shariʿa" and to allow the political institution sufficient flexibility to adapt itself to varying future situations.

Under the legal doctrine of "governance in accordance with the Shariʿa," the Sunni jurists thought of the *jihād* as a war for the expansion of Islamic territory—that is, the sphere in which the norms prescribed by the Shariᶜa would be paramount. In so doing, they offered a religious rationale for the historic practice of Muslim rulers, who are afforded an overriding personal discretion to determine, according to time and circumstances, how the purposes of God for the Islamic community might be best effected.

The Shiᶜi jurists did not regard the wars of expansion as motivated by the Qurʾan. In fact, it was the Shiᶜi scrutiny of the Sunni explications of *jihād* that gave rise to questions concerning right authority: Who can declare the *jihād*? While the majoritarian Sunni jurisprudence is always conditioned by the historic practice of the community, working out its ideas about *jihād* with respect to the reality of wars of conquest in the name of Islam, the minority Shiᶜi jurisprudence characteristically focused on the ideal.[27] As a minority living under Sunni dominance, Shiᶜites had no need to rationalize political power. Shiᶜite juridical tradition could remain adamant concerning the questions of right authority and just cause. The Shiᶜi jurists, therefore, questioned the motives of the Sunni caliphs with respect to the practice of war.[28] The original purpose of *jihād*, they contended, was not preserved under the Sunni rulers.

For the Shiᶜi, offensive *jihād*—*jihād* for the purpose of calling upon people to respond to God's guidance by accepting Islam—required the presence of the just, divinely appointed imam, not (as the Sunnites argued) just any de facto ruler under the "governance of the Shariᶜa"; or, in the absence of the imam, as is the case with the last of the Shiᶜite imams in concealment, the person deputized by him could authorize such a struggle. The Shiᶜite jurists made an explicit distinction between this offensive *jihād* and the defensive *jihād*, which would protect the welfare of the Muslim community against hostile aggression. The requirement of just authority (in the case of offensive war) was supposed to guarantee that the *jihād* against the unbelievers would be waged strictly for the cause of God. In fact, it is only the just imam who, by virtue of his divinely protected knowledge of Islamic revelation, could initiate the *jihād* against the unbelievers. More important, it is only the just leader who can avoid errors of judgment in critical matters like the shedding of blood and ensure that the *jihād* is truly in accord with the goals of Islam. Sunni jurists, although in agreement that there should be an imam (in the ordinary sense of a ruler and not a divinely appointed leader) to lead the *jihād* for the purpose of calling people to Islam, are in disagreement with the Shiʿi in regard to the necessity of the infallible Imam's permission for the initiation of such a *jihād*.

However, the question of obtaining the permission of the imam does not arise in defensive warfare, because defense, the Shiʿi argue, is a moral requirement founded upon such Qurʾanic passages as 2:190–91. Moreover, the Shiʿi jurists assert that from the fourth/tenth century on, when the last imam went into concealment, the obligation to engage in offensive *jihād* has lapsed until the messianic leader reappears in the future. But the imam's absence has no connection to the discharging of the obligation of self-defense. Whenever the Muslims are attacked by enemies, and they fear for the safety of the boundaries and peoples of Islam, it is their duty to undertake defensive measures and to defend themselves against those who threaten their security. This defense, as the Shiʿite jurists remind their followers, should be undertaken with the intention of repelling the enemy only. All forms of defense, against those who attacked Muslims, against those who want to kill and drive away people from their homes, and against those who rise up against a just ruler, were regarded as "defense" rather than as strict *jihād* in the meaning of furthering the cause of God against unbelief among the human race. It was also in this sense of defense that Muslims living in *dār al-ṣulḥ* (the "sphere of peace"), as a minority under non-Muslim government, and able to practice their religion freely, had the military obligation to fight in defense of *dār al-ṣulḥ*.[29] Evidently, the obligation of self-defense was regarded as universal enough to require Muslims, whether Shiʿi or Sunni, living under any government to undertake proper measures for self-preservation.

Sunni jurisprudence based its notions of *jihād* on the existence of an authority invested with political power to preserve and maintain the public order and to protect the Islamic norms from being infringed or tampered with from inside or outside. Consequently, Sunni jurists did not feel the need to pursue the discussion concerning the various types of *jihād* or the diverse justifications for it, because all types of warfare were afforded religious legitimation. By contrast, Shiʿi jurists presupposed their own lack of power. Hence, their indulgence in the exercise of defining the goals, the preconditions, the various types of *jihād*, and so on. Moreover, Shiʿi political jurisprudence was not justified in its theoretical formulations about *jihād* by the actual historical practice of the Muslim community. Consequently, there is a substantial discussion in the works of the Shiʿi jurists concerning moral and religious restrictions on the use of violence in making God's cause succeed—the knowledge of that being restricted to the infallible imam.

In the final analysis, from the point of comparative perspectives on the ethics of war, *jihād* in its Qur'anic ordainment made it possible for Muslims to assert that the only "just" war is one fought for religious purposes under the legitimate political authority.[30] The reason is that concern for peace, which has led to visions of a just society, has also required proscriptions on the use of force, in particular legal force to procure that peace. Just war tradition even in the West is generally connected with the desire to strive for and to achieve true peace by removing the causes of conflict. Accordingly, the choice to adopt violent or nonviolent approaches to confrontation in Islam has depended on the ultimate outcome of the conflict.

THE LAW OF REBELLION

The Prophet's injunction to avoid strife and wrongdoing has served as an important principle in the adoption of political quietism or pacifist activism in some sectors of the Muslim community. In general, the law in Islam prohibits rebellion under almost any conditions because it expresses a requirement of proportionality by warning that opposition to an unjust government should not result in greater discord than that which is being suffered. The government as an instrument for the common good, with its legitimacy hinging on the condition of providing means of fulfilling the religious-moral obligations of Islam under a just authority, was always an important consideration in conceding the right of rebellion. In situations of rebellion against the Muslim government, the law discusses the criteria relevant to rebellion (*al-baghy*) that serve to distinguish its participants from apostates and brigands. Muslim jurists define a *bāghī* (insurgent) as someone who commits an act of insurrection (*khurūj*), with a reason or interpretation (*ta'wīl*), while enjoying wide support or power (*shawka*). In the absence of a "reason" or "power," the party in question is treated as a common criminal and not an insurgent.

A rebellion may be justified because of what is ascribed to the Prophet who said: "If people see an oppressor and they do not hinder him, then God will punish all of them."[31] The tradition somehow requires a communitarian response to the oppressive situation in the society. Accordingly, the criterion of "power" (*shawka*) functions as a safeguard against an individual taking upon himself to correct the social and political ill. The insurgent group must demonstrate wide support in order to be recognized as having somewhat equal standing with the authority against which it is rising. The form of organization, leadership, and membership reduces the possibility of anarchy and lawlessness arising from a corrupt person inventing a justification and claiming to be a rebel. This requirement is consistent with the Islamic concern for the community and the protection of Islamic order. In the case of collective rebellion, the group itself functions essentially as a community and is concerned with the preservation of Islamic values rather than motivated by individual self-interest. The action is undertaken by public mandate, not by private initiative. It is only then, and only if the justification for rebellion provided by the legitimate group that wishes to oppose the state is valid and the imam concedes it, that the law rules that the imam should be liable for disorder, not the rebels. Additionally, even though both sides of the conflict may have some legitimacy, Islamic law acknowledges the likely power discrepancy between the state and the opposition by exempting the rebels from liability for any harm to property or life occurring during the course of rebellion.[32]

However, rebels should not use this power discrepancy as a way of justifying the use of any violent means necessary to achieve their goals. There are some among Muslim jurists who, taking the side of the insurgent group, argue that the justness of the rebellion renders considerations of moral restriction on the use of violent means irrelevant, thereby allowing acts of terrorism and the like. On the other hand, there are those jurists who support the state in reasoning that the legitimate authority of the state, that is, the imam, when compared with the lack of such authority among the rebels, has the right to put down insurrections using any means necessary as well.[33] Moreover, in terms of the balance of power, those engaging in guerrilla or terrorist practices commonly argue that their weaker position necessitates the use of such violent tactics in order for their resistance to the state to be possible.

These arguments embody the concern evident in the debates about the Qur'anic *jihād* and *jihād* in Islamic history where overemphasis on the importance of the justifications for war led to relative neglect of the limits on the use of violence to secure victory. However, in the law of rebellion in Islam the emphasis is on the means of resistance employed by rebels rather than on the ends they seek. After all, in essence, the law is actually engaged in regulating rebellion by Muslims living under an Islamic order. The rebels are not legally classified as

criminals and are required to observe moral restrictions in seeking
redress for injustices. Thus, the primary concern when rebellion occurs in the Muslim community is to find ways of reconciling the
contending parties and reestablishing order.

In sum, the law dealing with rebellion in Islam is comprehensive
and coherent, which does not negate the possibility of rebellion, but
encompasses it within a framework designed to be just and to promote
a stable community whichever adversary prevails. Since one cannot
resist an unjust tyrant unless such resistance would result in less harm
to the common good than that suffered under the unjust government
itself, the law takes the position that the means of such resistance must
be ordered toward preserving the common good as well. Therefore, it
views acts of terrorism as illicit in that they would tend to create more
societal disorder than that caused by the unjust government. Despite
the potential difficulty of implementing the right conduct, especially
the criterion of discrimination, in irregular warfare, Muslim jurists are
inclined to give more weight to the means of insurgency than to the
goals the rebels seek, by using the same principle of proportionality
that they invoke in the defensive *jihād*.

The law of rebellion in Islam, accordingly, points to the activist
response demanded by the Qur'an to eradicate "corruption on earth."
As a reaction to the recognized right of the people to prevent acts of
injustice, within the limits imposed by concerns over proportionality
and forewarning, a new opinion removing such a responsibility from
the people emerged. A number of Muslim scholars believed in the
postponement of the decisive judgment upon a Muslim's belief or
conduct until the Day of Judgment, when God Himself would deal
with such individuals and reward or punish them for their behavior.
This attitude led to some kind of moral complacency because what it
meant was that a Muslim retains his/her membership in the community even if he/she fails to uphold the moral conduct prescribed by
the faith. It also suggested that no one beside God can judge a person's
real faith and conduct. In support of this attitude, many traditions
attributed to the Prophet were circulated to justify the tyrannical rule of
a Muslim dynasty like that of the Umayyads. Most of these traditions,
although accepted by the community at large, directly contradict the
teachings of the Qur'an. Thus, for instance, the Prophet is reported
to have advised one of his close associates, Hudhayfa:

> "After me there shall be political leaders who will not be
> guided by my instruction nor shall they follow my custom

(*sunna*). Moreover, there shall rise among them men whose hearts shall be the hearts of devil as in the frame of human bodies."

Hudhayfa asked: "What shall I do when I find myself in such a situation?"

The Prophet replied: "You must listen and obey the political leader; even if he beats you on the back and confiscates your property, you must listen and obey."[34]

Such traditions were actually used to rationalize the concrete situation in the community and to argue for the prohibition of rebellion against an established state.

Nevertheless, such admonitions must be understood within the internal structures of the cultural values that require a connection between peace and justice and encourage the achievement of an ideal just social order ensuring that war, whether regular or irregular, will not be more destructive to society. Peace, which signifies not only the absence of warfare but also a perfect state of well-being and harmony, as Islam sees it, is the product of order with justice. Just as private individuals must show proper restraint in self-defense, public officials must also ensure that judicial rulings are reflective of justice and equity. While one ought not to despise the peace that comes from a simple avoidance of strife, one must always be aware that such a peace is uneasy and that conflict is always a possibility in oppressive situations.

PACIFIST ACTIVISM IN THE ISLAMIC LEGAL SYSTEM

Undoubtedly, Islam provides a complex relationship between the principles undergirding private acts of self-defense and the principles supporting public legal systems to promulgate order. It is important to bear in mind that even when concerns such as proportionality and self-preservation are present in different schools of legal-theological thought within Islam, these principles vary in scope, weight, and how they are applied in practice. With the existence of the Islamic legal tradition, which grants concessions to the accused beyond those of the presumption of innocence and the requirement to prove guilt beyond a reasonable doubt, it is inconceivable to propose a purely pacifist attitude inspired by politically quietist prophetic traditions, like the one cited above.

When the Qur'an and the Shari'a allow self-defense by appealing to the instinct of self-preservation, and when the agent who is empowered to save his life undertakes to do so without intending to harm or kill the attacker, then it is difficult to maintain a position opposed to bearing arms from the Islamic perspective. The alternative to that kind of "turn the other cheek" pacifism need not necessarily be *jihād*-oriented activism. Rather, on the basis of the historically autonomous existence of the Muslim community (autonomous from any sense of loyalty to de facto Muslim political authority), faithful to the divinely ordained Shari'a and aspiring to live in accordance with its norms, one might be able to speak about its pacifist activism inspired by the legal heritage of Islam.

Pacifist activism in this context is characterized by the demand in the Shari'a for balancing the violence with concern for proportionality. The Qur'an admits the human ability to cause harm to others and it therefore includes the "eye for an eye" limit on retaliation, although such retaliation is not commanded but merely permitted.[35] The principle of legality requires that no one accused of a crime can be punished unless he has been forewarned of the criminal nature of his conduct.

There are four purposes of punishment in Islamic criminal law: prevention, deterrence, retribution/revenge, and rehabilitation through repentance as a process of self-purification for one's crime.[36] Although deterrence is an underlying purpose in both private and public categories of crime, retributive justice and rehabilitation play important roles in *qiṣāṣ* ("retaliation") crimes that require the redressing of wrong by equalizing the crime, and *taʿzīr* ("chastisement," "deterrence") crimes for which discretionary punishment is instituted by the legitimate authority to deter the offender himself or others from similar conduct. Death penalty crime, which falls under the *ḥudūd* (God's "restrictive ordinances"), comprised acts directly prohibited by God for which a severe penalty such as capital punishment is sanctioned in the Qur'an.[37]

Islam proclaims that a crime may affect not only humans but God as well. There is a sense in which both humans and God may have claims in the same criminal act, even if the event seems to harm only one of them. Although the punishment of crimes against religion is beyond human jurisdiction, the juridical body in Islam is empowered to impose sanctions only when it can be demonstrated beyond doubt that the grievous crime included infringing a right of humans (*ḥaqq ādami*, a private claim). There are six offenses that are treated as crimes against religion and for which the law prescribes specific *ḥadd* ("defined") punishments:

1. Illicit sexual relations
2. Slanderous allegations of unchastity
3. Wine-drinking
4. Theft
5. Armed robbery
6. Apostasy (*irtidād*)[38]

The punishments laid down for them are:

> (a) the death penalty, either by stoning (the more severe punishment for unlawful intercourse) or by crucifixion or by the sword (for armed robbery with homicide);
>
> (b) the cutting off of hand and/or foot (for armed robbery without homicide and for theft, depending on the conditions under which the offender has committed the crime);
>
> (c) flogging with various number of lashes, depending on the circumstances and the methods used in establishing the guilt.

The underlying principle in the penal code is that the punishment should fit the nature of the crime and the character of the offender because the purpose of punishment is the prevention of any conduct prejudicial to the good order of the state. Here the supreme duty of the Muslim ruler is to protect the public interest for which the law affords him an overriding personal discretion to determine how the purposes of God for the Muslim community might best be achieved.

Because criminal law in Islam represented a system of private law that was conceived to fall under the purview of the established political power to ratify and enforce, prosecutions for offenses like false accusation of unlawful intercourse and for theft, crimes that include infringing a right of God and a private claim of humans, take place only on the demand of the person concerned, and the applicant must be present at both the trial and the execution. In the case of unlawful intercourse, the witness plays a crucial role. There should be four witnesses to the actual act of intercourse. Moreover, at the time of execution of the punishment, if the witnesses are not present (and, when the punishment is stoning, if they do not throw the first stones), the punishment is not carried out. If the thief returns the stolen object before an application for prosecution has been made, the prescribed punishment lapses; repentance of highway robbery before arrest causes the punishment to lapse, and any offenses committed are treated as ordinary offenses against the law (*jināyāt*) so that if the person entitled to demand retaliation is willing to pardon the offender, blood-money may be paid instead, or the punishment remitted altogether. In the cases of offenses against religion that are not sanctioned by specific punishments, like apostasy (for which there is no definite *ḥadd* punishment in the Qurʾan), the effects of repentance are even more far-reaching.

Overall, there is a strong tendency in the penal code to restrict the applicability of capital punishments as much as possible, except in the case of slanderous allegations of illicit sexual relations, with their wider social implications for community life. Even in the case of illicit sexual relations, which are regarded as detrimental to familial and societal good, the applicability of capital punishment is circumvented by the requirement of four witnesses for the unlawful intercourse itself.

The treatment of apostasy as an impingement on the right of God and humanity in Islam presents an interesting case of interdependency between the religious and political in the laws that govern the status of an apostate in the Muslim community.[39] Although classified as a capital offense (*ḥudūd* crime) in the Islamic penal code, apostasy was and remains the only crime that presented Muslim legal authorities with a serious dilemma of treating it as such. The verse in the Qurʾan that provides the jurists with the original ruling leaves no ambiguity as to its being a noncapital offense. The Qurʾan says:

> And, whosoever turns (*yartadid*) from his religion, and dies disbelieving—their works have failed in this world and the next; those are the inhabitants of the Fire; therein they shall dwell forever.[40]

Clearly, the problem was that while the Qurʾan favored an overall tolerance of religious pluralism, the social ethics delineated by Muslim jurists regarded that pluralism as a source of instability for Muslim public order. The so-called wars of "apostasy" (*ridda*) in the aftermath of the Prophet's death had served as a grievous reminder to the jurists to provide measures that would discourage those engaged in similar disruptive activity in the community.

It is important to bear in mind that, based on this early paradigmatic case of wars of "apostasy" (*ridda*), the use of the term in

Islam is problematic. To be sure, in its denotation the term carries the experience of the Christian church in dealing with public abandonment of the institutionalized religion. Hence, in the Christian-Western context, "apostasy" presupposes the existence of the church, which determines both the nature and the occurrence of apostasy, to institute appropriate punishment for an individual's public abandonment of an exclusive and institutionalized religion for another. On the other hand, the Arabic term *ridda* or *irtidād* (usually translated as "apostasy"), in an Islamic context, presupposes the existence of a Muslim political authority, which is solely responsible for determining that the act of *ridda* (meaning "rejection of," "turning away from," Muslim public order) has indeed occurred. It is important to bear in mind that the dichotomy between the sacred and the temporal did not exist in the state that was founded by the Prophet. In the early days of Islam, the Muslims were at once a political and a religious community, with the Prophet as head of state. In this position, he governed a territory and a people, dispensed justice, collected taxes, commanded the army, waged war, and negotiated peace. As such, turning away from Islam implied more than merely a change of religion. It meant resisting the political power.

Accordingly, in Islam, *ridda* crime necessarily falls under the jurisdiction of the political authority that is empowered to determine only the civil aspect of the crime. In the absence of the church and the ecclesiastical body, no one, not even the Prophet, has the power to negotiate the basic religious relationship between the divine and the individual human. Thus, when an act of *irtidād* ("rejection") occurs in the community, it is the responsibility of the civil authority to determine its criminality and to take appropriate measures to deal with it. Since its jurisdiction was restricted to the political authority empowered to protect the common good of the community, a number of Muslim jurists classified *irtidād* as part of the *ta'zīr* ("chastisement," "deterrence") crimes "which infringe on private or community interests of the public order," and for which punishment is instituted by the legitimate political authority to deter the offender from such conduct. Consequently, the burden is placed on the public authority to lay down rules that penalize all conduct that seems contrary to the public interest, social tranquillity, or public order.[41]

Hence, civil considerations surrounding the question of sedition have dominated in determining the act of apostasy in Islam. The ensuing harsh treatment of an apostate in Islamic law is promulgated without making an indispensable distinction between the freedom of religion granted by the Qur'anic insistence that no human agency can negotiate an individual's spiritual destiny, and the legitimate concerns of Muslim public order. As long as apostasy remains a private matter and does not disrupt society at large, there is no particular punishment in the Qur'an. However, when it violates the sanctity and the rights of society's members to practice their belief, then it is treated as a physical aggression toward the faith. At that point it is no more a case of apostasy; rather, it is treated as an act of sedition that has caused discord and threatened the unity of Islamic community. It is only in this case that "apostasy" is punishable by the severest penalties instituted in the form of necessary self-defense. The Qur'an treats it as a violent rebellion against God and the Prophet, and violent rebellion must be countered with violence if necessary:

> The punishment of those who take up arms against God and His Messenger and devote themselves to [corruption], creating discord on earth, is that they should be killed . . . or exiled.[42]

By now the problem of treating "apostasy" in the strict meaning of public abandonment of an institutionalized religion for another in Islam is self-evident. In the final analysis, a mere expression of religious dissent from the established community, according to the Qur'an, cannot constitute a criminal act punishable in this world. Muslim civil authority has the ultimate responsibility to use its discretionary power to assess the level of discord created by a public declaration of apostasy and to lay down the appropriate measures to deal with it.

The ordinary offense against the law, that is, homicide, bodily harm, and damage to property, is treated as a private and not as a public offense, although it is painstakingly regulated. Whatever liability is incurred through them, be it retaliation or blood-money or damages, is the subject of private claim. There is no prosecution or execution ex officio, not even for homicide, only a guarantee of the right of private vengeance, combined with safeguards against its exceeding legal limits. Pardon and agreeable settlement are possible, but repentance has no effect because the prosecutions are based on private claim. Unlike the crimes against religion, in the case of offenses against the law there is no tendency to restrict liability. The detailed regulations to verify culpability are undertaken to make sure that deliberate intent, quasi-deliberate intent, mistake, and direct causation are distinguished adequately without minimizing the gravity of the offense. At the same time, the juridical body responsible for administering justice undertakes to ensure that the exacted retaliation or blood-money will not exceed legal limits and will not be destructive to the parties concerned.

MARTYRDOM, THE PEAK OF ACTIVISM IN ISLAM

In the legal heritage of Islam, as discussed above, it emerges that a majority of the Muslim community maintains pacifist activism, "striving" (the literal sense of *jihād*) for peace by upholding the religious-moral law of Islam that promises lasting peace by redressing injustice. That being the case, our focus when considering Islamic views on quietism or pacifist activism should be on the view of the nature and requirements of a summons to struggle for justice in general. In this connection it is pertinent to raise questions about the violence that erupts in the form of willingness to end one's life in the name of God. How different is it from suicide, which would seem to be rooted in a tendency to lose the ability to ascribe meaning to life in light of the amount of suffering in it? Inasmuch as the decision to terminate one's life indicates a certain condition of human will, there is a tension in Islam between the prohibition of suicide and the affirmation of martyrdom.[43]

Affirmation of Islamic faith requires obedience to God. True piety is expressed in one's adherence to Islamic precepts. One should be ready to die for one's faith. That is the meaning of martyrdom in Islam. *Shahāda*, literally meaning "witness," implies the willingness of those who exalt the divine command to give their lives for divine purposes. It involves a kind of confrontation that necessitates resistance with courage and faithfulness even at the risk of one's life. But should one court death when those in power are insensitive to the common expectations cultivated in the tradition? Should one risk one's life when the procurement of justice is in doubt?

To begin with, Islamic denial of personal autonomy in the matter of suicide is based on the conviction that one's life is a trust from God that demands an ongoing relationship between the Creator and the caretaker. The primacy of the God-human relationship necessitates the maintenance of this life through human submission to the divine will. A human being is entitled to utilize the bounties of God only when he marches forward on the path of evolution prescribed for him by nature, that is, the path of faith, piety, and good deeds. Moreover, nature also requires him to seek the perfection of the self as a responsible member of the community of believers. There is no difference between actions toward the self and actions toward the other on this path of evolution. Suicide, as self-murder, is judged accordingly as an affront to God, the individual, and the community. Martyrdom, as self-sacrifice, is seen as virtuous because it bears witness to God's existence and strengthens the community. Moreover, martyrdom is regarded as heroic and admirable because it results from a voluntary, conscious, and selfless action.

Besides the language of voluntariness connected with self-sacrifice, there is also the language of duty and responsibility found in connection with martyrdom in Islam. It is here that one can sense the tension between a voluntary and an obligatory act of giving one's life. The zealous seeking of martyrdom when engaged in *jihād* appears to be in tension with the definition of it as a voluntary act of piety. Since participation in *jihād* is required by the Shari°a, could it give rise in the community to a desperateness to find opportunities to be a martyr? The process of self-justification toward the use of *jihād* as a means of attaining martyrdom has historically led to the adoption of extreme violent postures in the name of God. Those engaged in suicidal acts of terrorism continue to regard their violent acts as a struggle for the cause of God, in which death is seen as martyrdom. There is no doubt that the value of human life is totally connected with how one serves God. If by giving one's life one can serve God, then human life has no greater value than the purpose for which such a struggle is undertaken. On the other hand, the fundamental question of proportionality serves as an important criterion in determining whether the cause is worth such a self-sacrifice or sacrifice of other innocent human lives. The tactics of achieving the divine goal could not justify the indiscriminate destruction of human life, however irregular the warfare might be. Ultimately, the readiness to use violent means and even to wage war to meet and overcome the oppression of those already in power carries with it the burden of establishing the validity of one's own position, with the ever present temptation of excluding others as having a share in that truth. Violence in the name of religion necessarily involves the claim to exclusive validity for one's own position. Every perception of truth is accompanied by its own characteristic defects. A unique test of Islam as a religion that was led by the vision of ethical order through the use of force lies in explaining the supreme virtue of dedication to a goal beyond oneself to the point of readiness to give up one's life, that is, martyrdom in *jihād*, without falling prey to the spirit of exclusivity that led to the vision of the ideal community and that found expression in violent death.

QUIETISM RATHER THAN PACIFISM IN ISLAM

I have traversed a long way to demonstrate that Islam is not monolithic in its response to the central question about the relationship between Islamic ideals for an ethical world order and the obstacles that were encountered by those who brought to the fore methods of producing changes in social power. A serious commitment to social reform on the part of those who wielded authority "to command good and forbid evil" implied their readiness to use any means to overcome the forces that threatened its realization. This commitment as an active ingredient of the faith, I believe, reveals the Islamic views on activism or pacifist activism or quietism.

So far, I have intentionally avoided using the term *pacifism* in the way it has been used by pacifist Christian movements dedicated to a life of poverty and simplicity and opposed to bearing arms. The reason is obvious. Islam views human existence, caught up amidst contradictory forces of light and darkness, guidance and misguidance, justice and injustice as an ongoing and unending moral struggle for the creation of a just society on earth. Its attention is focused on problems of interpersonal justice. The fundamental doctrine of the impending Last Judgment, at which every individual would reap the fruits of his actions, good or evil, in his lifetime, clearly emphasizes the consequential nature of moral choice that is decisive in determining one's eternal fate. As such, pacifism in the sense of rejecting all forms of violence and opposing all war and armed hostility before justice is established has no place in the Qur'anic doctrine of human faith or its inevitable projection into not only identifying with the cause of justice but working for it on earth. Social justice accordingly took on implications more challenging to the established order and tended to be egalitarian justice for effective equality among the social classes found in Judaism and other Abrahamic traditions. In these traditions there was an active sense of the equal dignity and ultimate rights of the less privileged in society. It is this characteristic of Islam as an

Abrahamic tradition that negates pacifism in the sense of opposition to all forms of violence, including that generated by an insistence on justice and equality in interpersonal relations.

However, if pacifism is taken in its other signification, namely exhausting all peaceful means in order to resolve human conflicts, then its adoption in the Islamic community could be nothing more than a temporary decision to give peace a chance. Pacifist silence in the face of continuous violation of justice amounted to being an accomplice of those unjust forces, and that was regarded as a major sin of associating other beings to God.

On the other hand, quietism, which has been a strategy for survival in minority communities with the hope of regrouping and reasserting their ideals of justice, was a legitimate posture in Islam from its earliest days. In Mecca, Muslims constituted a minority and despite the fact that *jihād* (as armed defense) was ordained at this stage, quietism was adopted as a precautionary strategy to shield the true intent of the faithful community from the unbelievers. It signified the will of the community to continue to strive for the realization of the ideal Islamic polity by preparing the way without confrontation in the future. It was consequently a temporary measure until the achievement of God's purposes on earth became possible, either through an internal revival of individual believers or by the launching of the revolution under a divinely guided person to establish the rule of justice and equity. In view of the activist response demanded by the Islamic revelation that we have already seen, a posture of pacifist activism generated by a sense of dedication to the Shariʿa is an embodiment of the divine scales of justice for the Muslim community. However, there is one more attitudinal posture that has continued to influence large sectors of the Muslim community around the world, even today. This is quietism, more specifically quietist authoritarianism, the by-product of a predestinarian doctrinal stance advocated and disseminated by scholars who supported any de facto Muslim authority as a lesser evil than the general lawlessness created by sedition.

QUIETIST AUTHORITARIANISM AND ACTIVIST RADICALISM

The readiness to give up one's life for a goal beyond oneself presupposes a free human agent who can engage in risk/benefit analysis and decide to risk his life for a just cause. There is considerable agreement among Muslims that the precise direction in a matter involving endangering one's own life or the lives of others in the community should be determined with a renewed commitment to the activist precepts of Islam. It was not always possible to undertake the moral obligation of "commanding good and forbidding evil" without actively seeking to order society in a manner consistent with the guidance given to humanity by the Creator. Moreover, the existence of the legitimate authority invested with God's sovereignty to fulfill divine purposes was important in view of the Qur'anic injunction requiring obedience to God, to the Prophet, and to those invested with political authority.[44] In other words, as pointed out earlier, in Islam it was not possible to gain the authoritative and determinative guidance for the common good without considering constitutional questions as to who was authorized to determine a quietist or an activist direction and by what procedures.

It is important to emphasize that the question of legitimate authority in determining the goals of divine revelation and the means of implementing them has been central to Islam as a comprehensive social and political system. At no time did the Muslim community abandon its vision of a leadership qualified to create the Islamic polity. Indeed, religious leadership is the single most important issue that has divided the community and provoked debates about the justification for engaging in religiously sanctioned violence to establish or dethrone it. Political activism in Islam has been intimately related to the establishment of Islamic public order under the qualified leadership of a caliph or an imam. On the other hand, quietism as a legitimate tactic for the community living under adverse conditions was always determined by the religious leadership (either of the caliph/imam or the ulema, the jurist-theologians, who acted as juridical authority in the community) that was denied the right to head the Islamic polity.

There were precedents in the political history of Islam as well as in the teachings of the Qur'an for the exponents of both activism and quietism. A close examination of the arguments used to support one or the other posture reveals that the problem was related to government and obedience. The sole justification for the existence of the government, according to the Qur'an, was "commanding the good and forbidding the evil." This moral justification also made it morally as well as religiously obligatory to obey the government that undertook to implement that duty.

The Sunni and Shi'i division within the Muslim community was based on their respective views about the legitimate government under the caliph/imam. The problem faced by the Muslim community was a classic one in world history, namely, how to reconcile the discrepancy between the promised ideal and the existing real. In other words, how should the faithful respond to the injustices and distortions that had cropped up in upholding the duty of "commanding the good and forbidding the evil"?

The obvious question that arises in the minds of pious Muslims when they confront an unjust government that fails to command good and interdict evil, whether personally or collectively, is: Do Muslims have an obligation to take up arms to oppose or expunge tyranny and corruption within the community? In other words, Is obedience to the government that leads to disobedience to God to be tolerated? The response to the question of perceived injustices has depended on current sociopolitical circumstances and has been determined by the political and religious leadership.

Bernard Lewis in *The Political Language of Islam*[45] has traced the development of activist and quietist traditions in the political writings of the classical age. In earlier times, as he has shown, the question of obedience to the legitimate authority and the legality of those who exacted obedience in his name was critical for the community. In other words, the manner in which authority was acquired was important in determining the level of obedience that was owed to that authority. With the passage of time, more particularly when power was seized by force, the question of the legality of power was abandoned in favor of the manner in which power was exercised, because the reality was that political leadership had passed to those who possessed little legitimacy in their claim to obedience. The only source of their legal claim to obedience, as the Muslim jurists came to recognize and require of the community, was their respect for the Islamic legal norms. The concept of the sovereign being bound to rule according to the legal norms, the Shariʿa, meant that his supreme duty was the protection of the public interest. To this end he was given an overriding personal discretion to decide how the Islamic norms for the community might best be effected. This principle, as discussed earlier, is known as "government in accordance with the revealed law (*siyāsa sharʿ iyya*)." As a legal accommodation with existing political power, it became the precedent for activist pacifism, as discussed above.

Throughout this development Muslim jurists in their endeavors to rationalize the existing power had required obedience on the part of the Muslim subject. Thus, in addition to the numerous traditions

like the one cited on the authority of the Prophet, who advised Hudhayfa, his close associate, to listen to and obey the political leader
"even if he beats you on the back and confiscates your property," the
tenth-century Hanbali jurist Ibn Baṭṭa (d. 387/997) observed:

> You must abstain and refrain from sedition (*fitna*). You must not
> rise in arms against the imams, even if they be unjust. ʿUmar
> b. al-Khaṭṭāb, may God be pleased with him, said: "If he op-
> presses you be patient; if he dispossess you, be patient." The
> Prophet, may God bless and save him, said to Abū Dharr: "Be
> patient, even if he be an Ethiopian slave."[46]

There are other traditions that contradict these narratives attributed
to the Caliph ʿUmar and the Prophet himself. But their purpose in
the tenth century is obvious: to justify the authoritarian power of the
ruling sovereign and to give him unquestioning obedience however
unjust that sovereign might be. In fact, the majority of writers on
statecraft argued for the rights of authority and the necessity of obedience rather than the duty of challenging authority. Such challenging
on balance proved to be more harmful to the common good. Thus,
at times tolerance of injustice was necessary to avoid civil strife (*fitna*).

The use of the word *fitna* in Sunni tradition carries the notion
of quietist passivity and hence has a negative connotation as far as
Islamic teaching on just ethical order is concerned. Moreover, for the
Sunni majority, it is a term that evokes bitter recollection of the great
rift in the Muslim community shortly after the death of the Prophet
Muhammad. This conflict, later dubbed the "great *fitna*" (*al-fitna al-
kubrā*) or the "first *fitna*," pitted some of the closest associates of the
Prophet against each other and led to major schisms in the community.
The conflict was never fully resolved, but its memory in retrospect
left a deep impression among the Sunnis that the best stance in a
conflict situation was simply to adopt quietist passivity.

The alternative, namely fighting injustice and "forbidding the
evil," as Qurʾanic ethics required, was thought by these scholars to
lead to some scandal in the shape of a serious disturbance or strife.[47]
Thus, *fitna* was associated with undesirable change, and consequently
it implied reliving the political experiences connected with leadership
struggles, disputes, and conflicts of interest. It was to be avoided
at any cost, even if it meant sidestepping the Qurʾanic demand for

"commanding the good and forbidding the evil" and the ensuing defensive *jihād* to restore peace with justice.

Nevertheless, *fitna* as an experience of the first Muslim community has not, as an idea, entirely shaped the Muslim attitude of authoritarian quietism. Rather, actual social change and historical recollection together produced the consciousness of *fitna* as a delimiting and debilitating factor in social exigencies. The consciousness of *fitna* has grown and matured around a continual series of historical reinterpretations of the first civil strife in the light of new, emerging sedition. While the first civil strife has served as a prototype, other civil wars and disturbances have continually affected the Muslims' historical perception of it. The term *fitna*, therefore, acts and continues to act as a description, a justification, and a recipe for quietism, and even inaction.

Emmanuel Sivan has rightly alluded to this situation as a "trauma" in Muslim attempts to redress grave social and political injustices.[48] The apprehension involved in taking an activist stand looms so large in Sunni political understanding that even contemporary revolutionary ideologues like Sayyid Quṭb and Saʿīd Hawwa have had to go to great lengths to justify revolutionary activity if it might lead to some form of civil disturbance. The only way they could justify activism was to declare their disbelief in modern governments and Muslim societies against whom waging *jihād* was a legitimate step. Even that was a departure from the generally held Sunni position that the ruler, even if he be a sinner, must be obeyed as long as he respects the basic minimum. Some jurists, however, conceded that while a sinful sovereign must be obeyed, the same privilege might not be extended to agents of the sovereign who are sinful.

Sinful rule and tyrannical government, according to the authoritarian quietist view, are not the greatest evils, because the alternative to such a rule is chaos. Anything that disrupted the authority that was necessary to guarantee the unity of the community and to provide the legal basis for the execution of the most fundamental objective of government, namely, to enable Muslims to live the good Muslim life, was to be regarded as sinful deviation from the right tradition. Hence, through the centuries, quietism has been legitimized as a religious duty to maintain order in the Muslim community.

Yet this legitimization would not have been possible without a creed that viewed the divine being as the Absolute Sovereign, the All-Powerful God, who determined every action of humanity, leaving it completely helpless in the divine plan for human history. When God, as the Omnipotent Being, could do as he willed, so could the ruler, who was symbolized as the "Shadow of God on earth." All these ideas were part of the doctrinal development in Sunni theology and the related field of political thought.

For the exponents of an activist posture in the community the question of obedience and disobedience was posed in the context of early divisive civil wars that split the Islamic state and community, and ultimately the Islamic religion. The paradigm was provided by the second *fitna*, when Caliph ʿUthmān (d. 656 c.e.) was attacked and killed by Muslim Arab rebels. In the course of the argument two basic positions emerged. According to the one, ʿUthmān was both a rightful and just ruler, and his killing was therefore both a crime and a sin. According to the other, ʿUthmān was a wrongful and unjust ruler, and his killing was therefore a lawful and a necessary act. In time, and after a long and complex evolution, these two viewpoints became associated with two traditions: the one with the Sunni, the other with Shiʿite Islam. It would be an oversimplification to identify the Sunnis with the quietist and the Shiʿa with the activist tradition. The Sunnis, throughout their history, produced their own radicals. The Shiʿa evolved their own doctrines, decisions, and practices of passive submission.

To be sure, activist radicalism was at times invoked in specific legal terms to make disobedience to existing unjust regimes lawful, or to justify their forcible overthrow. However, the response to the armed revolt against unjust government in Shiʿism was offered by examining whether such an action was justifiable except under the leadership of a divinely appointed imam, or whether any qualified individual Shiʿite could undertake to fight the tyranny and corruption of his time when it reached an intolerable level. Historically the guidance of the Shiʿite jurists, whether leading to radical political action or otherwise, turned on their interpretation of the two basic doctrines intrinsic to an authoritative perspective that organizes the mundane existence of Shiʿite Muslims. These two doctrines are the justice of God and the leadership of righteous individuals. Undergirding social, political, and economic activity in the early centuries was the promise of Islamic revelation that only through obedience to God could believers accomplish the establishment of a just and equitable public order embodying the will of God. This promise was buttressed by the certainty that God is just and truthful. Divine justice demanded that God do what was best for humanity, and divine truthfulness generated the faith that God's promise would be fulfilled if humanity kept its covenant by working toward a truly godly life.

The proof that God is just and truthful was provided by his creating the rational faculty in human beings and sending revelation through the prophets to guide them toward the creation of an ethical world order. The indispensable connection between divine guidance and the creation of an ethical world order provided an ideological mandate for the interdependency of the religious and the political in Islam. It also pointed to some sort of divine intervention being necessary in the creation of a just society. Consequently, the focal point of the Islamic belief system envisions the Prophet and his properly designated successors as representing God on earth—the God who invested authority in them so that they might rule over mankind rightly. In other words, the linkage between the divine investiture and the creation of an Islamic world order became a salient feature of Islamic ideological discourse almost from the beginning.

However, the essential connection between the religious and the political became an underlying source of crisis in the Muslim community. The early history of Islam witnessed discontent among all Muslims. Some were moved by profound religious conviction and deep moral purpose to take activist political steps to confront injustices. The period, moreover, generated much discussion and deliberation regarding the duty of obedience to an unjust ruler who caused disobedience to God.

The idea of revolution to overthrow unjust authority favored by radical elements in the Shi'ite community took a different turn when the manifest leadership of their imams came to an end in the tenth century. With this end the activist ideology took on an apocalyptic cast: The revolution would come in a future time of fulfillment when the restorer of pristine Islam, the Mahdi, would appear. This belief in the future messianic role of the imam has served a complex, and seemingly paradoxical, function. It has been the guiding doctrine behind an activist political posture, calling upon believers to remain alert and prepared at all times to launch the revolution with the messianic imam who might appear at any time, and also behind a quietist waiting for God's decree, in almost fatalistic resignation, in the matter of the return of this imam at the End of Time.[49] In both cases the main problem was to determine the right course of action at a given time in a given social and political setting. The adoption of the activist or quietist solution depended on the interpretation of conflicting traditions attributed to the Shi'ite imams about the circumstances that justified radical action. Resolution of the contradiction in these traditions in turn was contingent on the agreement about, and acknowledgement of, the existence of an authority who could make the messianic imam's will known to the community. Without such a learned authority among the Shi'ites, it was practically impossible to acquire reliable knowledge about whether a government had indeed become evil, and whether a radical solution was an appropriate form of struggle against it.

CONCLUDING REMARKS

The historical development of Islam as a power-faith tradition with its ideology firmly based on creating the ethical order that embodied the divine will on earth provided a detailed and thoroughly developed vision of peace with justice. The basis for such a commitment to peace with justice was the act of faith that required an active response to the moral challenge of working toward the perfect existence. That perfect existence was conceivable by promoting the divinely ordained scales of justice in the religious-moral law, the Shari'a. Accordingly, peace was not possible in a society that self-righteously disregarded the evil of injustice. Struggle against injustice was the sole justification for engaging in *jihād*. Peace is an outcome of a society in which there is concern for justice and not just the absence of conflict.

However, Islam also acknowledged the existence of obstacles to the divine plan and its realization stemming in large measure from human volition and cognition. It pointed out the ways in which those who willfully rejected the faith and what it entailed in the moral realm conspired to defeat the divine purposes. To meet this challenge to the divine order, the use of force, even armed struggle, was sanctioned as a legitimate defensive measure to subdue those who were hostile to the establishment of justice. However, at no time was human life to be destroyed without justification, because the Qur'an commanded time and again: "Slay not the life that God has made sacred."[50]

Precisely at this crucial juncture in sanctioning violence, including the readiness to give up one's life for the religious cause, the role of the Prophet or the rightly guided imam, as the interpreter of the divine purposes for which such a sacrifice was inevitable, becomes indispensable. Without the Prophet or the imam, humanity, through its divinely endowed cognition of self-subsistent good and evil, could not expect to determine the level of, and the appropriate time for, such sacrifices to preserve God's purposes for creation.

To be sure, the Muslim community did not always live under what the Muslims came to regard as the ideal leadership of the Prophet and his righteous successors. The time came when Islam and Muslims became entangled with unjust rulers and their misrule and tyranny. These rulers frustrated the primary ideological demand of Islam, namely, the creation of the just order on earth. The Muslim community could choose either to oppose and overthrow these rulers or to tolerate them with patience until God changed its situation; or it could foster a distinct identity independent of its unjust political system, with an active affirmation that the revealed norms of the Shariʿa would be promulgated in an ideal Islamic polity.

The solution to individual cases of injustice through an aggressive response was an activist interpretation of Islamic ideology that served to incite some of the most radical revolutions in the history of Muslim peoples. The attitude of tolerance to disorder with a sense of resignation, on the other hand, was a quietist solution favored and institutionalized by those whose interests were served under the changing basis of power in the expanding Islamic empire. The third alternative, while maintaining sufficient ability to mobilize the force necessary to put down opposition to the promulgation of the divinely ordained legal norms, believed in social transformation through individual moral and spiritual reform. This was a pacifist activism that was expressed in terms of the expectations fostered by the Islamic revelation for the guidance of humankind and the practical policies of a cosmopolitan world.

It is important to emphasize that both the quietist authoritarian and the pacifist activist postures were potentially radical solutions, awaiting the right time and conditions to realize an adequately just society. In the final analysis, Islamic revelation by its very emphasis on justice and equity on earth calls upon its followers to evaluate a specific sociopolitical order and to defend and preserve it or to overthrow and transform it. The specific response to the existing social and political situation is elaborated within a cultural setting whose most powerful symbols are garnered to articulate the subtle and even complex religious ideas in the discourse that speaks to a community of ordinary people.

Accordingly, Islamic ideology is both a critical assessment of human society and a program of action to realize God's will on earth to the fullest extent possible. In such a strategy, absolute pacifism as understood by some Christian pacifist movements had no place in Islam. The Islamic ideal of social harmony and peaceful living was dependent on a faith in God that entailed the moral challenge of creating a just and equitable society on earth. Nevertheless, resort to violence in any form, without uncompromising adherence to the twin principles of self-preservation and proportionality, remained a central problem in Islam as its followers demonstrated readiness to wage war for a goal beyond acts of individual justice. In creating a total religious community, Muslim leaders were confronted by the temptation to a spirit of exclusivity that sought suitable expression in warfare. The readiness to use violent means, when other creative nonviolent methods of resolving problems of injustice have been suggested in Islamic revelation, has always raised the question in Islamic ethics: Is violence inevitable to transform human society? Not necessarily, if humanity responds to the divine call to heed its own sense of preservation. Ultimately, "submission" to God promises peace and security for which humanity has aspired from the time its first representative was put on earth. It is, undoubtedly, the search for peace and integral existence without "submission" that has proved to be fatal in human history.

NOTES

1. This article developed out of the two papers presented at two conferences held during 1993–94. The first part was presented at the "Conference on Quietism and Pacifism in the Western Monotheistic Traditions" at Washington University; and the second part was presented at the "Conference on Religious Perspectives on Pacifism and Non-Violence in Situations of International Conflict" at the United States Institute of Peace. I would like to acknowledge my appreciation of the suggestions offered by the readers of the early draft of the work, and of the incisive criticisms offered by my colleagues and friends Professors James Childress at the University of Virginia and David Little at the United States Institute of Peace.

2. David Little and Sumner B. Twiss, *Comparative Religious Ethics: A New Method* (New York: Harper and Row, 1978), pp. 54–55.

3. I assume that in the present context quietism refers to political quietism and therefore is not to be confused with the late-seventeenth-century devotional movement of that name within the Catholic Church in Italy and France. See "Quietism," in *The Encyclopedia of Religion*, ed. Mircea Eliade (New York: Macmillan Publishing Co., 1947) 12:153–55.

4. Pacifism in the sense of nonviolence in the context of visions of a perfect society based on social harmony and peaceful living is a relatively new term in the English language. However, pacifism in the meaning of a

nonviolent approach to confrontation, even in oppressive situations, has been present in the Abrahamic traditions as something divinely ordained in response to conflict. The corollary of such a requirement is the suffering of martyrdom (*kiddush ha Shem* in Judaism and *shahāda* in Islam connote bearing witness to the divine order) through sacrificing one's life. See "Nonviolence," in *The Encyclopedia of Religion*, 10:463–67.

5. Marshall G. S. Hodgson, "The World Before Islam," in *Venture of Islam* (Chicago: University of Chicago Press, 1974), 1:103–145, provides one of the most detailed introductions to Islam by undertaking the discussion of the Abrahamic roots of the Islamic tradition and highlighting the populist as well as confessional characteristics of Islam that it shares with the other Semitic religions.

6. 9:124. Translations are adapted by the author from A. J. Arberry, *The Koran Interpreted* (New York: Macmillan Publishing, 1955).

7. See our joint venture entitled *Human Rights and the Conflict of Cultures: Western and Islamic Perspectives on Religious Liberty*, co-authored with David Little and John Kelsay (University of South Carolina Press, 1988), for the justification of and restrictions in the use of force.

8. 2:178.

9. Muhammad b. Jarīr al-Ṭabarī, *Tafsīr* (Beirut: Dār al-Maʿārif, 1972), takes the word *fitna* ("dissension") to mean *shirk*, that is, a form of disbelief in which a person would ascribe divinity to things not worthy of such ascription. Other Qur'anic exegetes agree with Ṭabarī on this point. See, for instance, al-Bayḍawī, *Anwār al-tanzīl* (Cairo, 1887), p. 41.

10. 2:190–91.

11. See the article "Djihād" in *Encyclopedia of Islam*, 2d ed. (London: E. J. Brill, 1970), 2:538 for the opinions of Muslim jurists.

12. 9:29.

13. Discussion in this and the following section is based on my earlier research for "The Development of *Jihād* in Islamic Revelation and History," in *Cross, Crescent, and Sword: The Justification and Limitation of War in Western and Islamic Tradition*, ed. James Turner Johnson and John Kelsay (Westport, CT: Greenwood Press, 1990), pp. 35–50.

14. 8:39.

15. 9:33–34.

16. 3:104,110; 9:71.

17. 9:13.

18. 4:91–93.

19. 8:39.

20. 8:39–40.

21. 8:40.

22. 9:29.

23. 9:41.

24. 5:33.

25. 9:12.

26. 9:29.

27. In the chapter on the Shiʿite theory of political authority in my *The Just Ruler in Shiʿite Islam: The Comprehensive Authority of the Jurist in Imamite*

Jurisprudence (New York: Oxford University Press, 1988), pp. 105–17, I have discussed the intimate relationship between *jihād* and the question of right authority in Twelver Shiʿite jurisprudence.

28. There are a number of narratives related in the Shiʿite sources that question the legitimacy of the various *jihād*s of the Sunni caliphs as motivated by the Qurʾanic demand to make God's cause succeed. See Muḥammad Bāqir al-Majlisī, *Biḥār al-anwār* (Tehran: Kitābfurū shī-yi Islāmiyya, 1957), 100:18f.

29. *Dār al-sulh* as a spatial-religious conception conveys the essence of Muslim cognition of their immigration into non-Muslim countries. It provides a Muslim minority with the legal and ethical sources for furthering the ways in which it is necessary to conduct themselves as members of a family and a community in predominantly non-Muslim environments. Closely related to this concept is the notion of *dār al-ḥijra* (the sphere of immigration), which not only suggests that every corner of the earth is open to such immigration to seek God's universal bounty; it also considers any part of the earth as unrestrictedly and potentially capable of providing humanity with all the conditions necessary for directing it toward obedience to God. See my article "Islam and Muslims in Diaspora," in the *Bulletin of the Institute of Middle Eastern Studies*, International University of Japan, 7 (1993):109–46.

30. John Kelsay, *Islam and War: The Gulf War and Beyond, A Study in Comparative Ethics* (Louisville, Ky.: Westminster/John Knox Press, 1993), p. 2.

31. The tradition occurs in many variant forms, with a clear permission to enjoin the oppressor. See al-Nawawī, *Riyāḍ al-ṣāliḥīn* (Beirut: Dār al-Ḥadīth, 1974), p. 109.

32. Khalid Abou El Fadl, "*Aḥkām Al-Bughāt*: Irregular Warfare and the Law of Rebellion in Islam," in *Cross, Crescent, and Sword: The Justification and Limitation of War in Western and Islamic Tradition*, p. 162, cites all the relevant juridical sources on the issue.

33. Anwar Sadat's assassins relied on the righteousness of the duty of *jihād* to validate their questionable method of irregular warfare against the Egyptian state. See Johannes J. G. Jansen, *The Neglected Duty: The Creed of Sadat's Assassins and Islamic Resurgence in the Middle East* (New York: Macmillan, 1986), pp. 25–29.

34. Ṣaḥīḥ al-Bukhāri, Kitāb al-fitan, Ḥadīth #206.

35. 5:45.

36. Information in this section is derived from several articles that deal with Islamic criminal law in the volume *The Islamic Criminal Justice System*, ed. M. Cherif Bassiouni (New York: Oceana Publications, Inc., 1982).

37. N. J. Coulson, *A History of Islamic Law* (Edinburgh: University Press, 1964) and Joseph Schacht, *An Introduction to Islamic Law* (Oxford: Clarendon Press, 1979) provide the most adequate definitions of the terminology in the context of Muslim penal law.

38. There is a fundamental problem in rendering the Arabic word *irtidād* as "apostasy." The term *irtidād*, meaning "rejection" or "turning away from," was historically applied to the battles that were fought against those Muslims who had refused to pay taxes to the Muslim political authority after the Prophet's death. Hence, the *murtaddūn* were those who had rebelled against the established order. Compare this with the way the term *apostasy* is

understood in Christianity, where historically it suggests a whole range of different religious experiences of abandoning an exclusive and institutional-ized religion for another. In this sense, apostasy occurs when different reli-gions compete with each other in one public arena. *Irtidād*, on the other hand, occurs within the communal order, which is threatened by its public manifestation. At that point it is no longer simply a religious offense against which only God provides sanctions. Depending on the interpretation of the act, which should be undertaken by the political authority and not by the "church" or "ecclesiastical" body, the appropriate punishment is carried out. See "Apostasy," in *The Encyclopedia of Religion*, 1:353ff and n. 20.

39. I have dealt with the problem of the legal definition of apostasy in Islamic jurisprudence in my chapter "Freedom of Conscience and Religion in the Qur'an," in *Human Rights and the Conflict of Cultures*, pp. 53–90. Here, I am once again confronted with the complexity of the entire question of "apostasy" in Islam, more particularly in the light of consistent and obvious Qur'anic treatment of that offense as being beyond human jurisdiction. There is no doubt in my mind that the Qur'an supports freedom of religion and not just tolerance of religions other than Islam. Hence, it does not see itself in competition with other religions in winning converts. The *irtidād* or *ridda* of the Qur'an is, strictly speaking, "turning away" from God and, hence, punishable in the hereafter only, whereas the *irtidād* in jurisprudence, de-pending on its public manifestation and its adverse impact on the Muslim public order, denotes "turning away" from the community. Hence, the deter-mination of the gravity of the offense is strictly under the jurisdiction of legitimate Muslim authority.

40. 2:217.

41. A. A. Mansour, "Hudud Crimes," in *The Islamic Criminal Justice System*, ed. M. Cerif Bassiouni (New York: Oceana Publications, Inc., 1982), pp. 195–96.

42. 5:33.

43. For Islamic views on "suicide," see Franz Rosenthal, "On Suicide in Islam," in *Journal of the American Oriental Society* 66 (1946):239–59. For views on "martyrdom," see Todd B. Lawson, "Martyrdom," in *The Oxford Encyclopedia of the Modern Islamic World* (New York: Oxford University Press, 1995) 3:54–59.

44. 4:59.

45. Published by University of Chicago Press, 1988, particularly chap. 5.

46. ʿUbayd Allāh b. Muḥammad b. Baṭṭa, *Kitāb al-sharḥ wa al-ibāna alā usūl al-sunna wa al-diyāna* (Damascus, 1958), pp. 66ff.

47. See A. K. S. Lambton, *State and Government in Medieval Islam: An Introduction to the Study of Islamic Political Theory: The Jurists* (Oxford University Press, 1981), pp. 15–16.

48. Emmanuel Sivan, *Radical Islam: Medieval Theology and Modern Politics* (New Haven: Yale University Press, 1985), pp. 90, 96–97.

49. For detailed treatment of the messianic idea in Shiʿism, see my *Islamic Messianism: The Idea of Mahdi in Twelver Shiʿism* (Albany: State University of New York, 1981).

50. 6:152.

Is There a Tradition of Nonviolence in Islam?

MICHAEL N. NAGLER

Professor Sachedina has guided us with great subtlety through the moral reasoning of Islamic treatments of pacifism and nonviolence. There are interesting differences among Christianity, Judaism, and Islam from this point of view, but the impression I am left with is more of the fundamental similarities among the Peoples of the Book, the *Ahl al-Kitab*, and even to some degree among the other monotheistic systems I am familiar with, around the paradox of a fundamental injunction, "Take not the life which I have given, for it is sacred" side by side with a necessity—in this world of contradictions in which we find ourselves—to fight in self-defense and even more so for justice: "persecution is worse than slaughter."[1]

Since I can add little to Professor Sachedina's expert and informative survey (for one thing, my background is in Classics and then nonviolence theory), I would like to try to complement his description of the historical and theological facts by looking at them from another philosophical perspective. What I want to show is that the paradox just referred to is almost inevitable if one approaches nonviolence from the prohibitory point of view—as a "Thou shalt not"—but from another point of view there is a way out of the paradox. This alternative was best articulated by Gandhi, though one finds traces of it much earlier and in many other traditions; then it was adopted without hitch into an Islamic context—a rather demanding and orthodox Islam, in fact—by one of Gandhi's greatest followers, Abdul Ghaffar Khan.

I was particularly struck by Professor Sachedina's proposal to restructure the vocabulary of pacifism and nonviolence in application to Islamic experience, as I'll explain. The special issue of *Gandhi Marg* that was dedicated to nonviolence carried four articles, not surprisingly, on Islam.[2] On reading them I was struck by a statement two of the writers made that I have often heard from Jewish students in my nonviolence class at Berkeley: "Nonviolence is a wonderful thing but it doesn't apply to the Arabian peninsula (respectively, modern Israel)." They do not mean, of course, that Islam merits a special exemption from the norm that applies to mankind in general. As the Qur'an says, "Allah loves not aggressors";[3] a Hadith of the Prophet echoes, "those who commit violence—God has given them respite only until the day their eyes become glazed." They mean, nonviolence can work only under favorable circumstances.

I am going to dissent from this very commonly held opinion precisely because it leads to the paradox Professor Sachedina and others here have articulated and which besets Islam no less than other world religious systems. I am reminded of Pascal:

> Justice without force is a myth, because there are always bad men; force without justice stands condemned by itself. We must therefore put together justice and force, and so dispose things that whatever is just is mighty, and whatever is mighty is just.[4]

As long as you believe that nonviolence is not "mighty" you cannot be both nonviolent and just; that God asks humanity both to eschew violence and to fight for justice—particularly normative in Islam—puts us in an impossible dilemma, a real moral quagmire.

We are all aware how real the issue is for all of us: Islam, a culture and a movement now nurturing almost a fifth of the human race, is widely perceived, or stereotyped, as "fundamentalist" and threatening, as though we in the West need to fill what Professor Esposito calls the "threat vacuum" left by the end of the Cold War, to create a new demon, what one panicky journalist called a "global intifada," a kind of thinking that is creating incredible suffering and reinstalling the danger of global conflict we have just fortuitously avoided. Naturally, with this kind of thinking we fail to perceive that there is inherent nonviolence in Islam; conversely, by identifying the nonviolent currents in that faith we may be doing the most effective thing possible to dispel that stereotype.[5]

Of course the way we have framed the topic of this discussion, namely starting from quietism and pacifism, somewhat predisposes us to think about nonviolence in the philosophically negative light— as the absence of violence, and consequently of power. This leads to endless confusion, whether the task is to understand the inherent nonviolence in Islam or the nature of nonviolence itself.

Philosophically, Gandhi began from the opposite position. At a fairly early stage of his career he wrote instead:

The world rests upon a bedrock of satya or truth. Asatya or untruth also means non-existent, and satya or truth also means that which is. If untruth does not so much as exist its victory is out of the question. And truth being that which is can never be destroyed. This is the doctrine of Satyagraha in a nutshell.[6]

The implications of this statement have always seemed to me as revolutionary as the breakthroughs of quantum physics—and as little understood. It would be a grave mistake to think of this creed of Gandhi's as a mere philosophical abstraction. It was this principle which enabled him to carry on through massive apparent failures (which is where attempts at using nonviolence commonly break down), which enabled him to adapt nonviolence to the most unlikely situations and to use it against apparently overwhelming power, often with impressive success. It enabled him to understand that alongside a handful of situations in which we can see the force of persuasion operating toward greater justice, what Professor Mirsky calls the "nonviolent moment," are an infinite set of moments in which nonviolence is immanent and that we can release its operations if we make ourselves the right instruments to do so.

Politically, then, positive nonviolence, which does not start from a prohibitory norm but from a pragmatic need, which gets beyond the eschewal of what Professor Kenneth Boulding called "threat power" to conscious experimentation with "integrative power," was a distinct reality in the Indian freedom struggle.[7]

This brings us to one of the most spectacular demonstrations of nonviolent power the world has seen, namely the dogged resistance under intense provocation of an entire "army" of nonviolent volunteers, the Khudai Khidmatgars, or "Servants of God," inspired into being by the Pathan leader Khan Abdul Ghaffar Khan, who had come under Gandhi's direct influence in the 1920s. For this story, in the interest of time, let me refer you to Eknath Easwaran's *A Man to Match His Mountains*, available in Arabic as well as English.[8] I would just point out that since this book appeared the historical example of a trained, uniformed army of brave, formerly violent people resisting oppression without weapons or violence—and the Pathans knew how to use both—has become extremely important in the arguments for the creation of volunteer nonviolent international peace brigades. Many people have been working very hard on this idea, which some consider the most important format for large-scale nonviolence in the post-Cold War

environment. Once diplomatic means have failed and one must intervene in an advanced conflict, nonviolent interposition constitutes the
only alternative to the usual dilemma of force—which is more and more
often unworkable—or doing nothing. If Khan's example had been actively followed, the Pathans and others could have saved Afghanistan;
more to the point, we could be saving Bosnia right now.

But to return to our theoretical overview, instead of thinking
about nonviolence under pacifism (and when the two terms are on
the table, "pacifism," with all its disadvantages, predominates), we
should look at pacifism—the refusal to fight wars—under a rubric of
positive nonviolence. This is exactly what Badshah Khan was doing.
It is possible, to use Professor Mirsky's image, to "back into" positive
nonviolence from the mere abstention from violence, *if* you can cre-
atively face the need to find another kind of power. Most of the
Khudai Khidmatgars probably reached only the first stage of this
trajectory; but it is interesting to note that the Khan himself had
instinctively begun by village uplift, education, and other constructive
activities—activities that brought him somewhat into conflict with the
mullahs but not with the fundamental teachings of Islam—even before
he heard of Gandhi. For him the peace army came only at a later and
more critical stage; it was the flip side of "constructive programme,"
the less dramatic but more important mode of nonviolent work where
the Khan, appropriately, began his campaign.

This extremely important example of nonviolent action was part
of the Indian freedom struggle, to be sure, but it emerged in a distinctly
Islamic context—and a pretty "fundamentalist" one at that. Khan
himself, a plain-spoken man not given to theorizing, made this
straightforward statement:

> There is nothing surprising in a Muslim or a Pathan like me
> subscribing to the creed of nonviolence. It is not a new creed.
> It was followed fourteen hundred years ago by the Prophet all
> the time he was in Mecca, and it has since been followed by all
> those who wanted to throw off an oppressor's yoke. But we had
> so far forgotten it and when Gandhi placed it before us, we
> thought he was sponsoring a novel creed.[9]

Islamic scholars will, I believe, find nothing unreasonable in this claim.
Khan himself felt that what he was doing arose from his commitment
to the three Muslim principles of *amal*, *yakeen*, and *muhabat* (service,

faith, and love). More recently, an Islamic scholar has pointed out, "Four key concepts advocated by the Qur'an are *'adl, ihsan, rahmah, hikmah*; that is, justice, benevolence, compassion, and wisdom. . . . The very spirit of these key concepts would be injured by violence."[10]

If we stick to the positive orientation, however, many other elements of the Islamic tradition appear that are integral parts of nonviolence, though that is not always obvious at first. I will conclude by mentioning two. A Hadith from the prestigious *Sahih Bukhari* states, "Help your brother whether he is an aggressor or a victim of aggression." When the Prophet is asked how we can help the aggressor, he replies, "By preventing him from carrying out his aggression as best you can."[11] Notice how paradox is avoided by this application of "hating the sin but not the sinner." And finally this *Surah* reflecting a typically nonviolent emphasis on the moral character of an event rather than on political power derived from numbers: "If anyone takes a life, it is as though he slays all mankind. And if anyone saved a life, it would be as if he saved the life of the whole people."[12] As the Talmud puts it, "He who saves one life; it is as if he sustained the entire world."[13]

Islam, as a belief system with a specific scriptural foundation and an accompanying sacred history, took root in many different societies and cultures.[14] In none, I think it's fair to say, did Islam as such repress any existing developments that were toward nonviolence. There is no theological reason an Islamic society could not take a lead in developing nonviolence today, and there is every reason that some of them should.

NOTES

1. Surah 2:191.
2. *Gandhi Marg* 14 (1992).
3. Qur'an 2:191; see also 4:36, 5:67. My thanks to Professor Muhammad Siddiq for help with these references.
4. *Pensées et opuscules* (Paris: Hachette, 1976), p. 470, § 298.
5. I would recommend Prof. John Esposito's *The Islamic Threat: Myth or Reality* (New York: Oxford University Press, 1992).
6. *Satyagraha in South Africa* (Ahmedabad: Navajivan Press, 1928–1950), p. 260.
7. Kenneth E. Boulding, *Three Faces of Power* (Newbury Park, CO: Sage, 1989). Professor Boulding's work on power is going to prove its worth in years to come.

8. Eknath Easwaran, *A Man to Match His Mountains: Badshah Khan, Nonviolent Soldier of Islam* (Petaluma, Calif.: Nilgiri Press, 1984). The Arabic translation by the Palestinian Center for the Study of Nonviolence is unfortunately out of print.

9. Easwaran, *A Man*, 103.

10. Ashgar Ali Engineer, "Sources of Nonviolence in Islam," *Gandhi Marg* 14 (1992): 106.

11. 1116 § 45.

12. Qur'an 5:35.

13. Mishnah Sanhedrin IV, 5.

14. There is even a theory that strong commitments against violence were already in vogue among certain pre-Islamic desert communities having affinities with the Jains of northern India.

Quietism and Pacifism in American Public Policy: The Triumph of Secular Pacifism in the Religious State

EDWARD MCGLYNN GAFFNEY, JR.

And then the logic of war
    succeeded . . .
And I? Am I mad
    or maddened imagining
those who can't
    imagine this return
into violence? No
    tears, we hear,
no sense of terribleness
    or sorrow, nothing
only immense excitement
    when the attack
begins, blocks of light
    suddenly flattening
arc of laser-guided
    purple-tinged halos
around the open night.[1]

INTRODUCTION: LEGALISMS AND OTHER ISMS

Recently I was reading some of Larry Joseph's powerful poems, including the fragment cited above from a longer poem on the Gulf War. As I read this poem I realized that quietism and pacifism are not your usual isms pursued avidly by lawyers. Even after the end of the Cold War there are probably more lawyers in America committed to Communism than to quietism. And there are probably more of us afflicted with rheumatism than with pacifism. So it's risky business asking a lawyer to talk about the public policy implications of quietism and pacifism in America. But no lawyer I know of would shun the opportunity to say a few words about almost any subject, and I'm no exception to that general rule.

I would like to state at the outset that I find Professor Yoder's corrections of the label *quietism* persuasive.[2] Taking a leaf from his page, then, I will begin in the spirit of the rabbis constructing a midrash by attending first to the task of correcting the text assigned to me. I was told that I should write about "Religious Pacifism and the Secular State." But for the reasons that I offer in this essay I would like to rewrite my text to read "The Triumph of Secular Pacifism in the Religious State." Within this corrected title there is a term that I need to comment on: *pacifism.* I am, of course, aware that this term has a precise meaning in ethical theory to describe the position that war is never justifiable. Because of the importance of the justifiable war tradition in American politics, however, I will understand the term *pacifism* in the title to include an invitation to comment both on traditional "pacifism" in the strict sense and on the justifiable war tradition. I think it would be short-sighted to focus on only one of these traditions, but I will not mix up these two traditions in my essay. So that you will know when I am talking about one or the other, I will use the standard references to pacifism and the justifiable war tradition.

In this essay I write in a distinctively Christian way. To do so does not excuse me from offering a publicly accessible account of my religious convictions,[3] which I will also attempt to do in this essay by way of commentary on the justifiable war tradition[4] and by reference to commonly accessible historical materials. Yet I return to the point that for me to think about this particular matter of public concern entails not only the duties of a good citizen observing norms of intelligibility with one's fellow citizens, but specifically the religious convictions that serve as a frame of reference for the ethic of peace and war that I hold to be true.[5]

For some, of course, the very concept of an ethics of war is an oxymoron. Christian pacifists claim that the cross of Jesus mandates at least for his faithful disciples an important distinction between being willing to die for another and refusing to kill another. For others, however, the duty to serve one's country is morally justifiable, even as a Christian vocation. I wind up acknowledging that there may be some circumstances under which armed intervention might be necessary in a flawed world too often marred by hostility. But I reach this conclusion with greater hesitancy, reluctance, and much less frequency than many who are associated with the "just war" tradition. I think that the conditions for justifying warfare are rarely fulfilled, whereas some just warriors I know have rarely met a war they didn't like.[6]

You will note that I refer in this essay to the "justifiable war" tradition rather than to the "just war" tradition. By leaving open the question of whether any particular war was actually just, I intend to blur the line between pacifism and the justifiable war tradition.

One can, of course, appreciate why a secular Machiavellian, Metternichian political operative like Henry Kissinger would ignore the discourse of pacifism and the Christian doctrine of the justifiable war as quaint or remote from the center of power. I do, however, find it curious that religiously motivated thinkers do not take more seriously the claims that the biblical traditions still press upon our age. I find it strange that so many Christian theologians construct their ethical reflections on war as though the teachings of Jesus on nonviolence[7] or the manner of his death as the suffering servant of God[8] have little or no relevance to the attitude of his disciples toward the killing of others in the name of the nation state. For my part, I am willing to acknowledge that the reason for my hesitancy or reluctance to support most modern warfare is grounded in my attempt to remain faithful to the teaching of Jesus about nonviolence and to the normative consequences that I think flow from the manner of his death, not as a first-century freedom fighter, but as the suffering servant of God. By the same token, I do not claim that Christian just warriors are not faithful to those teachings, but leave that issue to them to decide.

As for those who do not share my beliefs in Jesus, I invite our brothers and sisters in Abrahamic faith, Jews and Muslims, to search within their own traditions for an appropriate way of bespeaking these concerns in their own voices.[9] As one who is well aware of the danger of the Marcionite heresy[10] in our own time, I hasten to add that I understand the biblical Word to include both the Hebrew Scriptures and the New Testament, and that although there is much of the New Testament that Jews cannot accept as normative, our conversations are constantly being enriched by the rediscovery of the Jewishness of Jesus.[11] And as one who has recently come to benefit greatly from dialogue with Muslims on matters of religious liberty,[12] I welcome the Muslim voice in this discussion as well.

The argument that I present here involves four questions. First, does American law impose any serious limits on the resort to war and on the conduct of war? Second, has the law favored some forms of pacifism over others? Third, has the law privileged secular pacifism over religious pacifism? And fourth, has modern warfare evoked a glorification of the nation state at war that religious believers might identify as a form of idolatry? The answers to these questions are complicated and have changed over time, but I suppose one could state that the answers to these questions, respectively, are not much, yes, yes, and yes. Although it would be a lot simpler if I were to conclude now, a common respect to the opinion of humankind impels me to state the case for my conclusions.

LEGAL LIMITS ON WAR

Does American law place serious limits on war? This question contains two subsets. Does American law place much restraint on going to war? And does American law place much restraint on the conduct of war? I will attend to each of these questions in turn, but first let me offer some metaphors from my days in Italy to image a reply to the general question.

Along the via del Gianicolo in Rome are a series of marble busts commemorating various military heroes, primarily of the Risorgimento. Fascist Italy conjures up images of brutal repression domestically under Il Duce, who did more than make the trains run on time. It recalls grand imperial designs on remote regions of the Mediterranean and Africa, including Ethiopia. And it evokes the memory of the courageous resistance of the *partegiani*.

There is, however, another dimension to the Italian spirit that is not captured on the Gianiculum hill. Who besides Garibaldi is remembered a hundred years later? Indeed, who besides Mussolini among the cutthroat Fascist bullies is now remembered even among the descendants of hardline *partegiani*? The attitude of which I speak—distrust of war—is celebrated in ethnic jokes about Italian militarism. One such joke suggests that, like the volume on *Good Irish Sex*, *The Italian Encyclopedia of War Heroes* probably ranks among the thinnest books ever written. Another ethnic joke suggests that Italian tanks were equipped with five gears, four in reverse and one forward in case the tanks are attacked from the rear.

Ethnic jokes are best told—and perhaps should only be told—as self depricating humor by members of a particular ethnicity. For example, Pope John XXIII once commented humorously on his military career as an Army chaplain in World War I. It speaks volumes about the Italian attitude toward war that Italy was on both sides of the Great War and wound up on the winning side. Sergeant Roncalli explained that his commendation—the equivalent of our Purple Heart or Medal of Honor—was actually not due to bravery on his part but to cowardice. During a pitched battle with the Austrians he saw that the enemy was outflanking the Italians and would soon overrun them, so he decided that that was not a particularly good place for him to stay. He got up from his position and started running as fast as he could to the opposite end of the battlefield. Several foot soldiers looked up in time to see a fat fellow with sergeant's stripes running by, and assuming that he had received orders to lead a reverse flanking manoeuver, they chased Roncalli to the opposite end of the field. The result was that the Italians now outflanked the Austrians on the right and moved in to end the battle swiftly. Angelo Roncalli was chagrined that the military leaders wanted to decorate him for bravery, but he decided to take the medal as a reminder that lots of lives were saved that day by his cowardice.

In the title of his gripping tale of World War II, *Catch-22*, Joseph Heller has contributed a phrase to the English language that captures the intractable dilemmas of modern warfare. More than that, Heller captured the marvelous way that Italians have chosen to survive the ravages of war on their motherland. Perhaps you recall the flags that Italians kept in reserve for whatever army happened to pass through their *paese*. Nazis would see the natives waving the swastika; Brits, the Union Jack; French, the tricolor; and Yanks, the Stars and Stripes. In this way—so hoped the natives—the "welcomed" conquerors would pass through quickly, leaving their village intact.

By contrast, Americans take their wars far more seriously than the Italians. We study war much more seriously. Our military academies are old, proud institutions. The United States Institute for Peace—a place to study nonmilitary solution to international conflict— is a recent innovation without the long pedigree of West Point and Annapolis. We glorify our wars to an extent that outsiders find remarkable. Perhaps the most notable example of a war that we ceaselessly glorify is the Civil War. Nearly 130 years after Appomattox we cannot even agree about the name of the war or who really won it. The fact that the enemy was literally ourselves is, of course, why we call it the Civil War. But even though the battlefields of this conflict meant savage slaughter that mounted up a death toll higher than any other

American war, we still cloak this bloodiest of our wars in the rhetoric of the gentlemanly tradition.

Does American law impose any serious limits on the resort to war and on the conduct of war? If so, which ones? From the wars against the Native Americans to the Spanish-American War, from World War I to World War II, from Korea to Vietnam, from Grenada to Panama, our leaders have rarely paused very long before plunging the nation into often dubious battle, often using dubious means for dubious ends. For example, the Spanish-American War marked the first effort to expand the American empire beyond the North American continent.[13] Rather than admit the obvious imperial purpose of the war, President McKinley said that it was necessary "to bring Christianity to the Philippines," some four centuries after the coming of the Spaniards to those islands. His vice president was more candid; ever ready for a fight, Teddy Roosevelt acknowledged that although "it wasn't much of a war," it had to be fought because it was "the only one we've got."[14] Of all the wars that we have engaged in, the Gulf War seems to me to be the one in which the justifiable war tradition was at least seriously debated in Congress before we resorted to war.[15]

Legal Limits on the Resort to War

Does American law place much restraint on going to war? This is the question of *jus ad bellum*. Both as a matter of logic and as a matter of public policy, this question is prior to the question about what the military may or may not do once the nation goes to war. The justifiable war tradition purports to set limits not only on the conduct of nations while they engage in war but also on whether they may use armed intervention at all as a legitimate means of reconciling an international conflict. All of the following conditions must be met before a war is thought to be justifiable in this tradition: (1) legitimate authority; (2) just cause; (3) right intentions; (4) reasonable hope of achieving desirable results; (5) proportionality between the desirable results and the evil inherent in all war; and (6) last resort.

The first condition of a justifiable war, that it be conducted by legitimate authority, is an important issue in American constitutional law. Who has the authority to commit the armed forces to war? The text of the Constitution does not resolve the issue. Article I, § 8 of the Constitution expressly grants to Congress the power to declare war and to regulate the armed forces, but Article II defines the Executive as the commander-in-chief. One plausible interpretation is that only the Congress may commit the nation to war, but that once a war has been initiated by a declaration of war, the president then has the duty as the commander-in-chief to "take care" that this act of Congress be "faithfully executed."[16] That interpretation of the text seems faithful to the original aversion to the concentration of governmental power in any one branch of our federal government, but it has been discarded in this century with the emergence of a strong managerial style in the Presidential Office.[17]

During the Vietnam War, several attempts were made to challenge the legality of the commitment of armed forces in Southeast Asia, but the Supreme Court declined to review all these cases, leaving the resolution of the legal question to the political branches.[18] Eventually, Congress accepted its own responsibility and stopped authorizing the expenditure of further funds to pursue any military activities in that arena. In 1973 Congress enacted over President Nixon's veto the War Powers Resolution, a political compromise which acknowledged the need for the president to have residual power to commit armed forces for a brief period, but which imposed reporting duties on the president and required the president to seek authorization from the Congress for continued military engagement.[19] As of this writing, President Clinton has not had an occasion to express his own views on the War Powers Resolution, but no other president since its adoption—Nixon, Ford, Carter, Reagan, or Bush—has ever acquiesced in the theory expressed in this resolution. For example, President Bush ordered a massive buildup of American troops in Saudi Arabia in Operation Desert Shield without consulting Congress; and right up to a fortnight before the commencement of Operation Desert Storm he maintained that he was under no duty whatever to consult Congress about actual hostilities against the Iraqis. In any event, none of the Vietnam era cases, and nothing in the War Powers Resolution itself, mandates that the nation must observe the other conditions for a justifiable war that are set forth above.

The question of *jus ad bellum*, moreover, is a dynamic one. That is, it may not be resolved once and for all during the stages preceding a war, but must be assessed rigorously and continuously in light of new empirical data pertaining to that war. Thus a war that might theoretically be justifiable at the outset could reach a stage where the war is no longer justifiable because it no longer offers any reasonable hope of achieving desirable results or because the evil inherent in the war has become disproportional to the desirable results of the war. I am unaware of any restraints that American law has ever placed upon our governors that would require them to reassess the legitimacy of any of the wars mentioned above once armed conflict had commenced.

On the contrary, the behavior of the courts during wartime has been lamentable, to say the very least. Judicial behavior in the face of presidential suppression of civil liberties was supine during both world wars of this century. The Supreme Court swiftly sustained the draft law enacted in 1917.[20] It also treated protesters against World War I with utter contempt, regularly sustaining convictions for political speech in opposition to the war.[21] After the war came to an end in 1918, the government continued to press for convictions of violators of the wartime laws, but juries refused to convict under these circumstances.[22]

Neither did the Court intervene to prevent President Roosevelt from a thousand days of our own infamy. I refer to the fact that our government not only rounded up Japanese-Americans and herded them into concentration camps euphemistically designated "relocation centers," but also closed down the pagodas and temples of the citizens whose property they had confiscated and whose other civil liberties they had shamefully abused. Ugly racial undertones that have not yet dissipated flow from the infamous wartime decisions against the Japanese.[23]

In all of these wartime situations the judges let the political branches suppress their political opponents, whether real or imaginary. Far from imposing limits on going to war by requiring that the conditions of a justifiable war be continuously reexamined, our political and judicial tradition has been supportive of unquestioned concentration of power once war has broken out. Which leads me to the second subquestion.

Legal Limits on the Conduct of War

Does American law place much restraint on the conduct of war? This is the ethical question of *jus in bello*. Even assuming that a nation is justified in resorting to war, the justifiable war tradition also sets limits on what the military may and may not do once hostilities have commenced. The central principle invoked in the theory is that the military is limited to the use of proper means, including an immunity for noncombatant civilians. Thus a classic example of what is prohibited is the indiscriminate killing of noncombatant civilians.

Even the war that enjoyed the broadest support both of ethicists and of the general public, World War II, proved to be a war with serious problems for this aspect of the justifiable war tradition. At the time of our entry into World War II, the overwhelming majority of Americans thought that this war was morally justifiable. Yet one of the tragedies of this war is that the Allies engaged in the very things we found so reprehensible in the conduct of our enemies. The *jus in bello* principle of discrimination, which requires differentiation between military targets and noncombatant civilians, was systematically abused on both sides. From the earliest stages of the war, Britain initiated and maintained a policy of indiscriminate bombing of civilian targets.[24] We tend to remember the bombing of London that commenced in August of 1940; we tend to forget that this was in retaliation for the British bombing of Berlin a month before. We tend to remember the Luftwaffe's bombardment of Coventry; we tend to forget the RAF block-bombing of Hamburg and Dresden. And by the end of the war, the United States emulated this conduct, unleashing on Hiroshima and Nagasaki the only use in history of nuclear weapons to annihilate entire cities manifestly populated by innocent bystanders to war.[25]

The principal difference between the Axis and the Allies on this score was that our war crimes were not tried at Nuremberg. Even when we acknowledged that our ground troops had committed an atrocity at My Lai, the courts-martial that followed were limited to the captain and lieutenant who were directly involved in the incident and did not reach any of the superior officers who were implicated in similar commands, much less the colonels and generals and admirals and chiefs of Staff and presidents who were directing a war that seemed in the minds of many to involve an official policy of indiscriminate killing of civilians in Southeast Asia.[26]

To sum up, the limits set forth in the justifiable war tradition under the rubric of *jus ad bellum* have sometimes been acknowledged in the debates that have sometimes preceded our going to war, but the law has not required the decision makers to attend to these limits very reflexively. The limits imposed on the military by the *jus in bello* restraints have been incorporated into the field manuals that the American military is expected to observe, but any serious account of the law of war would acknowledge that it has been reactive to the horrors of past wars and rarely offers serious moral guidance or real limits on the use of technology that has far outstripped the situations contemplated in the existing rules of engagement. Thus to speak of limits on American wars imposed by the *jus in bello* restraints is like talking about the NCAA putting limits on cheating in college sports. The rule books keep getting bigger and bigger, but the violations keep getting more sophisticated. For these reasons I am led to conclude that, on balance, the answer to my first question, "Does the law impose serious limits either on the resort to war or on conduct in war?" is more in the negative than in the affirmative.

WHAT COUNTS AS A CLAIM OF CONSCIENCE IN AMERICAN LAW?

The answer to this question has varied over time, so I will simply tell the story in narrative form. Conscientious objection to participation in war has been recognized since 1775, when the First Continental Congress enacted the following resolution:

> As there are some people, who, from religious principles, cannot bear arms in any case, this Congress intend no violence to their consciences, but earnestly recommends it to them, to contribute liberally in this time of universal calamity, to the relief of their distressed brethren in the several colonies, and do all other services to their oppressed Country, which they can consistently with their religious principles.[27]

After the adoption of the new Constitution, James Madison proposed a Bill of Rights to the first Congress. One of the proposals put forward by Madison was the following: "no person religiously scrupulous of bearing arms shall be compelled to render military service in person."[28] Although Congress did not adopt this language in what was to become the Second Amendment, the principal reasons offered for this result was that similar language was contained in the Bills of Rights of several of the state constitutions and that it was better as a matter of federalism to leave this issue to the states.

Since there was no military conscription at the time of the War of 1812 or at the time of the Mexican-American War, the issue of conscientious objection remained at the state level. With the enactment of a federal draft law at the time of the Civil War, the Congress of the Union enacted legislation in 1864 allowing conscientious objectors who were "members of religious denominations with articles of faith that prohibit the bearing of arms" to pay a substitute or to accept alternative service that entailed noncombatant duties.[29] The Confederate Congress made similar provisions for Southern conscientious objectors.

There was no draft in the Spanish-American War, but one was imposed when the United States entered World War I. In the Selective Draft Act of 1917, Congress exempted ordained ministers and seminarians from the draft, as well as "members of any well-recognized religious sect or organization at present organized and existing whose existing creed or principles forbid its members to participate in war in any form."[30] This provision, which clearly privileges members of some religious groups (for example, Brethren, Mennonites, and Quakers) over members of other groups which teach that some wars are justifiable and that others are not (for example, mainline Protestants, Catholics, Jews, and Muslims), was promptly sustained against an Establishment Clause challenge.[31] Weeks later, the Supreme Court unanimously sustained the legislation, merely noting in a curt paragraph the "apparent . . . unsoundness" of the claim that the exemption provisions offended either provision of the Religion Clause.[32]

After World War I, and without any congressional authorization, the Naturalization Service began asking all immigrants the following question: "If necessary, are you willing to take up arms in the defense of this country [the United States]?" In 1927 a Hungarian immigrant named Rosika Schwimmer stated that she could take the oath of allegiance without reservations, but that as an "uncompromising pacifist" she could not take up arms in the defense of any nation. The district court denied her application for citizenship, and in 1929 the Supreme Court sustained that result by a vote of 6-3.[33] In an opinion that was consistent with the stingy attitude toward free speech that had emerged during World War I, Justice Butler wrote that it was unlawful not only to refuse to bear arms in defense of the country but even to express an opinion against this duty that might influence others to "endanger" the safety of the country by refusal to perform their obligation of military service. In a wholly gratuitous aside, Butler suggested that religious scruples were not involved in the case because Madame Schwimmer had "no religion." Justice Holmes, a crusty Civil War veteran who had been severely wounded at Antietam and who had no patience with pacifism, nonetheless made a strong plea for protecting "freedom for the thought we hate," noting that he "had not supposed hitherto that we regretted our inability to expel [people] because they believe more than some of us do in the teachings of the Sermon on the Mount."[34]

The next critical year in the story is 1940, when the clouds of war had not only gathered again in Europe but had already burst open. Neville Chamberlain's "appeasement" of Hitler in Munich in 1938 proved no favor to the Czechs or the Poles in 1939. Just before France and Belgium were overrun the following year by German troops in Hitler's blitzkrieg, Chamberlain was replaced by Winston Churchill. The new prime minister immediately began urging President Franklin Delano Roosevelt to join the United Kingdom in armed resistance to the Third Reich. 1940 was an election year, and FDR thought that in seeking an unprecedented third term in office, it would be more astute to follow Wilson's example of feigning abstention from a European conflict, while waiting for the first opportunity after the election to get "involved." A year after FDR was reelected, the Japanese gave FDR the "incident" he had told Churchill he needed to enter the war. The pacifism of the 1920s and 1930s evaporated overnight[35] when FDR went to Congress for a declaration of war immediately after the "day of infamy." The country rallied overwhelmingly to the cry for revenge against the Japanese. In the war that ensued, little, if any, thought was given to rescuing the Jews and the other victims of totalitarianism, who were abandoned to their fate.[36]

In 1940 two major steps were taken to prepare for war, the Lend-Lease program to assist the United Kingdom with military weapons while we were still "neutral," and the enactment of a new draft law known as the Burke-Wadsworth Bill. This legislation originally copied the language of the 1917 act. Several religious leaders urged Congress to amend the bill so that the exemption would be available not only to members of traditional peace churches but to any pacifist member of a "well-recognized religious communion."[37] Leaders of peace groups pressed further, urging Congress to recognize nonreligious as well as religious objectors.[38] Congress acquiesced to the desires of the religious leaders, but not to the amendments sought by the peace groups, enacting the following statute: "Nothing in this Title shall be construed to require any person to be subject to combatant training and service in the armed forces of the United States who, by reason of religious training and belief, is conscientiously opposed to war in any form."[39] This version of the statute provided the basis for the momentous changes in public policy that were wrought by the Supreme Court in the Vietnam era. Before turning to those cases, let me conclude this section by noting that from the Revolutionary War to the modern period the exemption from compulsory military service was extended on a preferential basis to religious objectors over nonreligious objectors, and more particularly to pacifists over religious objectors who grounded their objection to war on the doctrine of justifiable war.

THE TRIUMPH OF SECULAR PACIFISM OVER RELIGIOUS COMMITMENT TO THE JUSTIFIABLE WAR TRADITION

My third question is whether the recent treatment of claims of conscientious objection to participation in war has privileged secular pacifism over religious pacifism. Understanding the term *pacifism* in this section of the paper to include all forms of objection to war, including both nonreligious and religious commitment to the doctrine of the justifiable war, I answer this question in the affirmative.

In the preceding section I concluded that the descriptive question as to whether American law in fact gave preference to religious objectors over nonreligious objectors must be answered in the affirmative. I turn now to the normative question as to whether American public policy should continue to do so. I have reached two conclusions. First, a sound case can be made on constitutional grounds, but not as a matter of statutory interpretation, that we should exempt both nonreligious and religious objectors to war. Second, an equally sound case can be made on constitutional grounds that the law must also recognize selective conscientious objection, that is, religiously motivated objection to war that is grounded in the justifiable war tradition.

The problem with my conclusions is that the Supreme Court did exactly the opposite, ruling in 1970 on statutory grounds that a nonreligious objector was entitled to relief under the terms of the draft law, and denying relief a year later to a devout Roman Catholic who was prepared to serve his country in a military capacity but who refused as a matter of conscience to participate in a war that his church had taught him to believe was violative of the justifiable war tradition. In other words, I have some explaining to do.

In 1965, with the call-ups for the Vietnam War in full swing, the Court decided three companion cases that presented a question as to the meaning of the term *religious training or belief* in the draft law.[40] The Selective Service System had denied CO status to Daniel Andrew Seeger, Arno Sascha Jakobson, and Forest Britt Peter, all three of whom professed no belief in God. At the time of the challenge, the statute included language defining "religious training and belief" both positively as "an individual's belief in a Supreme Being involving duties superior to those arising from any human relation," and negatively as excluding "essentially political, sociological, or philosophical views or a merely personal moral code."[41] Justice Tom Clark wrote for a unanimous Court that Congress did not mean the term *Supreme Being* to refer to "God," but merely as an indicator that an applicant should be granted CO status if his belief was "sincere and meaningful [and] occupies a place in the life of its possessor parallel to that filled by the orthodox belief in God of one who clearly qualifies for the exemption."[42] The Court decided that it did not have to reach the constitutional questions presented in the case, and disposed of the claim solely on statutory grounds.

What is wrong with extending CO status to atheists and agnostics? Nothing really, except that it is hard to believe that the Court was serious when it suggested that the result was well secured by the statute. As I mentioned above, peace groups back in 1940 had asked Congress to do exactly what the Court eventually did in 1965, but the point is that Congress refused in 1940 to extend objector status to nonreligious objectors.

Could the result in *Seeger* be justified on some other basis? I think that the answer is yes, but the problem is that the Court would then have to admit that it had answered the constitutional question incorrectly several decades ago when it first started looking at draft laws in this century. In other words, the central constitutional argument that I deem controlling is the one that the Court had dismissed summarily back in 1918: that the law may not prefer religious objectors over nonreligious objectors without violating the Establishment Clause. This principle now seems to be the very core of the historic purpose of that provision, which was enacted to overcome the history of penalties and disabilities imposed on nonmembers of the established or preferred religion in Tudor and Stuart England and in the American colonies.[43] The Court has recently recognized this principle as central to its Establishment Clause jurisprudence, but in a case involving disparate regulation of charitable solicitation, not exemption from the draft.[44]

In 1967 Congress responded to the *Seeger* case, amending the draft law to eliminate the reference to a Supreme Being but retaining the exclusion of "essentially political, sociological, or philosophical views or a merely personal moral code."[45] The federal courts lost no time in going to work on this version of the draft law. Several lower courts after *Seeger* in fact took up the very line of argument I suggested above. The leading case came from Boston, where an objector named John Heffron Sisson based his objection not on religious grounds but on philosophical and political grounds. Judge Charles Wyzanski obliged the objector, ruling that the draft act violated both the establishment provision of the Religion Clause by discriminating "in favor of certain types of religious objectors to the prejudice of Sisson," and the free exercise provision of the same clause by requiring "combatant service of a conscientious objector whose principles are either religious or akin thereto."[46] Judge Wyzanski wrote that the draft act "unconstitutionally discriminated against atheists, agnostics, and men like Sisson who, whether they be religious or not, are motivated in their objection to the draft by profound moral convictions of their beings."[47]

Within months, the Supreme Court agreed to review a similar case, *Welsh v. United States*.[48] Elliott A. Welsh II, a Los Angeles commodities broker, came before the Court having stricken the word "religious" from his federal form inquiring as to the basis of his objection to military service. He stated that his beliefs about war, which he characterized as "nonreligious," were formed by readings in history and sociology. On the basis of these facts one might have thought the Court would have had a difficult time finding this applicant's request for exemption from military service within the scope of the statute, even after the Court's fanciful interpretation of the term *religious training and belief* in the *Seeger* case. Not so. Without batting an eye, without even winking or putting his tongue in his cheek, Justice Black—who had served in Congress as a senator from Alabama—wrote that this phrase in the statute was meant to exempt "from military service all those whose consciences, spurred by deeply held moral, ethical, or religious beliefs, would give them no rest or peace if they allowed themselves to become a part of an instrument of war."[49]

All those folks are exempt from military service? Well, no, not those whose views as to the justification of war are religiously grounded. A year after *Welsh* the Court reached this result in a case rejecting the claim of Louis Negre, a devout Roman Catholic objector, that he was entitled to conscientious objector status on the ground that the Vietnam War did not meet the conditions that his church taught him were necessary for participation in war.[50]

It is not a digression from Louis Negre's story to state that the only place in all the documents of the Second Vatican Council (1962–1965) in which the bishops of the church used the noun *condemnation* is the passage that arrested Negre from going to Vietnam:

[T]his most holy Synod makes its own the condemnations of total war already pronounced by recent Popes [citations omitted], and it issues the following declaration:

Any act of war aimed indiscriminately at the destruction of entire cities or of extensive areas along with their population is a crime against God and man himself. It merits unequivocal and unhesitating condemnation."[51]

Despite an excellent brief arguing both free exercise and establishment concerns, and despite a valuable brief by Negre's attorneys, Richard Harrington and John T. Noonan, Jr.,[52] that was expressly relied upon in the lone dissent of Justice Douglas, the Court rejected both of his constitutional arguments that the statute violated the Free Exercise Clause by coercing Negre to act against his conscience and violated the Establishment Clause by preferring conscientious objectors over selective conscientious objectors.

There was some irony that one of the greatest civil rights advocates of the century, Thurgood Marshall, wrote an opinion for eight justices in *Negre* that the first of our civil liberties, religious freedom, was easily overborne by focusing on the "considerable difficulties of sorting" claims based on justifiable war theory and claims based on "nonconscientious dissent from policy."[53] Never mind that the Court in *Welsh* had gone a very long mile down the road toward privileging "nonconscientious dissent from policy." Never mind that the Court in *Seeger* had imposed a considerable administrative burden on local draft boards, whose members were now presumed to be familiar with Paul Tillich's concept of a "Ground of Being" or with Bishop John A. T. Robinson's version of Dietrich Bonhoeffer's "religionless Christianity." It boggles the mind that so ardent a champion of civil rights as Thurgood Marshall would actually raise considerations of administrative inconvenience that might obtain if selective service boards had to attend to claims pressed by selective conscientious objectors. One cannot imagine Marshall countenancing such a claim in the context of racial discrimination in the nation's schools or in the context of inequality in voting rights along racial lines, even though a plausible argument could be made by attorneys representing school boards and election authorities that various remedies devised to advance the goal of integration were difficult to administer.

Justice Marshall was in strange company with Justice Butler in the *Schwimmer* case when he dismissed the problem of the law's preference for absolute pacifists over those religious objectors who had reluctantly and prayerfully come to the conclusion that the conditions of the justifiable war tradition were not met in a particular war. Marshall was even in stranger company with himself, for he was soon to write a leading opinion that content-based discrimination is violative of the Free Speech Clause of the First Amendment.[54]

Justice Black fell silent in *Negre*. He added not a word, not a peep, in protest against the stunning departure from his broad, sweeping language in *Welsh* from the previous term. He expressly joined the portion of Marshall's opinion that purported to rely on the legislative intent of Congress to deny the exemption to serious objectors who grounded their views in the justifiable war tradition.

Nor came there a word in *Negre* even in a concurring opinion from Justice Brennan, the author of *Sherbert v. Verner*,[55] the ringing declaration of religious freedom in the modern period of the Court. Indeed, Brennan, the champion of constitutional entitlements, would soon write that conscientious objectors who performed their service to the country as an alternative to military service are not entitled to the same kind of benefits to which those who serve in the military are entitled.[56] Why so? Brennan could have offered the sound but modest argument that Congress had not decided to confer the educational benefit sought by the concededly valid conscientious objector. But that argument would not have worn well with other Brennan opinions conferring entitlements beyond any plausible interpretation of what the Congress hath wrought in statutes. So Brennan decided to depart from the Brennan who wrote *Sherbert* by trivializing the burden upon religious conscientious objectors and by escalating the government's interest far beyond the obvious economic one (cutting costs of educational entitlements) to a "substantial interest in raising and supporting armies." By writing in this way, Brennan exposed the Achilles heel of *Sherbert*, the ad hoc character of judicial interest balancing, a point of vulnerability upon which Justice Scalia later seized to reduce *Sherbert* to its facts and all but overrule it in *Employment Division v. Smith*.[57]

With its harsh ruling in the *Negre* case, the Court had come full circle, turning on its head a statute that was manifestly designed to give preference to religious pacifists over nonreligious pacifists (*Seeger*, *Welsh*) without invalidating the statute, and refusing to extend the same line of thinking it had employed on behalf of atheists and agnostics when confronted with a genuine case of conscience respecting the Vietnam War that arose within a religious community that takes the justifiable war tradition seriously (*Negre*). Which leads me to my fourth question.

ON THE WORSHIP OF MARDUK AND MARS: THE IDOLATROUS CHARACTER OF THE NATION AT WAR

My fourth question concerns how the phenomenon of modern warfare has contributed to a reification of the nation state at war that religious believers might identify as a form of idolatry. I am aware that my use of the biblical category of idolatry might obscure rather than clarify my argument for many in contemporary society. This criticism is, of course, valid for those of our contemporaries for whom the biblical world is alien. For them at least, it might be helpful to try to give at least some broad description of the concept of idolatry. In this paper I use the term to refer to any of the following: (a) the attitude that the nation state and its institutions are worthy of the ultimate respect and loyalty that believers reserve for God, (b) the claim on the conscientious convictions of the people by governmental institutions that renders these institutions the functional equivalent of idols, or (c) the tendency of those who serve in governmental institutions to command the sort of respect referred to in (a) and (b), no matter how they are functioning.

The category of idolatry, then, describes not simply a particular act of worship thought problematic in the ancient world; it is manifest in a variety of ways in which we do not let God be God, but place false substitutes in his place.[58] For example, as John Howard Yoder puts it, "Ethnocentrism is idolatry even when it does not shed blood. One might say that shedding blood makes more dramatic the basic ethnological meaning of idolatry (i.e., the idol is what you sacrifice to, what you will kill for)."[59]

Recognizing that each set of historical circumstances is unique, I am unwilling to conclude that all wars necessarily entail idolatry. Nonetheless it is my view that modern warfare discloses a recurrent pattern of exalting the position of the government to a level dangerously close to what the biblical tradition calls idolatry. We Americans are by no means the only ones who engage in this reification or, even worse, deification of the nation at war, but we have no immunity from this disease. In this sense at least, idolatry is no accident in war, but is endemic to most modern wars. When a nation state goes to war, it tends to absolutize its power and to behave like an all-encompassing deity. At the very least, national leaders tend to exaggerate the rightness of their cause. It is in this sense that I call attention to the hazard in what I have labeled the "religious state."

As suggested in the prior section, I am not troubled that nonreligious conscience should be honored in our republic. But I think that the lack of respect that the government has shown to religious conscience is a deplorable departure from the noblest traditions of our republic.[60] Because the danger of an all-encompassing state is real, I conclude that we must rekindle respect for religious conscience, whether based on a pacifist commitment or on the justifiable war tradition, as an important limit to the claims of governmental authority in our society.

CONCLUSION: THE DANGER OF SECULAR PACIFISM IN A RELIGIOUS STATE

In the spirit of feminist jurisprudence, which has called repeatedly for the enhancement of law through the reinvigoration of narrative in the process of its development, I conclude with an autobiographical sketch of my own faith. Although Roman Catholic teaching on the ethics of war is typically identified with the justifiable war tradition,[61] it has never been required in the manner of creedal or conciliar pronouncements of the church. Lutherans, by contrast, find this tradition embedded in their confessional documents.[62] Thus Roman Catholics are free to take spiritual nurture from peacemakers like Francis of Assisi, Teresa of Calcutta, and Dorothy Day of the Bowery. In this era of ecumenism I am most happy to report that people of other faiths, both Jewish and Muslim, have also shaped Roman Catholic thought on these matters far more than some would care to admit. In this respect at least, some of us Roman Catholics are like the Mennonites, who took a radical stand in opposition to violence at the time of the Reformation, and who believe that being in trouble with the state is one of the "marks" or sure signs of the church's authenticity.[63]

Although I take my stand generally against the necessity of violence to resolve disputes, this conviction does not mean that there are no circumstances under which I would support the use of armed intervention. For example, I think that military forces have served admirably for peacekeeping purposes in several instances since the end of World War II. As I write, the United Nations peacekeeping force in Somalia is securing the safe delivery of food necessary to keep millions of Africans from dying of starvation. Although multinational efforts like these are justifiable in my mind, I note that smaller countries like Czechoslovakia or Ireland may be better suited to the task of peacekeeping than large nations with an imperial past.

A recurrent temptation for those who live at the epicenter of an empire is to think of it as benevolent and to overlook its defects. Thus we might be tempted to conclude that ours was not an "evil empire" because it was not brutal in quite the same way the British Empire was with its colonials, the Portugese empire with its horrendous record on slavery, the Spanish and French empires with their exploitation of colonial resources without leaving behind many of the benefits of European "civilization," Fascist Italy's empire with its suppression of the Ethiopians, the Third Reich with its extermination camps, or the Soviet and Chinese Communist empires with their gulags and slave labor camps.

The parable in Luke of the two men praying in the Temple[64] cautions us, however, against smug boasting about these differences, when a humble posture of begging for mercy for our sins would be more in order.[65] Without such humility, it becomes very easy to exaggerate the benefits of our empire and to ignore the harm it has caused to others. In such a boasting attitude, we then tell ourselves the lie that, like ancient Rome, the American empire sustained the peace during its century of dominance. The boast about a *pax americana* unfortunately has the distinct disadvantage of being untrue. It fails to account for the three major wars in the second half of the American century: the Korean, Vietnam, and the Gulf War. And the boast masks all the difficulties in the administration of far-flung and diverse cultures that previous empires have experienced.

Whatever the truth about our own imperial era—a very complicated tale that I can only touch on briefly, and do not pretend to unfold within the confines of this essay—the biblical record takes a dim view of empires generally. Even the Davidic-Solomonic empire within Israel is not spared the criticism of the Deuteronomistic historian, who preserved the memory of an antimonarchical tradition that protested against the concentration of power with its ineluctable corollaries: high taxes, confiscation of property, impressed labor, coerced military service, and the death of the youth in battles to expand territorial control.[66]

The Bible does not have much good to say for the empires of Israel's ancient foes—the Egyptians, the Assyrians, the Babylonians, the Persians,[67] the Greeks, or the Romans—all of whom in turn dominated and oppressed the Hebrews. It is not exactly that all the biblical traditions concluded that if you had seen one empire, you had seen them all. To the contrary, the historical situation at the time of the writing of the biblical documents yielded very different attitudes toward various empires. Thus the Babylonians who destroyed Jerusalem and exiled its surviving inhabitants were viewed more negatively than the Persians who liberated Israel from the Babylonian captivity and who authorized the return of the faithful remnant to the land of Israel. For example, Deutero-Isaiah viewed Cyrus the Great (559-529 B.C.E.) as God's servant [*'ebed*], shepherd-king [*ro'eh*], and anointed one [*mashiah*] for his role in the deliverance of Israel from the Babylonian yoke.[68] During the first century of Persian rule, a similarly benign view of the Persians is reflected in the books of Ezra and Nehemiah.[69] Similarly, the Roman Empire in the middle of the first century of the common era—at a time free of expansionist wars or oppression of the church—was thought worthy of respect in a way that was clearly inappropriate after the persecutions of the church began later in the century under Nero and Diocletian.[70]

For all the precision of the nice distinctions about empires in the biblical literature, however, there is a marked tendency in the Bible to view imperial rule with scorn and disfavor. The prophets in particular engaged in a thorough critique of the hopelessness and numbness endemic to royal and imperial domination.[71] For example, "oracles against the nations" are found throughout the writings of the canonical prophets, both in prophets whose ministry was in the northern kingdom of Israel and in prophets whose ministry was in the southern kingdom of Judah, both in pre-exilic prophets and in exilic prophets.[72] Writing in Babylon (Baghdad), the capital or epicenter of a flourishing empire, the so-called Second Isaiah launched several polemical attacks on idolatry,[73] including a long taunt-song that satirizes the manufacture and worship of idols and an oracle that castigates both the imperial pretensions and the cult of the imperial deities that legitimated these empires.[74] Similarly, the well-known story of the futile construction of the tower of Babel was a parody of the pretensions of the Babylonian Empire.[75] The Israelites were taught repeatedly that they need not be in awe of the military might of their oppressors and that they must not worship the pantheon of their deities, mere statues that "have mouths but speak not, eyes but see not, have ears but hear not, have noses but smell not, have hands but feel not, have feet but walk not, and utter no sound from their throats."[76] At best, the nations were

God's instruments for purifying Israel of the temptation to be an imperial master. At worst, they were the prototypical heathens, infidels whose pagan ways Israel was prohibited from emulating.

In this biblical perspective, war seems regularly to entail what biblical religion calls idolatry. In ancient Israel the prohibition against worship of this sort[77] was designed to prevent the assimilation of Israel to the religion and culture of her pagan neighbors, in which the principal deity of the conquering empire was the god of war. A similar concern is reflected in the earliest period of the Christian church, when the religious oath of fidelity, "Jesus is Lord,"[78] was deemed incompatible with the claim of Roman law, "Caesar is Lord," that formed the *sacramentum*, or oath of office, of a Roman soldier.[79]

It was on biblical grounds such as these, accompanied by detailed knowledge of American political life and culture, that conscientious objectors in America have made it their business to contradict the belief of many Americans that, as empires go, the American empire has been mostly a blessing for the world. For these conscientious objectors, empires—ours or any other—inevitably entail the worship of a false god, a rival to the Father of Abraham and of Sarah, of Isaac and Rebekah, of Jacob and Rachel, of Moses and Zipporah and Miriam, and of Jesus. When a nation interposes itself as an object of veneration for its citizens, these people have insisted that faithful Jews and Christians and Muslims should refuse to bow down in adoration of that false god.

Is it possible for the nations to control the raging forces of war in the modern world? That is not simply a question for rational reflection but also a challenge to faith. I will conclude with the language of the Psalmist common to all three religious traditions of the Book. Existential despair in the ability of humankind to achieve the desired result of peace in our time by our own strength and will and imagination may be very close to a profound hope that God knows how in his sovereign moment to make wars cease to the end of the earth by shattering the spear and burning the chariots with fire.[80] In the face of the overwhelming evidence of human brutality and barbarism in this century, to maintain such optimism requires a quantum leap of faith. A discussion such as this encourages us to take that leap of faith, reposing our trust in the Lord as our sure rock and refuge,[81] not in the princes of this earth,[82] and most assuredly not in their horses[83] or their bows and swords.[84] With the Psalmist we can come to know that "It is better to take refuge in the Lord than to put confidence in mortals. It is better to take refuge in the Lord than to put confidence in princes."[85] If we live by this faith, we will refuse to bow down in idolatrous worship before the nations and their armies, including our own, because we will never confuse them with the power of our Lord.

And even if we are not ready to live by such a faith as this, I hope that these considerations will renew our respect for the consciences of those who are impelled to do so. In this way we will be accepting the challenge of the Williamsburg Charter to make real the American commitment to protecting the first of our civil liberties. In the language of the charter:

> As James Madison expressed it in his Memorial and Remonstrance, "The Religion then of every man must be left to the conviction and conscience of every man; and it is the right of every man to exercise it as these may dictate. This right is in its nature an unalienable right."
>
> Two hundred years later, despite dramatic changes in life and a marked increase of naturalistic philosophies in some parts of the world and in certain sectors of our society, this right to religious liberty based upon freedom of conscience remains fundamental and inalienable. While particular beliefs may be true or false, better or worse, the right to reach, hold, exercise them freely, or change them, is basic and non-negotiable.
>
> Religious liberty finally depends on neither the favors of the state and its officials nor the vagaries of tyrants or majorities. Religious liberty in a democracy is a right that may not be submitted to vote and depends on the outcome of no election. A society is only as just and free as it is respectful of this right, especially toward the beliefs of its smallest minorities and least popular communities.[86]

NOTES

1. "Lines Imagined Translated Into a Foreign Language," in Lawrence Joseph, *Before Our Eyes* (New York: Farrar, Straus, & Giroux, 1993), pp. 54–55. Used with permission of the author.

2. See John Howard Yoder, *The Politics of Jesus: Vicit Agnus Noster* (Grand Rapids, Mich.: Eerdmans, 1972).

3. In the words of the Williamsburg Charter, a bicentennial document celebrating religious liberty: "Arguments for public policy should be more than private convictions shouted out loud. For persuasion to be principled, private convictions should be translated into publicly accessible claims. Such public claims should be made publicly accessible for two reasons: first, because they must engage those who do not share the same private convictions, and second, because they should be directed toward the common good." "The Williamsburg Charter," *The Journal of Law and Religion* 8 (1990): 21.

4. See, e.g., Paul Ramsey, *War and the Christian Conscience: How Shall Modern War Be Conducted Justly?* (Durham, N.C.: Duke University Press, 1961); idem, *The Just War: Force and Political Responsibility* (New York: Charles Scribner's Sons, 1968); Ralph Potter, *War and Moral Discourse* (Richmond: John Knox Press, 1969); James Turner Johnson, *Ideology, Reason and the Limitation of War: Religious and Secular Concepts, 1200–1740* (Princeton, N.J.: Princeton University Press, 1975); Michael Walzer, *Just and Unjust Wars: A Moral Argument with Historical Illustrations* (New York: Basic Books, 1977); James Childress, "Just War Theories: The Bases, Interrelations, Priorities and Functions of their Criteria," *Theological Studies* 39 (1978): 427–45; James Turner Johnson, *The Just War Tradition and the Restraint of War* (Princeton, N.J.: Princeton University Press, 1981); and George Weigel, *Tranquilitas Ordinis: The Present Failure and Future Promise of American Catholic Thought on War and Peace* (New York: Oxford University Press, 1987).

5. I thus reject the view of Professor Bruce Ackerman that "No reason is a good reason if it requires the power holder to assert: (a) that his conception of the good is better than that asserted by any of his fellow citizens, *or* (b) that, regardless of his conception of the good, he is intrinsically superior to one or more or his fellow citizens." *Social Justice in the Liberal State* (New Haven: Yale University Press, 1980), p. 11. For refutations of Ackerman's view of "neutrality," see Michael John Perry, *Morality, Politics, and Law: A Bicentennial Essay* (New York: Oxford University Press, 1989); Perry, *Love and Power: The Role of Religion and Morality* (New York: Oxford University Press, 1991); and my essay, "Politics Without Brackets on Religious Convictions: Michael Perry and Bruce Ackerman on Neutrality," *Tulane Law Review* 64 (May 1990): 1143. In a letter to me dated Nov. 30, 1992, John Howard Yoder writes: "The argument of those who think that their frames of reference are 'public' or 'rational' or 'reasonable' are not less particular than those who confess an identifiable faith community loyalty."

6. In the letter cited in note 5 above, Yoder notes that there are two kinds of just war rhetoric: (1) a position with teeth: "if a war does not meet the criteria, you don't fight," and (2) a position that in effect means that "the criteria are never firm enough to say no to a real war; they provide a language for the debate but not a commitment to govern moral accountability." For a rare example of a religious community using the criteria of the just war to criticize the behavior of its own country at war, see "Resolution in Southeast Asia" in *Quest for Justice: A Compendium of Statements of the United States Catholic Bishops on the Political and Social Order*, ed. J. Brian Benestad and Francis J. Butler (Washington, D.C.: United States Catholic Conference, 1981), pp. 77–

79. See also letter of Cardinal Roger M. Mahony, chairman of the U.S. Catholic Conference International Policy Committee, to Secretary of State James A. Baker, urging the United States "in continued cooperation with the United Nations, the Soviet Union, Arab states, and other nations [to] stay the course of persistent, peaceful and determined pressure against Iraq. A resort to war in violation of these [just war] criteria would jeopardize many lives, raise serious moral questions and undermine the international solidarity against Iraq." Roger Mahony, "Just War Criteria and the Crisis in the Persian Gulf," *The New Oxford Review* 58 (Jan.–Feb. 1991): 7–8.

7. For example, Mk 8:34–37, 10:32–45; Mt 5:38–42; Lk 22:49–51; Jn 13:34, 14:27. See, e.g., Richard J. Cassidy, *Jesus, Politics and Society: A Study of Luke's Gospel* (Maryknoll, N.Y.: Orbis Press, 1978), pp. 40–47, 80–83; Oscar Cullmann, *Jesus and the Revolutionaries* (New York: Harper & Row, 1970); and Yoder, *The Politics of Jesus*.

8. For example, Acts 8:32ff.

9. For studies on these issues within Judaism, see, e.g., David M. Dakin, *Peace and Brotherhood in the Old Testament* (London: Bannisdale Press, 1956); Richard G. Hirsch, *Thy Most Precious Gift: Peace in the Jewish Tradition* (New York: Union of American Hebrew Congregations, 1974); and John Ferguson, *War and Peace in the World's Religions* (New York: Oxford University Press, 1978), pp. 78–98. For studies on these issues within Islam, see, e.g., S.A. Hague, *Islam's Contribution to the Peace of the World* (Lahore: Anjuman, 1932); Majid Khadduri, *War and Peace in the Law of Islam* (Baltimore: Johns Hopkins University Press, 1955); and Ferguson, *War and Peace in the World's Religions*, pp. 124–37.

10. Marcion was an influential early-second-century shipping magnate who opposed the inclusion of the Hebrew Scriptures in the canon of the Christian church and who denied the true humanity of Jesus. See Karl Baus, *From the Apostolic Community to Constantine* (New York: Herder & Herder, 1965), pp. 190–92.

11. See, e.g., Samuel Sandmel, *We Jews and Jesus* (New York: Oxford University Press, 1965); Robert Aron, *The Jewish Jesus* (Maryknoll, N.Y.: Orbis Press, 1971); Geza Vermes, *Jesus the Jew: A Historian's Reading of the Gospels* (London: Collins, 1973); Markus Barth, *Jesus the Jew* (Atlanta: John Knox Press, 1978); Samuel Sandmel, *Judaism and Christian Beginnings* (New York: Oxford University Press, 1978); Pinchas Lapide, *Israelis, Jews and Jesus* (Garden City, N.Y.: Doubleday, 1979); Eugene B. Borowitz, *Contemporary Christologies: A Jewish Response* (New York: Paulist Press, 1980); Pinchas Lapide, *The Resurrection of Jesus: A Jewish Perspective* (Minneapolis: Augsburg Press, 1983); Karl Rahner and Pinchas Lapide, *Encountering Jesus—Encountering Judaism: A Dialogue* (New York: Crossroad Press, 1987); John Dominic Crossan, *The Historical Jesus: The Life of a Mediterranean Jewish Peasant* (San Francisco: Harper, 1991); and John Meier, *A Marginal Jew: Rethinking the Historical Jesus* (Garden City, N.Y.: Doubleday, 1991).

12. See "Religious Freedom in America: Reflections by Muslims and Roman Catholics," joint statement prepared in 1989 by the Archdiocese of Los Angeles and the Islamic Center of Southern California under the auspices

of the Office of Ecumenical and Religious Affairs of the Archdiocese of Los Angeles, *Journal of Law and Religion* 8 (1990): 319–29.

13. In a letter to me dated Nov. 28, 1992, Doug Laycock reminded me that evidence of latent American imperial designs can be found as early as the War of 1812, when at least one eye was cocked on Canada. He also mentioned the Mexican-American War fought over the annexation of Texas, the squabble with Canada over the international boundary in the Northwest ("Fifty-four forty or fight"), and the doctrine of Manifest Destiny that fueled the wars against Native Americans and the annexation of their lands. Sometimes the expansion of the American empire was achieved through purchase rather than by military conquest (e.g., Jefferson's purchase of the Louisiana territory from France, Lincoln's purchase of Alaska from Russia).

14. Theodore Roosevelt, *The Rough Riders* (New York: Scribner, 1899). Finley Peter Dunne's famous Chicago bartender, Mr. Dooley, spoofed Teddy Roosevelt's braggadocio about his own involvement in the Spanish-American War. In his review of Roosevelt's *The Rough Riders*, Dunne wrote: " 'Tis 'Th' Biography iv a Hero be Wan who Knows.' 'Tis 'Th' Daring Exploits iv a Brave Man be an Actual Eye Witness.' 'Tis 'Th' Account iv th' Desthruction iv Spanish Power in th' Ant Hills,' as it fell fr'm th' lips iv Tiddy Rosenfelt an' was took down be his own hands." Finley Peter Dunne, *Mr. Dooley's Philosophy* (New York: R. H. Russell, 1900), reprinted in Robert Hutchinson, ed., *Mr. Dooley on Ivrything and Ivrybody* (New York: Dover Publications, 1963), p. 104.

15. After declaring during the campaign of 1916 that America would not enter World War I, President Woodrow Wilson sought a declaration of war from Congress less than a month after his second inaugural. Congress enacted this declaration by a vote of 82-6, with 8 abstentions in the Senate, 55 *Cong. Rec.* 261 (Apr. 4, 1917), and by a vote of 373-50, with 9 abstentions in the House, 55 *Cong. Rec.* 412 (Apr. 5, 1917). Jeanette Rankin was the only member of Congress to vote against both world wars in this century; she sought recognition from the Speaker to be heard on this matter, but was ruled out of order on the ground that "a roll call may not be interrupted." The declaration of war against the Imperial Government of Japan carried by a vote of 388-1, with 41 abstentions (several members were on their way to Washington when the vote was taken) 87 *Cong. Rec.* 9537 (Dec. 8, 1941). By contrast, the congressional resolution authorizing American participation in the Gulf War was much closer — 250-183 in the House, 137 *Cong. Rec.* H443 (daily ed. Jan. 12, 1991) and 52-47 in the Senate, 137 *Cong. Rec.* S403 (daily ed. Jan. 12, 1991)—and was preceded by far more extensive and deliberative debate. See, *e.g.*, 137 *Cong. Rec.* S100-76, S183-254, S259-99, S302-15, and S323-404 (daily ed. Jan. 10-12, 1991). The few pacifists who opposed American participation in World War I war were dealt with very harshly by the Wilson administration. See Peter Brock, *Pacifism in the United States, From the Colonial Era to the First World War* (Princeton: Princeton University Press, 1968).

16. U.S. Const. art. II, sec. 2.

17. President William Howard Taft initiated what may be called the managerial style of presidency. Before long the manager had become an

emperor; see Arthur M. Schlesinger, Jr., *The Imperial Presidency* (Boston: Houghton Mifflin, 1973).

18. In a series of cases designed to test the constitutionality of the Vietnam War, the Supreme Court declined to rule on these challenges, leaving the resolution of the matter to the political branches. See, *e.g.*, *Massachusetts v. Laird*, 400 U.S. 886 (1970) (attempt by Commonwealth to bring an original action in the Supreme Court to prevent its citizens from being sent to a foreign, undeclared war); *Velvel v. Johnson*, 287 F. Supp. 846 (D. Kan. 1968), *aff'd sub nom. Velvel v. Nixon*, 415 F. 2d 236 (10th Cir. 1969), *cert. denied*, 396 U.S. 1042 (1970) (private citizen lacks standing to sue the President; resolution of the war a "political question"); *Luftig v. McNamara*, 252 F. Supp. 819 (D.D.C. 1966), *aff'd*, 373 F. 2d 862 (D.C. Cir. 1967), *cert. denied*, 389 U.S. 945 (1968) (suit by serviceman being sent to Vietnam is a "political question"); *Mora v. McNamara*, 387 F. 2d 862 (D.C. Cir. 1967) *cert. denied*, 394 U.S. 960 (1969) (same); *McArthur v. Clifford*, 393 U.S. 1002 (1968); *Holmes v. United States*, 391 U.S. 936 (1968); and *United States v. Mitchell*, 369 F. 2d 323, *cert. denied*, 386 U.S. 972 (1967) (defense by draftee refusing to submit to induction). In August of 1973, towards the very end of the official involvement in the Vietnam War, Justice Marshall denied a request by a member of Congress for an injunction against the bombing of Cambodia, *Holtzman v. Schlesinger*, 414 U.S. 1304 (1973) (Marshall, Circuit Justice); on the view that the loss of life at issue in the case was akin to a death penalty case, in which a stay would normally issue to preserve the ability of the Court to address the issue presented to it, Justice Douglas, who had dissented from the denial of certiorari in *Mora v. McNamara* in 1969, then granted Holtzman's request for a stay, 414 U.S. 1316 (1973) (Douglas, Circuit Justice); several hours later Justice Marshall conducted a telephone poll of the other Justices, who ordered the injunction to be lifted, 414 U.S. 1321 (1973) (Marshall, Circuit Justice). Professor Tribe expresses the very tentative view that it is "by no means clear that federal courts should have refrained from addressing [the] issue" of the legality or constitutionality of the Vietnam War. Laurence H. Tribe, *American Constitutional Law* (Mineola, N.Y.: Foundation Press, 1988) 231, n. 5.

19. The War Powers Resolution, 87 Stat. 555, 50 U.S.C. §§ 1541-48; for a thoughtful discussion of this legislation, see John Hart Ely, *War and Responsibility: Constitutional Lessons of Vietnam and its Aftermath* (Princeton: Princeton University Press, 1993). For the view that the legislation is an unconstitutional delegation of congressional authority, see Allan F. Ides, "Congress, Constitutional Responsibility and the War Power," Loyola of Los Angeles Law Review 17 (1984): 599-655.

20. *Selective Draft Law Cases*, 245 U.S. 366 (1918).

21. See *Schenck v. United States*, 249 U.S. 47 (1919) (sustaining convictions under the Espionage Act of June 15, 1917, for distribution of a leaflet urging men who had been called and accepted for military service to view their conscription as "despotism in its worst form and a monstrous wrong against humanity in the interest of Wall Street's chosen few"); *Frohwerk v. United States*, 249 U.S. 204 (1919) (sustaining conviction for printing a newspaper, the *Missouri Staats Zeitung*, that included articles "declaring it a monumental

and inexcusable mistake to send our soldiers to France" and "speaking of the unconquerable spirit and undiminished strength of the German people"); *Debs v. United States*, 249 U.S. 211 (1919) (sustaining conviction of the presidential candidate of the Socialist Party for a campaign speech in which he said, "you need to know that you are fit for something better than slavery and cannon fodder"); *Abrams v. United States*, 250 U.S. 616 (1919) (sustaining conviction under the 1918 amendment to the Espionage Act that punished any urging of "curtailment of production of materials necessary to the prosecution of war against Germany").

22. See, *e.g.*, Christopher N. May, *In the Name of War: Judicial Review and the War Powers Since 1918* (Cambridge: Harvard University Press, 1989), 85, 184-86.

23. See Eugene Rostow, "The Japanese American Cases: A Disaster," *Yale Law Journal* 54 (June 1945): 489–533; Jacobus tenBroek, Edward N. Barnhart, and Floyd W. Matson, *Prejudice, War and the Constitution* (Berkeley: University of California Press, 1954); and Peter Irons, *Justice at War: The Story of the Japanese Internment Cases* (New York: Oxford University Press, 1983). For accounts of arson and racially motivated violence against Japanese-Americans, see *New York Times*, 11 Jan. 1945, A4; 21 Jan. 1945, A4.

24. In the letter cited in note 5 above, Yoder writes: "It is not the case, as Michael Walzer might let people think, that the step over the line to city bombing by Harris and Churchill, with Temple's support, was made reluctantly, or only occasionally, or in a supreme emergency. It was a formally stated policy, and in fact was the reason given for the fact that there were no planes available to bomb the rail lines to Auschwitz. Eisenhower even had great difficulty getting planes for Normandy." See Walzer, *Just and Unjust Wars*, pp. 255–61, 323–26. For a rare contemporary critique of the Allied policy of bombing civilian targets, see John Ford, "The Morality of Obliteration Bombing," *Theological Studies* 5 (1944): 261–309. Two years earlier Dorothy Day had written in a similar vein: "Love is not the starving of whole populations. Love is not the bombardment of open cities," in "We Cannot Keep Silent," *Catholic Worker* (Feb. 1942), as cited in *Catholic Agitator* 22 (April 1991): 2.

25. The fiftieth anniversary of the bombing of Hiroshima and Nagasaki was marked by several new historical studies probing the decision by President Truman to drop the atom bombs on these cities. In *The Decision to Use the Atomic Bomb and the Architecture of an American Myth* (New York: Knopf, 1995) Gar Alperovitz cites leading military authorities opposed to the use of the atomic bomb. For example, General Eisenhower voiced to Secretary of War Henry L. Stimson his "grave misgivings, first on the basis of my belief that Japan was already defeated and that dropping the bomb was completely unnecessary, and secondly because I thought that our country should avoid shocking world opinion by the use of a weapon whose employment was, I thought, no longer mandatory as a measure to save American lives." As cited id., 4. Similarly, Admiral William D. Leahy, who served both as the chairman of the Joint Chiefs of Staff in the War Department and as the chief of staff to Presidents Roosevelt and Truman in their capacity as commander-in-chief of the army and navy from 1942 to 1949, stated: "It is my opinion that the use of this barbarous weapon at Hiroshima and Nagasaki was of no material assistance in our war against Japan. The Japanese were already defeated and ready to surrender. . . . My own feeling was that in being the first to use it, we had adopted an ethical standard common to the barbarians of the Dark Ages. I was not taught to make war in that fashion, and wars cannot be won by destroying women and children." Id., 3. Truman defended his decision as necessary to saving American lives. On August 9, 1945 Truman wrote to the men and women of the Manhattan Project: "A grateful nation, hopeful that this new weapon will result in the saving of *thousands* of American lives, feels a deep sense of appreciation for your accomplishment." Id., 515 (emphasis added). That estimate corresponds to the contemporaneous military estimate that avoiding a full invasion of Japan in 1946 might save as many as 46,000 lives. By December 15, 1945, Truman stated: "It occurred to me that a *quarter of a million* of the flower of our young manhood was worth a couple of Japanese cities, and I still think they were and are." Id., 516 (emphasis added). Truman continually revised his estimate upwards. On April 28, 1959, he told students at Columbia University that "the dropping of the bombs stopped the war, saved *millions* of lives." Id., 517 (emphasis added). By definition the end of a war saves lives. Whatever the number of American lives that were saved by the swift end of World War II, the official explanation of the American policy to use nuclear weapons does not answer the objections of Eisenhower and Leahy that this decision was not necessary from a military point of view. See also Robert Jay Lifton and Greg Mitchell, *Hiroshima in America: Fifty Years of Denial* (New York: Putnam, 1995). For a theological reflection on the Hiroshima bombing, see Jim Harrison, *The Darkness of God: Theology after Hiroshima* (Grand Rapids, Mich.: Eerdmans, 1983); see also Peter Wyden, *Day One: Before Hiroshima and After* (New York: Simon and Shuster, 1984). Dorothy Day's lead essay in *The Catholic Worker* for September of 1945 remains one of the most powerful religious condemnations of the violation of the principle of noncombatant immunity: "Mr. Truman was jubilant. President Truman. True man. What a strange name, come to think of it. We refer to Jesus Christ as true God and true Man. Truman is a true man of his time in that he was jubilant. He was not a son of God, brother of Christ, brother of the Japanese, jubilating as he did. He went from table to table on the cruiser which was bringing him home from the Big Three conference, telling the great news, "jubilant," the newspapers said. *Jubilate Deo*. We have killed 318,000 Japanese. That is, we hope that we have killed them, the Associated Press, page one, column one of *The Herald Tribune* says. The effect is hoped for, not known. It is to be hoped they are vaporized, our Japanese brothers, scattered men, women, and babies, to the four winds, over the seven seas. Perhaps we will breathe their dust into our nostrils, feel them in the fog of New York on our faces, feel them in the rain on the hills of Easton." As cited in *The Catholic Worker*, vol. 62, no. 5 (Aug-Sept. 1995), p. 1.

26. The painful discovery of this truth by a British operative is narrated in a poignant tale in John LeCarré's, *The Secret Pilgrim* (New York: Knopf,

1991), pp. 209–45. "[M]odern comforts are few [in the Cambodian jungle], unless we include the American bombers that circle above . . . like patient hawks, waiting for computers to tell them what to destroy next: For instance, a team of oxen whose urine has been misread as the exhaust fumes of a military convoy; for instance, children whose chatter has been mistaken for military commands." Id. at 224. For a more technical account of the violations of *jus in bello* principles, see Richard Falk, *The Vietnam War and International Law* (Princeton, N.J.: Princeton University Press, 1968); and see Telford Taylor, *Nuremberg and Vietnam: An American Tragedy* (Chicago: Quadrangle Books, 1970); Taylor was the U.S. Chief Counsel at Nuremberg.

   27. Worthington Ford, ed., *Journals of the Continental Congress, 1775* (Washington, D.C.: Government Printing Office, 1904–37), 2: 189. The basic narrative of the law in this section of the paper is contained in *Toward Benevolent Neutrality: Church, State, and the Supreme Court*, ed. Robert Miller and Ronald Flowers (Waco, Tex.: Baylor University Press, 3d ed. 1987), pp. 104–09. For a more comprehensive treatment of the theme, see Ralph Potter, "Conscientious Objection to Particular Wars," in *Religion and the Public Order*, ed. Donald Giannella (Ithaca: Cornell University Press, 1968), pp. 44–99.

   28. *The Debates and Proceedings in the Congress of the United States*, ed. Joseph Gales (Washington, D.C.: Gales & Seaton, 1834), 1: 451.

   29. *The Statutes at Large, Treaties, and Proclamations of the United States of America from December 1863 to December 1865*, ed. George P. Sanger (Boston: Little, Brown and Company, 1866), 38th Cong., 1st sess., 1864, sec. 17, p. 9.

   30. Selective Draft Act, 40 Stat. 76, 78 (1917). In the election year of 1916, Woodrow Wilson knew it would be more astute not to urge the country to go to war; instead he promised not to send American boys to "distant lands to die of foreign fevers and foreign shot and shell," as Justice Black was later to describe the Vietnam War. Shortly after his inauguration in 1917, however, Wilson urged Congress to declare war against Germany and its allies in order "to make the world safe for democracy." See *The Papers of Woodrow Wilson*, ed. Arthur S. Link (Princeton, N.J.: Princeton University Press 1966–   ) 41: 525.

   31. *United States v. Stephens*, 245 F. 956 (D. Del. 1917).

   32. *Arver v. United States [Selective Draft Cases]*, 245 U.S. 366, 389 (1918).

   33. *United States v. Schwimmer*, 279 U.S. 644 (1929).

   34. Id. at 655 (Holmes, J., dissenting).

   35. In a letter to me in December 1992, Dale Lasky notes that some (e.g., Langdon Gilkey, who resolved in 1940 never to fight in another war) soon found themselves on the war front out of conviction, while others (e.g., Reinhold Niebuhr, who participated in founding the Fellowship of Reconciliation in the 1920s) gradually came to the conviction in the late 1930s that Hitler would not be undone by pacifism; see Niebuhr, "Why the Christian Church is Not Pacifist" (1940), reprinted in Robert McAfee Brown, ed., *The Essential Reinhold Niebuhr: Selected Essays and Addresses* (New Haven: Yale University Press, 1986), pp. 102–119.

   36. David S. Wyman, *The Abandonment of the Jews* (New York: Pantheon Books, 1984).

37. See, for example, testimony of Roswell Barnes, Associate General Secretary of the Federal Council of Churches, before the House Committee on Military Affairs, cited in Potter, "Conscientious Objection to Particular Wars," p. 48, n. 16.

38. See, for example, testimony of Abraham Kaufman, Executive Secretary of the War Resisters League, id.

39. Universal Military Training and Service Act, 62 Stat. 612 (1948).

40. *United States v. Seeger*, 380 U.S. 163 (1965).

41. Selective Service Act of 1948, 62 Stat. 604, 613 (1948).

42. *United States v. Seeger*, at 166.

43. See Chester Antieau, Arthur Downey, and Edward Roberts, *Freedom from Federal Establishment: Formation and Early History of the First Amendment Religion Clauses* (Milwaukee: Bruce Publishing, 1964); Thomas Curry, *The First Freedoms: Church and State in America to the Passage of the First Amendment* (New York: Oxford University Press, 1986).

44. *Larson v. Valente*, 456 U.S. 228 (1982); see also *Employment Division v. Smith*, 494 U.S. 872 (1990) (ruling that singling out religion for disparate regulation violates the free exercise principle).

45. Military Selective Service Act of 1967, 81 Stat. 100, 104 (1967).

46. *United States v. Sisson*, 297 F. Supp. 902, 906 (D. Mass. 1969).

47. Ibid. at 911.

48. 398 U.S. 333 (1970).

49. Ibid. at 344.

50. *Negre v. Larsen*, 401 U.S. 437 (1971), decided sub nom. *Gillette v. United States*.

51. "Pastoral Constitution on the Church in the Modern World," art. 80, in Walter Abbott and Joseph Gallagher, eds., *The Documents of Vatican II* (New York: Herder & Herder, 1966), 294; see René Coste's commentary on this text in Herbert Vorgrimler, ed., *Commentary on the Documents of Vatican II* (New York: Herder & Herder, 1969), 5:356–58.

52. Noonan is now a circuit judge who was commissioned to serve on the Court of Appeals for the Ninth Circuit by President Reagan.

53. *Negre*, note 50 above, at 455–56.

54. *Police Dept. of City of Chicago v. Mosley*, 408 U.S. 92 (1972).

55. 374 U.S. 398 (1963).

56. *Johnson v. Robinson*, 415 U.S. 361 (1974).

57. 494 U.S. 872 (1990). Congress responded to the *Smith* case by enacting the Religious Freedom Restoration Act, 42 U.S.C. Sec. 2000bb et seq., which created a statutory right to the same standards governing free exercise of religion that the Court had recognized in *Sherbert* and had abandoned in *Smith*.

58. See Os Guinness and John Seel, eds., *No God But God: Breaking with the Idols of Our Age* (Chicago: Moody Press, 1992).

59. Letter cited above in note 5.

60. "The right to freedom of conscience . . . is the foundation of, and is integrally related to, all other rights and freedoms secured by the Constitution. This basic civil liberty is clearly acknowledged in the Declaration of

Independence and is ineradicable from the long tradition of rights and liberties from which the Revolution sprang." "The Williamsburg Charter," 8 cited above in note 3.

61. For a comprehensive effort to locate this tradition within Roman Catholic teaching, see Weigel, *Tranquilitas Ordinis.*

62. Article 16 of the Augsburg Confession (1530) provides that a Christian may wage war justly (*jure bellare*). For a commentary on this article of the Confession, see George Wolfgang Forell and James F. McCue, "Political Order and Vocation in the Augsburg Confession," in *Confessing One Faith: A Joint Commentary on the Augsburg Confession by Lutheran and Catholic Theologians,* ed. Forell and McCue (Minneapolis: Augsburg Press, 1982), pp. 322–33.

63. In Mennonite terminology, it is counted as one of the seven "ordinances of the true church" that its members suffer persecution for the sake of truth and righteousness, but exercise no dominion over the consciences of others with sword or force or violence. See *Spiritual and Anabaptist Writers,* ed. George Williams and Angel Mergal (Philadelphia: Westminster Press, 1962), pp. 251–54.

64. Lk 18:9–14.

65. In the letter cited in note 35 above, Lasky reminds me that Reinhold Niebuhr's distinction between equality of sin and inequality of guilt is pertinent here. See Niebuhr, *The Nature and Destiny of Man* (New York: Charles Scribner's Sons, 1949), pp. 219–27.

66. 1 Sm 8.

67. Although it is generally agreed that Persian imperial policy was more benign than that of their predecessors, their fiscal policy with respect to their provinces was every bit as onerous. See John M. Cook, *The Persian Empire* (London: Dent, 1983), pp. 78–79; Richard N. Frye, *The History of Ancient Iran* (Munich: C. H. Beck, 1984), pp. 116–18. For a popular commentary on the biblical literature of this period, see Peter R. Ackroyd, *Israel under Babylon and Persia* (Oxford: Oxford University Press, 1970).

68. Is 42:1–4; 44:28; 45:1; 44:24–28. For a thoughtful commentary on these passages, see Claus Westermann, *Isaiah 40–66: A Commentary* (Philadelphia: Westminster Press, 1969).

69. See Joseph Blenkinsopp, *Ezra-Nehemiah: A Commentary* (Philadelphia: Westminster Press, 1988).

70. Rom 13 and Rv 13. In the letter cited in note 5 above, Yoder writes: "One point where I do not follow . . . Barth and Cullmann and others is in playing Rom 13 and Rv 13 off against each other, as if a given government could be assigned to either of two compartments. If Romans we obey, if Revelation we disobey. Both are true at the same time; at the same time it is idolatrous and it claims to keep the peace. This is true generally, and it is true when the apostles were writing. We are not supposed to categorize or credential good governments." See Karl Barth, *Rechtfertigung und Recht* (Zürich: Evangelischen Buchhandlung, 1938); and Oscar Cullmann, *The State in the New Testament* (New York: Scribner, 1956), pp. 50–85.

71. See, e.g., Walter Brueggemann, *The Prophetic Imagination* (Philadelphia: Fortress Press, 1978), pp. 44–79.

72. Am 1–2; Is 13–23; Jer 46–51; Ez 25–32. In a letter to me in December of 1992, Walt Rast notes that "the language in many of these oracles is so similar that one could conclude that there was a prophetic consensus against imperial power and their use of coercive force."

73. Is 40:19f, 41:6f, 42:17, 44:9–20, 45:16f, 46:1f, 46:5f.

74. Is 44:9–20; 47:1–15. The imperial deity of the Assyrians was Ashur. For an insightful comment on idolatry in the ancient world, see Christopher R. North, "The Essence of Idolatry," in *Von Ugarit nach Qumran: Beiträge zur alttestamentlichen und altorientalischen Forschung [Festchrift für Otto Eissfeldt]*, ed. Johannes Hempel, Leonhard Rost, and William Foxwell Albright (Berlin: A. Töpelmann, 1958), pp. 151–60.

75. Gn 11:1–9. See Joseph Blenkinsopp, *The Pentateuch: An Introduction to the First Five Books of the Bible* (New York: Doubleday, 1992), p. 91 (dating the text in the exilic period). Fred Niedner agrees that, even if this text is not exilic in origin, it certainly reflects a spoof on empire-building.

76. Ps 115:5–7.

77. E.g., Ex 20:3.

78. 1 Cor 12:3; Phil 2:11.

79. See Tertullian, *On Idolatry*, chap. 19, as cited in Adolph Harnack, *Militia Christi: The Christian Religion and the Military in the First Three Centuries* (Philadelphia: Fortress Press, 1981), pp. 54, 76; and see Roland H. Bainton, *Christian Attitudes Toward War and Peace: A Historical Survey and Critical Reevaluation* (Nashville: Abingdon Press, 1960).

80. Ps 46:9.

81. Ps 31:3.

82. Ps 118:8–9.

83. Ps 20:7, 33:17, 147:10.

84. Ps 44:6.

85. Ps 118:8–9.

86. "The Williamsburg Charter," 7–8 (cited in note 3 above).

Toward a Common Heritage

J. PATOUT BURNS

During the discussions at the Washington University Conference on Pacifism and Quietism in February 1993, the presenters, commentators, and other invited participants engaged one another on the basis of the papers that had been presented on campus during the previous year and that were then distributed in advance of the meeting. A few months later, at the United States Institute of Peace consultation in July 1993, many of the same experts engaged these issues once again. As in other such discussions, moments of insight and mutual understanding were separated by digressions or inquiries that proved fruitless. More suggestions were made than could be explored. The following analysis attempts to report the first, eliminate the second, and pursue some of the third. The editor, and in this case author, draws together suggestions and observations made by many. Unlike the other participants, he alone has had the advantage of reviewing all the contributions in revised form and of drawing out the implications of the views expressed in the conferences. Thus he alone takes responsibility for the final form in which their views and suggestions are here presented.

I will begin with a review of each of the contributions and attempt to summarize the position of each of the religious and legal traditions. I will then try to evaluate each from the viewpoint of the others and to determine points of agreement and conflict. Finally, I identify eight issues that emerge from the discussions as crucial points of contention or opportunities for agreement.

The order of consideration here is different from the order of presentation of the papers. Because the Christian contributors present a clearly articulated challenge to embrace pacifism, that viewpoint will be considered first. Then the Islamic position, which enjoins quietism under certain circumstances, will be reviewed. Finally, the Jewish stance, which rejects pacifism but may allow quietism, will be examined.

CHRISTIAN CONTRIBUTION

John Howard Yoder bases an argument for Christian, and indeed Jewish, pacifism on a discernment of divine purpose in the history

200

of Israel and the Christian church. At the time of the conquest of Judea by the Babylonians at the beginning of the sixth century B.C.E., the prophet Jeremiah delivered the instruction that the Jews were to go and live among the nations—they were not to seek sovereignty again. Subsequent attempts to regain and maintain nationhood failed because God did not grant lasting victory over the power of Rome to the Maccabees, the Zealots, or finally Bar Kochba. Instead, Judaism survived and prospered in a Diaspora culture characterized by Torah observance, the synagogue, and the rabbinate but not by national sovereignty. Thus Yoder would argue that rabbinic attempts to construct a religious law for warfare are anachronistic: Such systems either address a dispensation that is no longer divinely sanctioned or attempt to anticipate the Messiah's future reign of justice and peace.

Jesus, Yoder argues, affirmed the divine dispensation under which Israel lived during his ministry; he refused to lead a struggle for national liberation and taught his followers not to seek an earthly kingdom. Within the first two generations, Christians realized that only the return of the Messiah would inaugurate a government of divine justice and peace on earth. They refused to participate in the revolts against Rome and distanced themselves from the Jewish efforts to reestablish a nation. Instead, they affirmed divine control over the processes of human history; they strove to follow the teaching and example of Jesus, which were based on love of one's neighbor, and therefore renounced the power of violent coercion—in particular, killing or threatening to kill—typical of rule over persons who do not voluntarily assent to the governors' values and sanctions.

Furthermore, Yoder's historical analysis indicates that subsequent Christian attempts to acquire and exercise state sovereignty have generally resulted in both compromise with the exigencies of power politics and infidelity to the example and teaching of Jesus. He shows, however, that on certain occasions Christians have accepted and fulfilled the duty of governing according to their pacifist principles. Thus he calls not for a renunciation of all social power but for its exercise according to the standards of the Gospel.

This Christian pacifism, therefore, is based on the affirmation that God controls the historical process even through unwitting human agency and that the divine purpose does not require that either Jews or Christians wield the power of the state in order to mold human society into the divinely ordained social order. Instead, Christians are called to follow the way of life established in the teaching and example of Jesus. In new situations, they attempt to discern the proper course of action under the continuing guidance of the Holy Spirit in their churches. Reflecting on the life, death, and resurrection of Jesus, they affirm that God's ways surpass human understanding, that the calculation of probable outcomes and consequences can never become the Christian method of making moral decisions. Instead, they commit themselves to follow faithfully the divine commands and guidance; they trust in providential control of the outcome.

Judaism of the Diaspora rather than the Davidic Kingdom provides Yoder's model for Christian existence. He criticizes the Constantinian revolution because it made empire a privileged vehicle of divine purpose and sacrificed the Christian way of life in order to exercise and maintain imperial power. True Christians, however, will usually expect to live as a minority group in a society that does not accept their radical faith; they may serve and influence the larger culture in ways that are compatible with their commitment to the way of Jesus. They may even, when called upon, take up the reins of government, but they may not violate the teaching and example of Jesus in order to exercise that state power effectively. In particular, they must not violate Jesus' command to love one's neighbor in order to protect their persons, communities, or property from harm. Because their lives are under God's providential governance, such resistance to evil might work against a divine action that would correct and edify the community. Their suffering of oppression and even martyrdom, moreover, will make a positive contribution to the historical process, which a violent response could not.

As John Howard Yoder attacks the principle that the nation or empire is a privileged actor in human history, Walter Wink questions the myth of redemptive violence: the belief that violence can overcome evil and inaugurate a reign of justice and peace. In place of coercive force as a means of opposing evil, he explains, Jesus taught and practiced a form of resistance that effectively unmasks the presumptions of violence and can even liberate both oppressed and oppressor from its power. Jesus did not preach passivity in the face of oppression; instead, he exercised a form of resistance that does not mirror and multiply the evils of coercive violence.

Walter Wink extends his analysis by suggesting a transformation of the Christian justifiable war doctrine so that it does not offer an escape from the demands of the teaching and example of Jesus. Focusing the criteria of moral judgment on the reduction rather than the justification of violence, he argues, would create a new Christian discourse in which pacifists would be called upon to exercise creativity in opposing violence and ethicists to cease accommodating Christian standards to the demands of imperial politics.

John Langan's response is directed to John Howard Yoder's historical analysis. The Constantinian theology that made the power of empire a privileged vehicle of divine purpose in history has, he asserts, been gradually discarded as a consequence of the Enlightenment. Christianity is no longer called upon to provide justification and sanctification for the exercise of military power by the modern secular state. Democratic capitalism, moreover, has resulted in the dispersal of the various forms of coercive power that were once concentrated in a sovereign ruler and backed by military might. Even in a minority status, therefore, Christians must exercise many forms of power that put them "in charge," albeit in a limited way. Through the rise of democratic capitalism, Langan argues, Jews and Christians have been granted real, though limited, state sovereignty. Thus in modern society, the exercise of coercive force is unavoidable. He questions, moveover, the distinction between warfare and other more subtle but effective forms of violence.

Yoder's consideration of military power and state sovereignty, Langan contends, has been too narrowly conceived. Instead, he calls for a broader analysis that does not separate the use of violence from other methods of social control and coercion. Such an analysis, he seems to believe, would result in a more general understanding of the Christian application of power that would be closer to the justifiable war doctrine than to the pacifist renunciation of coercion.

ISLAMIC CONTRIBUTION

Like the other Abrahamic faiths, Islam affirms the revelation of divine standards for a just social order. It also obliges its adherents to strive for the realization of that order in their lives, their communities, and the world as a whole. Unlike the form of Christianity represented by Yoder and Wink, however, Islam asserts that the use of coercive force may be necessary and appropriate for carrying out this divine mandate. Thus, according to Abdulaziz Sachedina's analysis, Islam excludes a principled renunciation of violence. Since war's only purpose is to

achieve the divine will, however, quietism may be justified or even required in specific circumstances, such as the absence of the necessary
divine guidance or the force required to achieve the divine will.

Sachedina undertakes a careful analysis of the various provisions
for the use of violent force found in the Qur'an. The Muslim community is clearly required to defend both its own existence and its right
to obey the divine law. As leader of the community, the Prophet was
required to repel any attack on the just social order established by
the divine law. Historically, this involved control over the Peoples of
the Book who rejected the moral code of Islam. This command might
be extended to the use of coercive power to make the cause of God
succeed in the face of other forms of hostility. Both these provisions,
however, look to the protection of the moral order, the just ordering
of society. While the Qur'an requires that force be used to protect the
social order, Sachedina argues, it does not justify coerced conversion
to Islam. Submission to God must be freely given; its refusal can be
punished only by God.

The responsibility for securing a just social order within the
Muslim community provided a basis for waging war against forces
that threatened this moral order. Victory in wars of conquest subse-
quently led jurists to expand the Qur'anic justification of war and to
abrogate the limits it had set on the use of force as a means of effecting
religious conversion. The actual success of the territorial expansion
placed the Qur'an's teaching on the use of force in a new social
setting, in which protecting the community against overt hostility and
persecution was no longer the primary concern. Instead, establishing
the divinely revealed social order throughout the world became the
justification for subduing other peoples by force of arms. Thus the
objectives of expanding the realm of submission to God and extending
the blessing of the Islamic social order to the entire world were used
to inspire Muslims to undertake offensive wars of conquest in God's
cause. The Sunni jurists, speaking for the dominant group within
the community, built this justification of violence on the Qur'an's
command to strive so that the cause of God would prevail. They
transformed warfare from a defense of true religious practice into a
means of calling the nations of the earth to submit to divine revelation.

The Shi'ite jurists, by contrast, were in a minority status and
thus were not faced with the problem of controlling and justifying
the use of power by the conquering caliphs. Accepting the role of
critics of the establishment, they insisted that offensive warfare—war

to make the cause of God prevail—required a secure understanding of the revealed will of God. Those who took up arms for other motives risked spilling innocent blood and thus falling under the divine wrath, which the Qur'an warned would be visited on aggressors in the judgment after death. Neither an unjust ruler nor an ordinary teacher could guarantee that the expansionist effort would be uncorrupted by human ignorance and perverse desires. The jurists concluded that only an imam whose knowledge of divine revelation and whose personal goodness or justice protected him from error in judging what the divine will required in a particular case could authorize an offensive war, a war to call the nations to Islam.

During these early centuries, the difference between Sunni and Shi'ite stances toward the obligation to expand the realm of submission to God by warfare reflected a disagreement over the legitimacy of political power and its relation to divine authority. This dispute took shape in contrary evaluations of the early conflicts and struggles for control within the community. The Sunni jurists, relying perhaps on an understanding of divine omnipotence, accepted the actual ruler as properly authorized by God. Every ruler of the Muslim community participated in the divine sovereignty and was thus endowed with the responsibility for determining when offensive warfare was required and for obliging the faithful to fight not only for the defense but also for the expansion of the realm of obedience to God. Their Shi'ite counterparts refused, however, to grant such authority to every ruler on the sole grounds that he had been allowed by God to secure political power. Instead, they required the directive of a truly religious leader, the authorized imam or his deputy, to guide the community's striving to achieve the divine will.

These conflicting stances toward the legitimacy of political authority led, paradoxically, to parallel condemnations of rebellion against an established regime. The Sunni jurists adopted a quietist stance toward established government as long as it recognized and protected true religious practice. Since they believed that the function of government is to secure the divinely revealed order in society, they were willing to tolerate some injustice within the community on the grounds that encouraging sedition in the name of religion would lead to even greater civil strife, disorder, and injustice. While in principle they were willing to approve rebellion against an unjust ruler, the Shi'ite jurists continued to insist that only a divinely guided imam could provide the trustworthy interpretation of God's will that would justify rebellion or warfare against an unjust ruler. Once the imam was hidden from the community, the Shi'ite faithful adopted a modified quietist stance. Their activism turned into an expectant apocalypticism that looks for the coming of the Mahdi, the religious and military leader who will guide the restoration of a pure and pristine Islam.

In interpreting the teaching of the Qur'an on the use of violence for the protection and spread of Islam, Sachedina distinguishes between the religious and moral orders. As a religious stance, both unbelief and certain forms of immorality fall under divine rather than human sanction—they are to be punished by God in the final judgment. As a refusal to submit to divine sovereignty, therefore, infidelity cannot be attacked nor can faith be spread by coercive force. When unbelief threatens the stability of the just social order, however, it becomes a moral problem and thus falls under the responsibility and coercive authority of the Islamic community and its leaders. Yet even in punishing crimes that attack both God and humans—such as illicit sexual relations, homicide, and apostasy—Islamic practice carefully restricts the application of force, especially capital punishment. The ruler is required to guarantee and regulate the satisfaction of private, rather than public, claims for retribution. The requirement of prior warning and abundant witnesses, as well as the promotion of negotiated settlement, all tend to forestall the exaction of harsh penalties. Nor does the ruler enforce the claims of God; he can only protect the stability and order of the community. No human agency can negotiate an individual's spiritual destiny; God will act on Judgment Day.

Sachedina's analysis demonstrates the ambiguity of Islam's developing stance toward the use of coercive violence. Establishing, defending, and expanding the just social order commanded by God can require the use of warfare, both within the community and against peoples who do not accept the faith when it is offered to them. In this sense, the Qur'an neither enjoins nor even permits a principled renunciation of violence. Yet this very understanding of warfare as obedience to the divine will also established strict conditions for its justification and implementation. Clearly the Prophet himself and, for the Shi'i, the just and learned imam could interpret the divine will for the community and authorize a particular rebellion or an offensive war. In the absence of such a manifest authority, however, the Shi'i were unwilling to entrust the divine power to a de facto ruler whose religious legitimacy remained ambiguous. In this Shi'ite view, therefore, the community was restricted to an expectant activism, prepared to take the offensive against enemies both foreign and domestic when the divine command was delivered by the Mahdi. In the meantime, individuals should strive to realize the divine justice in their own lives, even if they cannot establish it in society. The Sunni, in contrast, accepted the legitimacy of any actual ruler who professed to govern according to Islamic law. On this basis they justified an activist, even offensive, stance toward the non-Muslim world. Yet they adopted a quietist stance even more radical than that of the Shi'i within the Islamic community.

For the most part, this development of Islamic law looked to the situation in which the Muslim community constituted an autonomous religious polity. In subsequent centuries, however, the majority of Muslims lived under governments that neither claimed to rule according to Islamic law nor were granted religious authority by the faithful. In this new context, the obligations and responsibilities of the individual believer and the religious community were modified once again. In the absence of a religious ruler, offensive war for the expansion of the realm of submission to God was neither enjoined nor justified. The protection of social order and justice, however, might be religiously required. If a non-Muslim government established a society that allowed the practice of religion, the Muslim was not obliged to strive against it; indeed he might be required to defend it by force of arms against external enemies and internal sedition. Even when the government oppresses and persecutes the Muslim community, moreover, quietism may be adopted as a temporary measure until the force necessary to resist the injustice becomes available.

Islam makes a firm commitment to a divinely revealed social order that ought to be realized throughout the whole world. The religious order, in which infidelity is punished by divine sanctions, may be distinguished from the moral order, in which injustice falls under the human authority established by God. Although state power may not be used to force religious belief, it may and even must be exercised to enforce the moral order based on that belief. As a consequence, under proper conditions Muslims accept the obligation and responsibility to use coercive force not only to defend but to establish and extend the social order decreed by God. The obligation to undertake offensive wars for the spread of Islam has generally lapsed because of the absence of the requisite ruling authority. Even the command to defend the true social order has been suspended because of the uncertainty of the outcome of rebellion against injustice. Warfare cannot, however, be renounced in principle on the basis of the Qur²an's revelation or its juridical interpretation.

Michael Nagler's response addresses precisely those divinely imposed obligations that Abdulaziz Sachedina's presentation clearly articulates. He argues, on the basis of Gandhi's doctrine of nonviolence and Abdul Ghaffar Khan's adaptation of this theory to Islam, that an active pacifism is the more effective means of establishing the divinely mandated social order of justice and peace. Nagler accepts the Islamic commitment to defense and even extension of the rule of God's law but argues that after Gandhi's discovery of the power of nonviolence, the Qur²anic prohibition of aggression must be given greater weight. Khan's program, he asserts, demonstrates that the obstacles to activism in the quest for social justice, particularly the questions of legitimate and learned authority, do restrain the faithful from seeking justice except by a consistent application of the liberating and persuasive power of nonviolence.

In one sense, Nagler reverses the order of analysis. After distinguishing the religious from the moral order, Sachedina demonstrated that the jurists had extended the human authority operative in the moral order into the properly religious realm so that they might justify the success of coercion as a means of calling nations and peoples to submit to God's law, to Islam. Nagler suggests that Gandhian nonviolence, as developed by Abdul Ghaffar Khan, actually draws upon the religious power of the believer to address the conscience, which, Islamic teaching asserts, guides each human being to choose good and reject evil. In this way, pacifism persuades to justice and draws to faith.

JEWISH CONTRIBUTION

Michael Broyde clearly distinguishes between three different standards that might be operative for Jews in different political and religious situations. Under direct divine command, the people might be required to wage particular wars, even wars of extermination. A religiously established government acting under revealed law would be able to wage offensive as well as defensive wars, through the operation of the Sanhedrin and the consent of the people. In the absence of such a religiously authorized state and government, the revealed law restricts Jews to defensive wars and to the use of force for protecting innocent life. Jewish law would also recognize a similar right to the defensive use of force by non-Jews and thus by secular governments.

Thus Broyde explicitly addresses the situation of a Jew living in a state that does not have a religiously established government—the situation Yoder describes as prevailing since the fall of Judea in the early sixth century B.C.E. Jews and, by extension, any other citizens may be obliged to take part in defensive wars for the protection of their state when it is actually under attack, even at the risk of grave harm and loss of life. A person may also have an obligation, subject to certain conditions, to intervene for the protection of innocent life even when the entire state of which he is a citizen is not at risk. The state does not have the right, however, to impose such an obligation, to require its citizens to put their own lives and goods at risk in order to save the lives or property of other individuals or countries. In contrast, an ethnically Jewish government—even if not religiously established—could oblige its citizens to participate in a preemptive strike against a power that is threatening but not yet attacking the Jewish community.

A secular government, even in an ethnically Jewish community, may not oblige its Jewish citizens to participate in an offensive war. In the absence of the kind of religious authorization that is not currently operative, a Jew would be forbidden to act as an aggressor or to take innocent life. Even service in a defensive or protective war in which the proper limits of violence are not observed could not be compelled by any government, since the harming of the innocent may never be directly intended. Finally, in a war undertaken to protect innocent life, the application of force must be strictly limited to what is necessary to deter aggression. A Jew, and by extension a non-Jew, would be obliged to refrain from participating in wars that violate these standards.

The laws of warfare developed in rabbinic writings do not provide a theoretical basis for the renunciation of force. Rather, these standards sanction and even require the use of force under certain circumstances, particularly the defense of country and of innocent life under attack. Yet this rabbinic law strictly limits the application of violence and requires selective conscientious objection when its restrictions are systematically violated.

By Jewish law, according to Broyde, both secular and religious governments may adopt a quietist restraint of force when recourse to violent resistance against aggression would prove futile and entail even greater danger to the nation or people. Such a renunciation was actually practiced after the final revolt against Roman rule and did preserve the people—though not without significant loss—into the modern period.

Everett Gendler questions Michael Broyde's development of an ethic of defensive warfare that is not subjected to the strict limitations on the application of force that are operative in nongovernmental interventions to protect innocent life. In particular, he urges that rabbinic standards require that the taking of innocent life be actively prevented rather than tolerated as unintentional or inadvertent. In addition, Gendler asserts that the weight of the Jewish tradition establishes a preference for the use of nonviolent means of resisting aggression whenever such tactics might prove effective, not just when a violent response would be futile and counterproductive.

Like Michael Broyde and Everett Gendler, Yehuda Mirsky focuses on the situation of Jews living under a government that is not established by the authority of Jewish law. Unlike them, however, he clearly distinguishes the Jewish people from a Jewish state and focuses his attention on the obligation to preserve the people itself. Thus he argues that, as a religious tradition, Judaism cannot be pacifist because it is committed to the historical existence of a particular people as the carrier of a religious faith essential to the created universe as a whole. Without identifying the two, he suggests that the Jewish community of faith might be considered a deep metaphor for the divine presence and its operation in the world. Since the destruction of the Second Temple in 70 C.E., therefore, the primary legitimating cause of warfare according to Jewish law has been the preservation of the existence and religious identity of the people. Sometimes, war might also be justified to resist injustice and to establish a good social order.

Under certain circumstances, nonviolent forms of resistance to forces that endanger the Jewish people, however, might actually be preferred. If a particular threat is in conflict with the foundational values of a culture, that dangerous structure or institution might be attacked through nonviolent means that appeal to the fundamental commitments shared by both the oppressing and oppressed segments of the society. In this way, the civil rights movement in the United States appealed to foundational constitutional principles and widely held religious convictions to attack particular laws and practices. When, however, injustice is integral to the structure of a society, when the common humanity of persecutor and persecuted is systematically repudiated, when oppression aims at annihilation rather than subjugation, then nonviolence would not only prove ineffective in protecting the endangered but would be tantamount to cooperating in the destruction of the oppressed. Faced with intended extermination, the threatened people would be obliged to resort to whatever force was available.

Relying on his analysis of the cosmic significance of the Jewish people, however, Mirsky insists that its physical survival must be subordinated to its religious identity. Even for the purpose of saving life, Jews may not agree to perform an action that undermines the identity of the community, such as murder, idolatry, and certain forms of sexual immorality. In such instances, Jews are required to accept martyrdom: to lay down their individual physical lives in defense of the community's religious character and its role as a symbol of the divine presence in human history. Such martyrdom is not to be sought; it is rather to be accepted as the only form of resistance still available to assert the existence and peculiar mission of the people, which is the true object of the persecutor's attack. If another way—violent or nonviolent—could be found to preserve both individual lives and communal identity, it would have to be preferred to martyrdom.

In her commentary on Yehuda Mirsky's analysis of the cosmic significance of the Jewish people, Naomi Goodman argues that nonviolent resistance effectively asserts the community's identity and religious commitment, even in the face of overwhelming force. She then extends this thesis by claiming that even in less desperate situations, pacifism would be a more appropriate and effective means of affirming the faith and realizing the historical mission of the Jewish people.

The contributors focusing on the Jewish tradition largely agree that it does not provide a foundation for a principled pacifism. The supposition that God requires the initiative and action of human agency to protect the existence of the Jewish people, which is itself a necessary religious good, would seem to preclude a universal renunciation of the use of violence. Yet the same religious character that places such value on the existence of the historical community itself imposes significant limits on its resort to violence and may even establish the priority of nonviolent means of resolving conflicts and protecting the people.

In agreement with Yoder's analysis of the situation in which Judaism finds itself now without a religiously established government and national state, Broyde and Mirsky assert that offensive warfare cannot be authorized. Yet both would uphold the right and obligation to defensive warfare to protect the existence of the people. Broyde makes a clear distinction between such defensive warfare and the intervention to protect innocent life that is immediately endangered by an attacker. He argues that a secular government may compel its citizens to fight in a defensive war and may accept the unintentional killing of noncombatants in such wars. Gendler challenges Broyde's analysis of these rules of engagement, asserting that force should be applied only to protect the innocent, not to punish the guilty or prevent anticipated future attacks. In either form, the rules of defensive war or protection of innocent life would be applicable even to a government that was not established and sanctioned by Jewish law, whether or not the state was ethnically Jewish. By Mirsky's analysis, these rules would also be binding on a Jewish community that did not enjoy national sovereignty: The obligation to secure the physical existence and religious identity of the people would apparently rest on the individuals and on the social organizations available to them.

In certain situations, the protection of the community's physical existence and its religious identity might require the renunciation of force or a preference for nonviolent means. Giving up forcible self-defense might be used to win tolerance within a society, a stance adopted by Jews in the later Roman Empire, in Christian Europe, and in Muslim states. As a witness to the overriding value of peace and the hope of the messianic age, Jews might also give priority to nonviolent means of resolving disputes. Broyde, however, seems to argue that the anticipated efficacy of such means provides the only basis for preferring them. None of the commentators appears to disagree with Mirsky's assertion that in the face of a determined program of annihilation, all means of preserving the community's religious identity and its physical existence must be employed, including killing the oppressors and sacrificing the lives of individual Jews.

The four commentators seem to be agreed in ruling out offensive wars of national honor and aggrandizement under the current dispensation, in which a religiously established Jewish government does not function. Naomi Goodman calls attention to the conscientious rejection of offensive war by that movement within the Israeli military which refuses to serve outside the State of Israel. Michael Broyde observes that the Jewish citizen of a secular state might appropriately claim the status of a selective conscientious objector on the grounds of being forbidden to participate in military action that is aggressive, fails to safeguard the lives of innocent noncombatants, or otherwise exceeds the legitimate use of force.

Yehuda Mirsky's analysis is particularly helpful because it makes explicit the link between the religious identity and the physical survival of the Jewish people. This connection might imply that, at least from the perspective of Jewish law, peoples who do not carry this particular religious faith would not be obliged to preserve their own physical existence and ethnic identity, though they would have the right to do so. Thus Jewish law might provide a basis for quietism when only non-Jewish lives are threatened.

THE SECULAR STATE

Edward Gaffney's survey of the history of the treatment of pacifists by the government of the United States indicates a recognition of religious pacifism that recent judicial activism has extended to cover nonreligious objections to the bearing of arms. Yet neither the legislative nor the judicial branch of government has been willing to acknowledge the conscientious right of religious citizens to judge the morality of particular military actions and to refuse to serve in those wars that cannot be justified according to the established teachings and practices of widely espoused religious traditions. This refusal, he implies, violates the right to free exercise of religion established in the First Amendment to the United States Constitution.

In this refusal to recognize the citizen's right to selective conscientious objection, Gaffney discerns claims of sovereignty that the Abrahamic religious traditions should brand as idolatrous. In the practice of warfare, he explains, modern states, like ancient empires, tend to set themselves up as objects of veneration for their citizens. Claiming absolute sovereignty, they reject ethical standards that are independent of and superior to their own executive decrees, legislative decisions, and judicial orders. They refuse to recognize citizens' rights of appeal to principles of a higher or more universal order as a basis for refusing to implement particular governmental policies and shielding themselves from commands that they consider manifestly evil. In particular, secular governments deny their citizens the right to refuse to support and serve in those wars that do not meet religious criteria authorizing and limiting the use of force. Gaffney concludes that, as was done in the case of Louis Negre, such government claims must, on occasion, be resisted.

In his lecture during the conference, Peter Steinfels presented a detailed criticism of contemporary pacifism. During the era between the two world wars, most European pacifists consistently failed or refused to recognize the danger presented by Hitler's program of militarization and expansion into Central Europe. Once the onslaught began, they concluded that resistance by the unprepared Allies to such overwhelming power was futile and therefore unjustified. He showed that during the debate preceding the Gulf War in 1991, American religious leaders regularly overestimated the efficacy and understated the violence of economic sanctions; they blamed their governments for arming Iraq and permitting the conditions that had led to the invasion of Kuwait. Few were willing to recognize the actual danger or accurately appraise the probability of meeting it successfully by nonmilitary action.

In rejecting military force as an appropriate means of responding to injustice, Steinfels argued, many religious and secular pacifists experience great difficulty in truth-telling. In a fundamental revulsion from violence, they appeal to the justifiable warfare doctrine to prevent a recourse to arms. Seizing on its requirement that war must be a last resort, they advocate alternative courses of action whose expected efficacy they then exaggerate. They often argue that because the defenders have also contributed to injustice, they cannot use force to restore order. In many instances, these ideological analyses manifestly misrepresent the realities of the situation.

In contrast, religious pacifism appeals to a transcendent faith and interpretation of reality rather than arguing for the efficacy of nonviolence within a secular framework. Although Yoder's own historical analysis demonstrates that a pacifist approach can be effective, the Christian pacifist commitment is based not on that effectiveness but on faith in the divine action revealed in the life and teaching of Jesus. In the same way, the Jewish position advocated by Steven Schwarzchild attempts to anticipate the messianic age. Proponents of pacifism or quietism who cannot base their arguments on such transcendent claims because they or their audience reject religious faith as a basis for public policy must argue either against the efficacy of warfare or for the efficacy of nonviolence. In either case, according to Steinfels' historical analysis, they regularly distort reality.

CONCLUSION

The principled pacifism presented by John Howard Yoder challenges both Christians and Jews to accept a divine dispensation in which they are not normally granted state sovereignty and are forbidden to use coercive violence to advance the divine cause on earth or even to protect life and property. Walter Wink, Everett Gendler, Naomi Goodman, and Michael Nagler assert that the nonviolent resistance practiced and taught by Jesus and Gandhi actually responds to aggression and oppression more effectively than does war. Neither of these positions has been generally accepted or implemented by any of the three Abrahamic traditions. Judaism allows, and when necessary even requires, the use of force to defend the religious identity and physical existence of the people. Christianity encourages a nonviolent response to coercion, according to the example of Jesus. Though it accepts the right to self-defense on the basis of natural law, its specifically religious argument for defensive violence is based on the duty to protect one's neighbor, even at risk to oneself. Islam requires active resistance to uphold a just social order and true religious practice against active hostility or persecution. All three traditions, however, would seem to permit—and even encourage—the use of a nonviolent defense, as long as its anticipated success is as likely as an armed one.

Each of the traditions sets strict limits to offensive warfare: It might be mandated or forbidden depending on the circumstances. Broyde's analysis of rabbinic law shows that it obliges Jews to impose the observance of the provisions of the Noachide covenant on all peoples. It does not forbid wars of conquest, as long as they are approved by religiously established authorities and procedures, including the consent of those whose lives will be at risk in combat. At present, however, the requisite procedures cannot be followed because the ruling bodies of the Jewish community are not religiously established and authorized. Hence, Judaism currently has no means of legitimating an offensive war of conquest. Islam justifies offensive war only in the cause of God, for the expansion of the realm of submission to the divine law. Strictly speaking, such war is undertaken in defense of justice, and that justice is based on specific divine revelation rather than on natural law. Sachedina explains that this offensive warfare can be mandatory only upon specific authorization by a just and learned leader who can interpret the divine will in the particular circumstances. His exposition seems to imply that this duty has been used as a cover for wars of conquest that are neither required nor allowed by a proper interpretation of Islamic law. As with Judaism, the authority which Islam requires to justify offensive war is currently absent or inoperative. Christianity, as represented by the justifiable war tradition here championed by Langan and Gaffney, does not authorize wars of conquest, though it may permit and even require a nation to initiate hostilities for the purpose of defending violated justice. The right in jeopardy, however, would be based on natural law rather than Christian revelation.

Each of the religious traditions specifies the authority that is necessary to declare an offensive war legitimate or even mandatory. The absence of the required religious or social institutions, therefore, may limit a state or people to defensive war against aggression. Jewish law specifies action by the Sanhedrin or its equivalent in a religiously established state. The government of the contemporary State of Israel is not generally recognized as fulfilling this condition; indeed some Jews believe that only the messianic intervention can confer religious authority on government. In Islam, the Sunni jurists have erected a justification of offensive war on the belief that an actual political ruler who professes support for Islam thereby gains the religious authority to undertake offensive war and to oblige the faithful to fight in the cause of God. The Shiʿite jurists, in contrast, set more stringent conditions for the legitimation of war-making authority. Some, like their Jewish counterparts, await the appearance of the Mahdi. Nearly all contemporary governments, even in nations whose population is overwhelmingly Muslim, neither claim nor are granted the religious authority necessary to wage offensive war according to Islamic law. The Christian position on legitimate authority has been divided. Pacifists would argue that any Christian government that undertook offensive war would be abandoning the teaching of Jesus and would thereby delegitimate itself. The justifiable war tradition, in contrast, has generally followed a line of argument not unlike that of the Sunni jurists, granting war-making authority to the actually established government, as long as other conditions are fulfilled. Gaffney's analysis of the practice of a modern secular state, however, seriously questions its authority under the provisions of the warfare theory espoused by each of the Abrahamic religious traditions. A government that refuses to allow its citizens to challenge the justice of its decision to undertake a particular war and to refuse to serve in unjustified military action on the basis of religious conviction would, in Gaffney's view, forfeit the authority to oblige its citizens to bear arms in any of its wars. Thus all three Abrahamic faiths share a hesitation to grant political leaders the religious authority to oblige their subjects to participate in offensive warfare. This caution might be grounded in their common rejection of idolatry, here understood as the claim of absolute sovereignty over life by any human institution.

Each of the religious traditions does offer a certain degree of support to practical pacifism, to a reliance on nonviolent and noncoercive forms of conflict resolution. Each reserves ultimate control over human life and death to God alone and concedes a strictly limited authority to human agents of God to risk or destroy life. Moreover, each tends to make the religious subject responsible before God for decisions and actions; it thereby sets a further limit to the religious authority that might be conceded to the state or other social institutions.

Indeed, in their specific provisions, each tradition encourages nonviolent means of resolving disputes. An Islamic war to call the nations to submit to God must be preceded by announcing the revelation and granting the opportunity to freely embrace its prescriptions. Unlike Islam, Jewish law makes a clear distinction between the detailed prescriptions that apply to Israel and the more general Noachide law that other nations may be required to follow. Moreover, the rabbinic law governing warfare requires that an opponent be allowed to submit or to resolve the conflict by negotiation. The example of Jesus' own refusal to resort to coercive violence as well as the explicit criteria of the justifiable war theory tend to make warfare a regretted necessity in a sinful world, according to Christian teaching. Like Judaism, Christian tradition also distinguishes the requirements of the natural law, which might be imposed on all, from the stricter moral standards set for Christians; it requires the state to enforce only the former and only to the extent compatible with public order.

Thus it would seem that all three religious traditions should support a practical pacifism that outlaws offensive wars, especially for conquest, and attempts noncoercive or nonviolent means before resorting to arms in defense of justice. Each might also embrace Gandhi's ethic of nonviolent resistance or Jesus' strategy of unmasking and disarming oppressive force. Support of such programs would be based, however, on the high value each sets on human life as a divine gift and on the anticipated efficacy of nonviolent means of protecting it. Neither Judaism nor Islam, nor even the dominant Christian bodies, have endorsed the principled renunciation of coercive power that Yoder discerns at the heart of Jesus' teaching and practice.

CHALLENGES

The contributors to this investigation of pacifism and quietism in the three Abrahamic faiths have revealed certain areas in which further interreligious dialogue might be pursued in expectation of fuller agreement or at least mutual understanding. The following are not listed in order of importance.

First, a strenuous review and critique of the legitimacy granted to secular governments by religious communities seems to be necessary. The law of each tradition envisions a nation whose military decisions are guided or influenced by religious principles. In fact, however, the overwhelming majority of adherents of each tradition live under governments that do not claim religious establishment or authority. Broyde, Sachedina, and Gaffney, as well as Yoder, have questioned the propriety of lending religious authority to political powers that repudiate the religious restrictions upon that authority.

Second, Mirsky's suggestion that the Jewish people serves as a deep metaphor for the presence of God in the world might be applied to other religious communities. Islam seems to regard itself as an agency for God's cause of establishing a just society. Christianity trusts a divine promise that it will be preserved against hostile forces. Mirsky's observation is based on the religious identity of the community and thus could imply that the form of the religious community's life should concretely manifest the divine presence and operation in the world. Each tradition might then examine whether approval of offensive or even defensive warfare is compatible with its role of manifesting the divine it worships. This is essentially Yoder's argument for Christianity. Steven Schwarzchild, whose influence pervaded the discussions at Washington University, developed a parallel thesis for Judaism. Abdul Ghaffar Khan presented a similar challenge to Islam.

Third, and closely related to the second point, the religious ethic of obedience to revealed law, along with the techniques of interpretation and application of that law, might be examined in each tradition. Judaism has developed different forms of fidelity to Torah. Some Christian communities have embraced a natural law morality to interpret the teaching of Jesus, while others use a method of communal discernment that trusts in a continuing divine guidance. Islam, according to Sachedina's analysis, remains wary of the power of human reason to discern the divine intention.

Fourth, all three faiths advocate or accept martyrdom, in which the faithful risk or give up their lives in witness to the sovereignty of God. As this tradition of self-sacrifice has been adapted to support self-sacrifice in warfare, it might also be developed as a foundation for the type of pacifist intervention and interposition practiced by Abdul Ghaffar Khan. Still, Mirsky's distinction between injustice that is contrary to the foundational commitments of a culture and that which is integral to a corrupt system must be considered in any attempt to implement such a plan.

Fifth, the implications of the justifiable war tradition might be more fully developed and implemented as public policy. Each of the three traditions would seem to require some form of selective conscientious objection, the right to abstain from participation in wars that are judged unjustified by their religious communities. A shared insistence on this right and coordinated procedures for reaching judgment in individual cases might be attempted, as an exercise of responsible participation in democratic government.

Sixth, Peter Steinfels demonstrated the difficulty that pacifists have historically experienced in honestly assessing the danger posed by aggressive nations. He suggested that their belief in the divine control of the historical process and divine reward or punishment in an afterlife helps religious traditions to face realities more squarely and honestly. When the pacifist program is advanced in a secular culture, however, it can rely only on the greater efficacy of nonviolent means in opposing aggression and reaching long-term resolution of conflict. While this would imply that the principled religious pacifism or quietism will not be adopted by a secular state, its adherents might assist their secular counterparts to a realistic and truthful assessment of the dangers involved and of the hope of measurable success.

Seventh, Islam's commitment to the establishment of the just social order revealed in the Qur'an, even by force of arms, could create an ongoing instability within and among nations. It would impose the obligation to defend the practice of a law that is actively challenged by contemporary secularism. The threat of warfare by a religiously established Muslim state in defense of its observance of Shari'a might convince other nations to tolerate societies that are organized on religious principles abhorrent to their own religious or secular ideology. Forms of Islam developed by the jurists also required the faithful to bring other peoples into submission to the Shari'a, even through force of arms. The resurrection of such a Muslim state would certainly lead to international conflict. Other nations could be expected to defend their own contrary forms of social organization, thus leading to active warfare or armed truce. Sachedina's analysis suggests that the issue could be attacked at the point of transition from the Qur'an to the jurists, who legitimated the practice of armed conquest for the expansion of Islam. As was noted in the first point above, he also signals the more general question of the religious authority of the secular governments that have ruled Muslim peoples for centuries, with little reference to Shariʿa.

Eighth, the exchange between Yoder and Langan on the forms of coercion suggests that pacifists and quietists may have focused too narrowly on military action. Langan argues that killing and the threat of destruction can be recognized as points far along a continuum of coercion. Yoder's appeal to the ethic of Jesus would seem to question other forms of violence and forcible control. A more generalized theory of power and the conditions for its exercise might be profitably addressed.

These points are among those which might be investigated in further scholarly and religious discussion of pacifism and quietism in the three Abrahamic faiths.

DATE DUE

APR 2 3 2003			
			Printed in USA